TRUE
PROFESSIONAL

JAMES ODDY

TRUE PROFESSIONAL

THE CLIVE SULLIVAN STORY

pitch

First published by Pitch Publishing, 2017

Pitch Publishing
A2 Yeoman Gate
Yeoman Way
Worthing
Sussex
BN13 3QZ

www.pitchpublishing.co.uk
info@pitchpublishing.co.uk

A CIP catalogue record is available for this book from the British Library.

ISBN 978-1-78531-310-3

Typesetting and origination by Pitch Publishing

Printed in the UK by TJ International Ltd, Cornwall

Contents

‘Do you not know that in a race all the runners run, but only one gets the prize? Run in such a way as to get the prize. Everyone who competes in the games goes into strict training. They do it to get a crown that will not last, but we do it to get a crown that will last forever. Therefore I do not run like someone running aimlessly; I do not fight like a boxer beating the air. No, I strike a blow to my body and make it my slave so that after I have preached to others, I myself will not be disqualified for the prize.’

1 Corinthians, 9:24-274

For Clive, Colin and Roger.
Thanks for the memories.

Foreword by Rosalyn Sullivan

CLIVE was, primarily, my husband, the man I loved, and dad to Anthony and Lisa. But he had another love and that was rugby league. Although he had a full-time job, rugby was what he lived for.

I feel very lucky to have such lovely memories of wonderful times with Clive at Hull FC and Hull Kingston Rovers. Winning a Challenge Cup medal for both Rovers and Hull FC was a dream come true for Clive and I feel privileged to have been part of this.

Clive wasn't the easiest to live with when he had an injury – and he had his fair share – but I always tried to keep him positive.

I was quite surprised when James approached me regarding writing a book about Clive so long after his death and I can imagine Clive would have had some tales to tell. What is wonderful is that the men who played with him have told these tales. Clive would have been so surprised and honoured at the interest shown since his death. The people of Hull and the rugby world never forget him, which is a great thing for me, Anthony and Lisa. The grandchildren are so proud of their grandfather even though they never met him.

I would like to say thank you to the people of Hull, as when Clive died they mourned with me and have kept his memory alive with the stories they tell of him.

Acknowledgements

THIS book is and was very much a labour of love. Like most things of that nature, it was a long and winding process with plenty of bumps along the way.

As such, I must first and foremost thank Paul and Jane and Pitch Publishing as a whole, for their continued support and patience along the way. Thank you Duncan Olner for your excellent design work and salvaging images for the book.

The book wouldn't also be possible without the generosity shown to me by the Sullivan family. Rosalyn, Anthony, Lisa, Sharon and Mark were always helpful, considerate, generous, friendly and approachable. The superlatives just don't exist to describe such a wonderful family.

The book became both easier and harder to write as I got to know them more. It was sad to think that a father, husband and brother has been lost to them, but their memories and pride in him convinced me that the story needed to be told.

A huge thanks also needs to be given to Roger Pugh, Bill Dalton, Dave Windass, Donald McRae, Anthony Clavane, Phil Caplan, Martyn Saddler, Tony Collins, Tony Hannan, Tony Cope, Brian Lavery, Andrew Cudbertsons and Luke G. Williams. All provided information, opinion and inspiration at different times.

All the players interviewed did so free of charge yet were wonderfully generous with their time and anecdotes. They continue to be heroes for all generations, not just the one they belonged to.

Thank you to Zane Johnson for your editorial work and feedback along the way, and putting up with my non-stop nagging. You did a great job.

Thank you to my wife for being so patient, and my parents for making sure I had books and watched rugby league as a kid.

A World Cup

THE Stade de Gerland in Lyon, France, was not the most obvious choice for the Rugby League World Cup Final. Even in 1972, when the French were much more of a force in the international game than in 2017, Lyon was a long way from the game's heartlands in the south of the country.

When Great Britain and Australia emerged into the vast stadium, led by captains Clive Sullivan and Graeme Langlands respectively, they were met with nearly empty stands. The official attendance was said to be 4,000, leaving large pockets of concrete stand exposed in a venue capable of holding over 40,000. Aside from the location, the French had also had a largely disappointing tournament, dampening what little interest might have remained. Even the chill of this mid-November afternoon was unappealing, making the grey of the terraces appear even bleaker on BBC's television coverage.

The crowd present made so little noise in the opening quarter that the broadcast's only atmosphere was provided by players talking to one another and the referee, whose shrill whistle echoed around the stadium.

Intensity, though lacking in the stands, found its home on the field. The tournament only featured four teams – Great Britain, Australia, New Zealand and France – in a round-robin format, after which the top two would face off in the final. Britain and Australia had been, by far, the best of the tournament; Britain had gone undefeated, winning their first game against the Australians 27-21 in the much more welcoming city of Perpignan, located on the south coast.

Perpignan's Stade Gilbert Brutus only had around 7,000 in attendance, but this almost filled the stadium, creating a boisterous atmosphere as the French spectators got behind the British underdog.

Australia were the tournament's clear favourites. They had won the World Cup in 1970 in the UK (Rugby League World Cups have not always had the most regular of schedules). Their triumph came in a brutal final at Headingley 12-7, during which Australia's scrum half Billy Smith and Britain's centre Syd Hynes were both sent off for fighting; the image of the pair consoling one another as they left the field is etched into rugby league memory.

The final whistle brought more carnage as British winger John Atkinson punched Australian full back Eric Simms, resulting in a mass brawl broadcast live on afternoon British TV. The scuffle led to a local councillor describing the sport as 'degenerating into street corner brawls', due to the 'crude violence and lack of sporting content'.

The 1972 British team had only one player left over from the previous tournament. Oddly enough, it was Atkinson. This was partly due to a slate wiped clean by coach Jim Challinor, but many key players were missing due to a variety of circumstances. Castleford enforcer Mal Reilly, the loose forward, had left the British game to carve a fearsome legacy for Manly in Australia, making him ineligible for British selection. The sensational Mick Shoebottom, nicknamed 'the Lionheart' due to his commitment, was also ruled out.

After playing at stand off in the 1970 final, Shoebottom was nearly killed by a stray boot from Salford's Colin Dixon at Leeds in 1971. Paralysed for a period, he eventually recovered sufficiently to be able to walk, but rugby was out of the question. Roger Millward, in superb form for Hull KR and expected to be Britain's main playmaker, suffered a variety of unfortunate injuries and thus was ruled out.

The Australians themselves were not the same team as seen two years previously. They had been through an overhaul with only a few key players still involved. The mercurial Bob Fulton, born in Warrington but raised Down Under, remained along with John O'Neil, the huge South Sydney prop, and teak-tough loose forward Gary Sullivan.

New to the Aussie class of '72 was the infamous Arthur 'Artie' Beetson, an icon of the Aboriginal community. He was a strapping back-rower renowned for a combative attitude both on and off the field, which led to numerous bust-ups, sendings-off and the love of the rugby league public in Australia. He had been involved with the national team since the 1960s, but for '72 he was set to be a key player.

Despite the lack of continuity between the two squads, the rivalry between the British and Australia had not subsided. Both sets of players had a great deal of mutual respect for each other, highlighted when they shared beers moments after the 'crude violence' of the 1970 final. But, the British/Australian rivalry never truly dies regardless of the sport, be it rugby union, rugby league or cricket.

Both classes of '72 were eager for the first meeting. The two teams had scoped each other out around Perpignan in the lead-up to the first meeting, the British noticing the huge size of the Aussie team in the outside backs alone, with the forwards even bigger. According to the British players, they were riled even further because they felt the Australians also carried themselves with an air of superiority and arrogance.

Finally, the two sides met. The match in Perpignan featured some brilliant running rugby; Fulton bagged a hat-trick in a losing effort. John Atkinson, Phil Lowe, Dennis O'Neil, Mike Stephenson all scored. But the best try went to captain Sullivan. Steve Nash, at scrum half, collected the ball inside his own ten-metre line after a scrum, raced to the halfway mark, and fed full back Paul Charlton in support. Charlton passed to centre Chris Hesketh in space, who sent a looping ball out to winger Sullivan, who showed blistering pace to go over untouched from 20 metres out.

Sullivan had been something of a surprise pick to captain the side. Despite being on the international scene since 1967, he didn't make the cut for the 1970 World Cup team with Leeds's Alan Smith picked instead of him. Still, Sullivan showed an obsessive will to win, a consistently excellent try-scoring ability, and a strength few could match either physically and mentally.

Competitive while remaining disciplined on the field, Sullivan was ready and willing to produce crunching tackles and do the dirty work of carting the ball upfield, often resembling an extra forward rather than a fleet-footed winger. Yet he was also capable of producing a sudden burst of pace, a piece of magic that an opposing side could never anticipate. He had the ability to lift the spirit and intensity of his side, and he was always willing to lead by example.

Off the field, he was quiet, even shy, according to those who knew him. A gentleman, he was well-liked and respected by his own fans and teammates at Hull FC and the fans and players of the opposition. That gentle nature fled him as he stepped out on to the park. A ruthlessness came over him that matched even that of the Australians.

He was also a black Briton, the first to skipper a British sports team. England's soccer team would have to wait another 23 years until Paul Ince donned the armband, while the Welsh rugby union team would not even pick a black Briton until 1986 when winger Glenn Webbe was selected. Yet such was Sullivan's standing in the sport that his selection for captain garnered very little comment, either in or out of the rugby league bubble.

While the 1970s had certainly seen some progression in terms of race relations around the world, it was also the decade of sitcoms like *Love Thy Neighbour,* in which a working-class white man comes to terms with having a black neighbour. Even more sinister, the 1970s saw the rise of the neo-fascist National Front, also headquartered in Hull, which exploited racial tensions across the country. Even as a man born and bred in Wales, Sullivan still represented a break in aesthetic from the typical captain.

The mood in the camp was buoyant following the win over Australia in Perpignan. The next challenge was the French, who had beaten New Zealand 20-9 in front of 20,000 fans in Marseille in the tournament's opening game, in the famous Stade Velodrome.

Yet Britain triumphed again, winning 13-4 at Grenoble, Sullivan again scoring to add to two from Hull KR's loose forward Lowe. Lowe was in superb form and his athleticism was drawing envious glances from a number of clubs across the world.

New Zealand, who had only just lost to Australia 9-5, were up next. Britain went on to produce one of the most complete performances in their history, hammering their opponents 53-19. Sullivan scored again, and John Holmes, the young Leeds stand off, got two tries and ten goals in a record-breaking haul. Holmes had taken over goal kicking duties from a rested Terry Clawson, and the stand off berth from Dennis O'Neil. He produced a performance of such youthful vigour that he retained his place against Australia in the final.

The British had gelled wonderfully, both on and off the field. For this, credit is split between Sullivan and coach Challinor, for creating the kind of environment where Britain, as underdogs, could play carefree, expressive rugby league. Players like Holmes could slot in and express themselves in an era when half backs and scrum halves tended to be much more freewheeling in their play than today's organisers.

This isn't to say that the underdog tag was fully deserved, either. A quick look at the roster shows the team's astounding quality; all 13 players would have long and successful careers, and it was the perfect opportunity to right the wrongs of 1970. The paper talk of the time seems more a reflection of British self-deprecation and lack of confidence in sporting prowess than earned worry.

Going into the final, however, the British Lions had every reason to believe they had one hand on the Paul Barrière Trophy. Their perfect record in the tournament meant that they could win the trophy with a draw. Australia would need to win.

The game was scrappy, dissimilar in aesthetic to the try scoring seen in the meeting a few weeks earlier. Instead, it was a war of attrition. Both sides ripped into each other with an aggression that seeps through the footage. It wasn't just the forwards, either; both sides' flair players mixed it up with brutal tackles and runs.

Eventually, Britain broke the deadlock. Clawson, one of the toughest props of his or any era, was also a superb goal kicker. Referee Georges Jameau penalised Australia for an incorrect feed at the scrum around 20 metres out and to the left of the posts, and Clawson, with his distinctive toe-poking style, slotted the ball over to put his side up 2-0.

The lead would not last. Australian hooker Elwyn Walters fed prop Bob O'Riley, who pivoted and popped the ball up for an on-rushing O'Neil. Making a mockery of his 'Lurch' nickname, O'Neil showed a brilliant turn of pace, and went at the gap between Lowe and Sullivan. Lowe attempted the tackle, textbook around the legs, but O'Neil evaded, and the falling Lowe prevented Sullivan from attempting the tackle himself.

Loose forward George Nicholas then tried an ankle tap, but it did little to prevent the marauding prop. O'Neil finally crashed over in the corner with full back Charlton having made a futile last-ditch tackle attempt on the line. The score had moved to 3-2 and O'Neil was mobbed by his teammates, while a visibly annoyed Sullivan looked on. Winger Ray Branighan, or 'Braaaaanighan' as commentator Eddie

Waring anointed him, then slotted over the touchline conversion to make it 5-2.

The Aussies were in the ascendancy and looking to land another telling blow with Britain on the ropes. However, the Lions's defence was resolute and it would clearly require a moment of brilliance to prise it open. Unfortunately for the British, their opposition had plenty of players capable of such an act.

Scrum half Dennis Ward launched a high kick down the left flank about 20 metres out. Sullivan and centre Hesketh turned to chase it. However, Aussie full back and captain Langlands was facing the right direction and had read the play superbly, outpacing them. With an outrageous swan dive, he plucked the ball out of the air and scored, winding himself in the process.

The crowd was suddenly alive – standing, clapping, cheering – with the thrill of such a well-worked and exhilarating try and the score stood at 8-2. Or, it should have been. Langlands had just completed what was dubbed 'the greatest try never scored' as the referee Jameau incorrectly ruled him offside.

It was a major turning point but the Australians still hammered the British line. The ball worked its way across the line to O'Riley. Half-tackled by Nicholas, O'Riley attempted to offload the ball. Instead, it slipped forward out of his grasp, and bobbled into the waiting hands of Sullivan on his own 15-metre line.

Sullivan picked up the ball on the run, showing his superb hands, and ran hard, seemingly straight at the Australian players, attempting to quickly regroup. The crowd, already fans of Sullivan and aware of what he could do, rose to their feet.

'Can he go?' asked Waring.

Suddenly, Sullivan sidestepped, smoothly, around opposition winger John Grant. Sullivan did not miss a step, but Grant slipped in his attempt to match the change of direction. Sullivan was now in the clear down the wing.

'I think Sullivan will go … everyone's shouting, go, go, go!' Waring announced, and the crowd began to roar with Sullivan's advance.

Some of the Aussies almost kept up, including O'Neil, as Sullivan ate up the metres. Just as O'Neil bore down upon him, Sullivan pulled away. The sun hung low enough in the winter afternoon for the flashbulbs of the pitch side photographers to visibly pop as Britain's captain crossed the try line. Then, Sullivan turned to huge prop David Jeanes, who was in support.

Clawson missed the resulting kick so the score remained 5-5 as both sides went in at half-time. The game still had plenty of drama left in it but Sullivan had lit it up with one of the most thrilling, timely, and fondly remembered tries in the history of the British national team.

As it stood, Britain would win the cup, but 40 minutes was a long time to keep the Australians at bay.

While Fulton was seen as the big danger man, the diminutive Ward, the lightest man to ever wear the green and gold of Australia, was not to be underestimated. He received the ball from the play-the-ball, slowed and dummied, and then cut through the British defence, leaving a heap of defenders in his wake. Charlton raced up to meet him, and hit Ward hard, but the ball had already found Beetson, tearing up the inside in support.

Thinking quickly, Stephenson attempted to punch the ball out of Beetson's grasp, but 'Artie' made it under the posts.

The game scoreboard read 10-5 as Branighan kicked the easy conversion. The clock ticked on and it looked as if Britain were set to lose another close final. With seven minutes remaining they were only around 15 metres from the opposition try line and were growing increasingly desperate.

Lowe threw a wild pass out to the right wing, which found air and nothing else, and the ball trolled along the ground. Sullivan scooped it up and quickly sidestepped the onrushing defender. He then straightened up, sidestepping another tackler, and the crowd's excitement grew. A posse of Australians eventually brought him crashing to the turf, but not before he off-loaded the ball.

It found back rower Brian Lockwood, another uncompromising forward of sublime skill. Lockwood ran hard at the defensive line, then pivoted and saw Stephenson running at pace on his inside. Lockwood popped the ball up into the onrushing hooker's hands. Stephenson then went over the line as more flashbulbs popped, though unclear pitch markings led to Stephenson placing the ball further away from the sticks than was needed. Despite this, the ever-confident Clawson still kicked the goal to leave the game 10-10.

After the final whistle an additional 20 minutes was played and if the Lions could keep the scores tied, they would win. Even so, with both sides exhausted after one of the toughest 80 minutes of rugby league ever seen, Great Britain came the closest to winning. Centre Josh Walsh made a break up the field and found Hesketh obstructed. Hesketh kicked the ball forward and gained a penalty around 25 metres out. The kick was a tough one, even for Clawson, so although it had the length, it sailed wide.

Ultimately, with both teams out on their feet and players cramping up, the referee blew his whistle and, with the score at 10-10, the cup belonged to Great Britain once again.

The Australians graciously congratulated the winners, and a few players swapped shirts in the aftermath. The mutual respect that was a major source of the rivalry between the two teams – and indeed, the two countries – remained after 100 minutes of brutal warfare.

Finally, after the weeks in France away from work and family, focused on nothing but the tournament, Sullivan was handed the trophy at pitchside. This was not the choreographed and stage-managed presentation of modern-day sport, yet Sullivan's joy as he shook the hands of the various officials and held the trophy overhead was captured by many cameras, and by the television broadcast as he was lifted by his teammates and carried from the pitch. The meagre support inside the arena applauded the new World Cup winners.

Clive's wife, Rosalyn, was watching the BBC broadcast back in their home in Hull. She could see what becoming a World Cup-winning captain meant to him, a reserved man committed to being the best he could. 'The look on his face when he won the World Cup,' Rosalyn recalls. 'I could tell how happy he was.'

A Proper Introduction

THE 1972 World Cup campaign is a great microcosm of the career of Clive Sullivan, MBE. He acted as a superb captain for a superb team, one of the brightest players of a squad filled with stars. His speed, skill, stamina and support play were top notch. His defensive discipline, reading of a game, ability to motivate and lead by example were displayed in abundance. When it mattered, he ran plays that directly resulted in Great Britain winning their last major international honour in the 13-a-side code.

For rugby league fans in the UK, it was a joyous occasion. The immensely well-liked Sullivan was the perfect talisman for that achievement, a man who united the country over a game prone to intense tribal loyalties.

But, following the signal of the French public, the British public (outside of the code's hotbeds) was rather indifferent upon the team's return. The squad was not met by scores of press members clamouring for interviews, or requests for endorsements and sponsorships. Sullivan – as the photogenic captain, proven try-scorer, and most thrilling player – should have become an overnight sensation. He received an MBE and an appearance on *This Is Your Life*, the Eamon Andrews-fronted 'surprise' television documentary. Unfortunately, the episode appears to be lost, but it still starred Clive on prime time British television.

But the glamour and attention did not last. He returned to Hull and went back to his day job with rugby league for Hull FC squeezed in-between normal life with his young family.

Sullivan still had many good years left in rugby league, which was glad to have him. But his stardom did not ascend to the heights it deserved following one of his and British sport's most defining moments.

The indifference of the media and the general public morphed over years into forgetfulness. Sullivan is still revered in Hull and respected across the whole rugby league community, but saying his name to most of the general public does not generate the flickers of recognition that the likes of Bobby Moore, Ian Botham, Henry Cooper and Johnny Wilkinson elicit.

As the 1972 World Cup is a microcosm of the career of Clive Sullivan, so, too, is Sullivan's career a microcosm of rugby league as a whole. To this day the sport is still only given national attention begrudgingly. No matter what blend of finesse and toughness the players exhibit, they are acknowledged and respected only fleetingly. Their honours are not deemed prestigious enough to be remembered, as they deserve to be.

Sullivan deserves to be remembered. That generation of rugby league players – still rooted in their local, working-class communities when they played – deserves to be remembered.

He would like to have been remembered as a great, committed rugby league player and an approachable, friendly father and husband off the field. Yet, regardless of how little he would have welcomed the tag, he should also be remembered as a trailblazer. The black British community recognised his historic and, at the time, unprecedented successful leadership as captain of a British sports team by naming him as one of the 100 Great Black Britons in 2000 following a public poll.

Yet, why Sullivan and his team were and are not given their full due is a complicated and somewhat controversial topic. Some would say it was due to a southern media antipathy for 'The North' and the working communities and their culture, of which rugby league is a key part. Some say that those northern communities are not the best at self-promotion and self-reflection of their achievements. Some claim that it was just that generation of rugby league players' bad luck to be in their primes when other sports – such as cricket, boxing and soccer – also experienced golden periods. Some may say it was due to Sullivan being a Welsh rugby union convert, who deserved to be ignored by union acolytes for his 'crime' of professionalism.

It could be a combination of all of the above, plus hundreds of other variables.

Regardless of exactly why this imbalance exists, this book seeks to readdress the value of such moments. It seeks to place Sullivan, the city of Hull, the north, and rugby league where they deserve to be, back in the public consciousness.

It has not been easy. Many of the generation of players whom played with Clive have either passed away or are not well enough to now speak of their experiences. Clive himself died tragically young, depriving the game of his insight, charisma and experience. The communities that produced these players – and the wives and children that supported them – have, in most cases, fallen away and dispersed, along with the industries that supported them.

Also, rugby league has not always been blessed with the type of amateur and professional statisticians that document other popular sports. This leads to some unavoidable gaps in detail regarding try-scorers, goal-kickers and attendance figures.

Yet the game has always had a resilient, communal spirit, and I am indebted to that spirit. I am indebted to the committed historians who have given countless hours to compiling dusty old newspapers featuring match reports, such as Bill Dalton, Roger Pugh, Tony Collins and Phil Caplan. A special mention should also go to Joe Latus, who wrote a biography of Clive in 1972, entitled *Hard Road to the Top*. Though the biography only features half of Clive's career, it has been an invaluable resource, even WITH Latus's bias as a Hull FC director, having had major involvement with the club throughout Clive's time with the team.

I am indebted to Clive's former teammates who were willing and able to speak to me. And I am most certainly indebted to Clive's family, who supported the project from its earliest stages. Rosalyn Sullivan in particular, as someone who has a unique perspective on the pressures and strains of a rugby league player away from the field, was wonderfully helpful and supportive throughout.

Above all, I am indebted to Clive Sullivan. I just hope the book does him justice. He deserves it.

Setting the Scene

LIKE most rugby league cities, Hull was known for a trade. Castleford, Featherstone, Wakefield and St Helens were pit villages. Leeds and Bradford were mill towns, dealing in textiles. The clutch of towns around Dewsbury and Batley were the 'heavy woollen district'. Warrington was a hub of steel production, specialising in wire, giving Warrington their distinctive nickname, 'The Wire'. In the case of Hull, situated on the east coast of Yorkshire, it was fishing.

It is no great mystery why fishing would rule the economy – the river Hull runs almost down the middle of the city. It leads out towards the Humber Estuary, which in turn runs 25 miles out into the vast, unforgiving North Sea.

All of these tough, physical industries helped to produce townspeople who were robust and rugged enough to play one of the toughest team sports ever played, the 13-a-side code of rugby league football.

The adage 'you could shout down a pit in Featherstone and find a new prop forward for the first team' sounds absurd to those unfamiliar with the game's origin, but the game has for most of its history been played by the working-class residents of the towns where it flourished. These trades, often extremely dangerous but always physically punishing, helped to foster a sense of community, camaraderie and locale. This was reflected in the passionate support given to the local rugby team, and the pride the players had in wearing their team's colours.

Perhaps most importantly for rugby league in its early days, these industries also created a steady income for towns folk to spend on leisure pursuits, not least of which was live sport. Journalist and historian

Anthony Clevane states, 'The industrial revolution had been driven ... by the local trinity of home, work and leisure.' Rugby league was the perfect marriage of these, as local teams reflected their place of origin, usually featuring heavily people from the local area, and watched by those of the same.

In Hull's case, that sense of camaraderie, togetherness and community was magnified by the fact that men would be away for weeks at a time at sea or trawling the estuary, while the families left behind would support and protect one another.

This led to a unique and distinct culture which featured heavy amounts of superstition, both from trawlermen and their families. Much of this culture sought to ward off death and danger in a profession in which it was prevalent, but it also helped to further cement the already tight bonds and build a language that is almost impenetrable to outsiders. The obscure traditions of these fishing communities included wearing items of green clothing, avoiding hauling in from the portside (left) of a ship, and not washing any clothes on a sailing day.

To an outsider, the superstitions seem peculiar, and the source of their creation unknowable. But they were strictly adhered to and taken seriously by those whose greatest friend – and indeed, worst enemy – was the sea.

The river, which runs down its centre, was vital for establishing the city, and remains a key part of its identity to this day, even though the fishing industry is now all but non-existent. That industry, with its own unique sensibilities, alongside something of a geographic isolation from the rest of Yorkshire, provided the town with its unique character and uniquely strong passions, not least of which was sport.

The river was also a vital dividing line between two rugby league sides. No other town has sustained and supported two vibrant and successful rugby league clubs for such a prolonged period. Leeds briefly had an all-conquering Hunslet RLFC and a solid Leeds RLFC, but Leeds eventually overtook their city rivals, and the two have never really been on a level playing field since.

The story of both clubs is fascinating, and, like the formation of the code, has been written about extensively elsewhere. However, it is important to understand the history of each of these famous clubs before Clive Sullivan cut his figure into the scene as a raw teenage winger.

Hull FC were formed in 1865. The public-school boys network, playing forms of soccer with modified rules, was the bedrock of the early days of the FC club. Rugby was only adopted formally in 1870. It is worth noting that while FC would go on to have the famous black and white hooped strip, they started out in the cherry and white hallmark of their neighbours and rivals, Hull Kingston Rovers.

It would take 17 more years for Rovers, or KR, to be formed. Formed from slightly more working-class stock, it was apprentice boilermakers who decided to set up a rival club on the iconic Hessle Road of West Hull. Hessle Road was to be key in both teams' history, though it would become synonymous with Hull FC.

Both teams started out playing rugby union until the famous split of the northern union occurred in 1895. In essence, northern teams, which were seeing huge crowds, wished to pay their players – most of whom worked in the pits, factories and trawlers – for giving up their time away from work. This offended the sensibilities of the midlands- and southern-based Rugby Football Union, who whole-heartedly endorsed amateurism in the game. Crucially, many of those advocating the continued need for amateurism, being from more lofty stock with greater personal wealth, did not have to trouble themselves with working for a living.

At a fateful meeting at the George Hotel in Huddersfield on 27 August 1895, 21 clubs resigned from the union and formed the Northern Rugby Football Union, one of which was Hull FC. Hull KR followed in 1897. Rugby league had officially arrived in Hull.

Around this time, the clubs also switched sides of the river, with FC taking up the expired lease on KR's Hull Athletic ground, thus transferring to their long-term home on the west of the city. Likewise, KR moved over to the east side of the city, living nomadically for a time before settling in Craven Park.

The move to rugby league worked out particularly well for Hull FC in the early years. They reached three consecutive cup finals from 1908 to 1910, although they went down all three times in defeat, to Hunslet, Wakefield and Leeds, respectively.

They finally won the cup in 1914 with star signing Billy Batten in the side. Batten's signing highlighted the prosperity and pre-eminence of the Hull FC side as they parted with a record £600 for the British and

Hunslet outside back. Batten was a prolific points-scorer and one of the sports very earliest superstars, capable of playing full back, centre or wing. Newspapers at the time also passed comment on his unusual habit of not drinking or smoking regularly, a rarity at the time for most men, be they athletes or not.

After a dispute over wages with Hunslet, Batten was offered to both of the Hull clubs as well as Huddersfield, Oldham, Wigan and Leeds. Such was the nature of professional sport at the time that he was also attracting interest from soccer teams, with Manchester City offering him £200 a year to switch codes and Manchester United offering £4 per game. Ultimately, Batten picked Hull FC, his wages allegedly rising from around 50 shillings per game to an astronomical £20. It proved a small price to pay for a player of such skill.

A league championship, a Yorkshire Cup triumph and more visits to the Challenge Cup Final followed the signing of Batten, as the team, now in black and white and firmly settled in the Hessle Road community to the west of the city, embraced the new brand of fast-flowing rugby league football.

The present-day RFL is often criticised for its trigger-happy attitude towards trying new concepts and quickly abandoning them. Yet the Northern Union and the Northern Rugby Football League were not hesitant to alter the rules of the game. The code was built upon the idea of entertainment, and by the time Batten was showcasing his skills, the game's rules had long differed from rugby union. The removal of rucks, line-outs and flankers, leading to 13-a-side teams, were all intended to encourage the kind of spectacle Batten and his contemporaries could provide.

Batten eventually moved on to Wakefield for £350 in 1924 after notching 89 tries in 226 games. He was an overwhelming success, and he helped the FC club set their stall out as one of the more exciting sides in this fledgling sport.

Hull KR, entrenched in the east of the city, had also taken wonderfully to the new code, appearing in the 1905 Challenge Cup Final in a losing effort to Warrington. They then picked up championships in 1923 and 1925 as well as a Yorkshire Cup at the start and end of the 1920s. The club, nicknamed 'the Robins' due to their distinctive red and white-hooped shirts, had some wonderful players, particularly in the 1920s, like stalwart Gilbert Austin. The outside back made 346 appearances for KR and made his debut on the same day as Hull-born Frank Bielby, a rampaging back rower who retains a lasting place in fans' hearts.

Unfortunately for both sides, they then entered something of a barren spell. The 1930s and '40s saw neither pull up any trees as teams from Lancashire and in particular West Yorkshire dominated the Challenge Cup, although FC did pull off another Yorkshire League Championship victory in 1935. The whole of the 1940s saw neither side pick up any silverware, although it goes without saying that the events of the Second World War impacted not only on both Hull teams but organised sport across the board.

This is not to say that the teams during this time period lacked decent players, but, understandably, the disruption and shifting priorities caused by the war made rugby league no more than a fleeting concern. Hull, with its vast civilian fleet, was one of the most heavily-blitzed cities in the country, spending over 1,000 hours under bombardment. By the time the dust cleared, there were 1,200 civilians dead, 3,000 injured, and just under half the population, around 150,000 people, were left homeless. Many of the city's schools, churches, pubs and hospitals were destroyed. Hull could not take much more of war.

While rugby league was not a priority, it found its place as an escape. When the war did come to an end, people were keen to return to some form of normality, and FC could provide something like it: they returned to the finals in 1946, losing 10-0 to Wakefield at Headingley in the final of the Yorkshire Cup. The result was a disappointment, but it marked a return to competing at the sharp end of leagues and cups for an area accustomed to success.

This quest for continued success led to Hull FC signing, for over £1,000, the prolific centre Roy Francis in 1949. This would prove to be crucial both for the continued resurgence of FC and, in the decades to follow, the tactical progression of the 13-a-side code. On the field for FC, he was a classy addition, notching 61 tries in 130 games, but by 1954, after a spell captaining the side, he had more or less retired. He did make six more appearances over the next two seasons, but he focused more on his new role as team coach.

Francis did not seem like the type to bring about a revolution in the sport. He was not an immediate success in the professional code, after being signed by Wigan in 1936 from Welsh amateurs Brynmawr RUFC after only a handful of appearances in rugby union. He eventually moved on after three patchy seasons to Barrow as the war loomed into view. However, as was the norm during the war years for players, he 'guested' for Dewsbury. His talent truly blossomed under the management of another rugby league visionary, Eddie Waring.

The West Yorkshire side reached three consecutive championship cup finals, winning two, with Francis crossing for a try in all three games. His talent for contributing with scores in the biggest games was further evidenced with two tries in the 1942 Yorkshire Cup Final triumph over Huddersfield, in one of Dewsbury's most successful sides to date.

The story of Roy Francis has many similarities with that of Clive Sullivan, and his own life and career would intertwine with his fellow countryman. Roy overcame the stigma of switching from rugby union, the culture shock of moving from Wales to Yorkshire, and the issues of being a black man in pre- and post-war Britain. Francis and Sullivan also both had spells in the armed forces before making their marks on the game of rugby league and the city of Hull.

As the league teams recovered and regrouped following the war, so did the fishing industry. The city still maintained a major fishing fleet, which saw hundreds of boats coming in and out of the docks, providing if not affluence, at least a regular, secure source of income.

The Hessle Road community and that fishing fleet, already the main foundation of the FC club, helped to produce a further key part of the re-emergence of the team as a major force on the playing field.

In 1930, Reg Whiteley, unsurprisingly a trawlerman by trade, and his wife Clara had a son named Johnny Whiteley. The Hessle Road area, described by historian Alec Gill as 'the spinal cord of Hull's fishing community', was at its zenith at the time. The city had 250 trawlers by the time Whiteley was eight, as Icelandic fishing grounds had also long been added to the original North Sea hunting ground.

The bustling area, with numerous pubs and community shops such as bakeries and butchers, also contained the St. Andrew's fishing dock. The dock also provided work for those not going to sea. Its work, while not quite as perilous as a life at sea, was still tough, demanding work; with ships not spending much more than a day in the dock before heading back out.

'Bobbers', who landed the trawlers, generally began work at 2am, emptying the 'fish rooms' of on average around eight ships.

Jobs such as filleting, cleaning and restocking the vessels had to be done, and done quickly, to prevent any fish caught from spoiling and fish uncaught from being snapped up by rival fleets. This work was done almost round the clock in all weathers, with fillet knives freezing on dockside chopping blocks. When this happened, they froze so solidly that they had to be hammered free.

Once filleted, the fish would be then placed on trains which delivered them all over the country. The railways themselves were the biggest employers of people in the Hull fishing community; such was the size and scale of the operation and the volume of fish being brought ashore and transported up and down the UK. Academic and writer Brian Lavery points out, 'Hull had arguably the biggest fishing fleet on earth. Grimsby could argue but they didn't go as far as Hull.'

Yet as Lavery says, more so than almost any other trade, the whole fishing industry was extremely dangerous, 'Although it was a massive industry and made gigantic profits, it also exploited the men to an alarming degree. It's estimated that 6,000 men died in a century, that's one every week. Can you imagine if you had a factory where someone died every week? You'd have it shut down. They were running essentially a side winder fleet. As it suggests, you ship from the side of the boat. Which is fine in the North Sea. But when you go out into the really bad weather, it's difficult enough to keep your boat stable anyway.

'It was more difficult to fish those areas in those boats. Because of something like the silver cod trophy, which was won by the biggest haul of the year averaged out in the year, it encouraged skippers to take more risks. But skippers did want to come home as well. But there were skippers who'd take risks. As I said in my book, you get old skippers or bold skippers but you don't get old, bold skippers.'

* * * * *

The Hessle Road area, however, was still cramped and crowded. Whiteley grew up around the destruction of the war, as many of the homes and streets were bombed out and not all were rebuilt quickly. He quickly sought refuge in sport, although at first couldn't settle for his first choice of rugby league. The last key component of the Hessle Road community was now very much Hull FC's ground, the Boulevard, with its intimidating threepenny stand being home to the hard core supporters who jeered and heckled opposition fans and players. For a young man such as Whiteley, it was not hard to see why rugby league held such a high appeal.

However, Whiteley was forced to play soccer, turning out as a goalkeeper for the Fish Trades team as the Second World War also decimated the area's amateur and junior rugby league set-ups, which were either disbanded or offering irregular fixtures unsuitable for such an energetic and athletic young man as Whiteley.

Come 1946, however, the junior rugby was back up and running, and Whiteley was the stand-out operator of a clutch of brilliant talent for Hull boys clubs, a group of players who had been moulded playing unorganised street rugby, along with football and boxing. Whiteley himself was a proficient young boxer, but Hull boys club policy at the time required him to choose which sport to continue with, and rugby league was still his sporting passion.

Unsurprisingly, after leaving school at 14, Whiteley worked in the fishing trade, as a filleter on the docks, but a career in sport was his only focus. As he himself recalls, 'We had 28,000 people who were involved in the shipping industry in one way or another [in Hull.] All my cousins were skippers. My dad was a fisherman. Everyone around me was a fisherman. All I wanted to do was play rugby. And I fulfilled my destiny; I did what I wanted to do.'

Before he could achieve that, however, he served a spell in the army for his national service commitments, where he did get the opportunity to box a few more times.

That single-mindedness to make it in rugby league remained when he returned to the city. Once demobbed from the army, both Hull FC and Hull KR were after his signature, with Whiteley unsurprisingly choosing his beloved Black and Whites, appearing as a trialist in an 'A' team game against Huddersfield. Such was his evident talent, he signed permanently in December 1950 and made his first-team debut that same month against York.

It was the start of a near 20-year association with FC as he became the heart of a club regaining its confidence and chasing its prior glories.

An able centre, he was most effective out of loose forward, becoming the ultimate exponent of the art of a position, which blended the toughness and physicality of forward play and the creativity of stand off play.

While the role of a loose forward has now evolved in the modern game into that of an extra prop forward and metre maker, in Whiteley's time it fulfilled a different purpose. It was a link between the forwards and half back and stand off, a mixture of brain and brawn. Whiteley was an imposing physical presence and says his attitude to the game was, 'I wasn't a hard hitter; I used to think with my brain to get out of trouble.'

He can still eloquently describe the role as he performed it in Francis's 1950s Hull side. 'First of all, you looked after your scrum half, you got across him and defended him. You cover defended, the ball was played and you'd stick your head up and have a look. Your backs would move in and I would always get across the ball. I'd break; the second row would get behind me. If our winger got the ball, and got beat, then I'd be there to tackle the opposition winger into touch.

'Occasionally I'd pick the ball up to move everyone out one. From the tackle, I'd be first receiver. I had good hands, I was 6ft 2in and 15 and a half stone and I was quick. I used the ball to move people. I was a ball player. And the difference between a ball player and a player who thinks he's a ball player is the former can change his mind. If I say go through that gap and that gap closes, you don't get the ball. If I think I'm a ball player, then you're getting the ball if it closes or not. A ball player has all the time in the world. And if I thought I'd get someone into trouble, I'd absorb the tackle and we'd start again.'

Ultimately, Whiteley would find work as a brewery drayman rather than in the fishing fleets, his strength, fitness and professionalism had an enormous impact on rugby league both locally and nationally. Indeed, aside from his skills and game IQ, what so many spoke of when praising Whiteley was his incredible stamina. He was as fast and strong at 80 minutes as he was in the first. The drayman job may have played a major part in this, involving a serious amount of running and lifting, which supplemented his on-pitch training for FC.

This fitness and commitment to the cause led to him gelling superbly with Francis.

He said, 'I was his blue-eyed boy from day one, because I'd run up mountains. I was already an international when he came [and became coach.] Roy was a novice when he started. We signed a brand-new side on, really, as Roy came along. Train, train, train. That was my forte.

'I'd train every day. I'd been a PTI in the army, like Roy. He came out with all that knowledge he got in the army. And he'd push you. That was right up my street. We were two of a kind, but he was up 'ere [he held a flat hand above his chest and then lowered it to his thigh] and I was down 'ere. I've never met anyone like Roy Francis in my life. I've met every type of person but not one like Roy Francis. Colin Hutton, who coached Great Britain and a good side [Hull KR], we both together, unanimously, agreed there's never been another Roy Francis.'

Whiteley, who had been capped in 1954 for Great Britain, became captain of FC for the 1956 and '57 seasons as Francis's team really came together. The likes of Workington-born prop forward twins Bill and Jim Drake, talented second row Michael Scott and Welsh hooker Tommy Harris, along with Whiteley, built a fearsome and legendary reputation as a pack of forwards.

Yet, the side had plenty of skill, as full back Peter Bateson, centre Colin Hutton and prolific winger Ivor Watts feasted on the opportunities, the platform that pack created. Whiteley himself, while being a presence in the creation and prevention of tries, also proved prolific in scoring three pointers, the amount then awarded for a try. He never failed to score more than ten tries a season for ten years, his most impressive season being when he crossed for 22 in 1955/56. In total he bagged 156, placing him seventh on the all-time Hull FC try-scorers list. It's a phenomenal total for a forward in the era of muddy, heavy pitches, with an old-fashioned leather ball which would soak up the mud, sweat and water.

Unfortunately, the side didn't quite achieve its full potential, although they still challenged consistently for honours, never falling out of the top ten league placements for eight years.

They also reached nine cup finals in nine years, although only walked away victors in two of them. In 1956, Whiteley's most formidable year, they beat Halifax 10-9 at Maine Road in Manchester, Colin Hutton kicking a last-minute penalty to secure the league championship. Whiteley himself was praised for an all-action, disruptive performance against a quality Halifax team.

After losing a year later final against Oldham, they bounced back to win it in 1958. It was a complete performance against Workington with a 20-3 triumph. According to newspaper reports from the time, the writer's name unfortunately lost, the rugby and manner of victory was highly praised. 'The open-style, classical handling, which Roy Francis brought to the Boulevard, was too much for the bewildered Workington, whose vaunted defence crumbled gradually,' it was written.

Unsurprisingly, Francis was beginning to be linked with moves away from the team, with lucrative offers allegedly coming from the likes of Halifax and even Hull KR. He remained, however, and came close to adding more trophies to the cabinet.

The Challenge Cup, the Holy Grail for every rugby league player, was to elude them all, however. It was let slip as they lost consecutive finals in 1959 and 1960. First came Wigan, in a game they underperformed in, crashing to a 30-13 loss. The following year, a team badly ravaged by injury lost out 38-5 to Wakefield.

The 1959 season also saw the emergence of a rival to Bateson's full back spot in 20-year-old Arthur Keegan. Keegan was signed out of West Yorkshire's amateur rugby scene, originally hailing from Dewsbury, and would constantly compete with Bateson for the key position, as one would have a run of games before being replaced by his rival. Keegan was to provide a valuable link from the 1950s era into the '60s.

It's worth pointing out that during this era, the 'coach' did predominantly that, he coached the players on the training field, while a board of directors or the chairman would make final decisions on selection. Francis's innovative, professional fitness regimes and intelligent teasing out of a player's best qualities was well suited to this method to a certain extent. But, reading back over first-hand accounts of the period, there was clearly a degree of tension between Francis and the board, headed by Ernest Hardaker.

Fans of the period, as in modern-day sports, often held the coach accountable for all the losses and bad performances, rather than the board that would ultimately decide the 13 who would take to the field. This dynamic would prove to be difficult for the forward-thinking Francis as the seasons marched on and create serious issues for his eventual successor as the club and the city entered the 1960s.

While that glorious side of the '50s were growing old together, new players were recruited. One of the most exotic was a Tongan centre named Nan Halafihi, who would make his debut late in the 1959 season.

The club also signed a young stand off, locally born and bred Terry Devonshire. Devonshire would go on to play centre to Clive Sullivan, and the pair became firm friends off the field, Devonshire acting as Sullivan's best man. Devonshire's signing heralded the start of a new crop of young players making their way into the professional game who would go on to play major roles in the 1960s Hull FC side.

'I started playing rugby at school,' Devonshire, still lively and witty in older age, recalls. 'Then [I] played at Craven Street Youth Club. We won everything. Hull got in touch, when I was 17, asked me to go training with them. Craven Street had a cup final, before Hull vs Wigan [played at the Boulevard.] We got beat, 10-9. They kicked five goals and I got three tries. We were all sat at the side [afterwards] and Roy Francis came round and said, "Which one is Terry Devonshire?" He said, "See me after the match."'

Devonshire signed, and, in the first season of the new decade, David Doyle-Davidson, another player who would have a long association with the club, also joined as a junior. But the player who was to have one of the biggest impacts on both sides in Hull did not come from the most obvious of sources.

Clive Sullivan Arrives

BORN in Cardiff's Splott district on 9 April 1943 to Dorothy Sullivan, Clive Sullivan was the younger brother of Brian and the elder brother of Yvonne and Elmyra.

Being a single parent household, money was never particularly abundant, although the Sullivan home was by all accounts a settled and loving one, which helped all four children to prosper. Indeed, Splott was the kind of area described as 'respectable' working-class, in which a collective sense of community and self-preservation helped make up for a lack of finances. If this kind of community were based in the north of England then it would have invariably been a rugby league playing area. As it was, however, Wales had not only remained a rugby union region, but rugby union was the country's national sport.

As with children such as Johnny Whiteley and his Hull boys team, all the Sullivan siblings spent a great deal of time engaging in street games and sports, on and around the waste ground and cobbled streets of Splott. All four children proved prodigious runners – Brian in particular – and they were so proficient that they began racing competitively.

A local event, the Whit Festival, offered a solid amount of prize money for winners of certain short distance races, and, after Brian was deemed simply too good to compete, five-and-a-half-year-old Clive took his place. Despite being a year and a half younger than the rest of the field, Clive trounced them, and the money provided a welcome source of pocket money for the younger Sullivan brother.

While the age gap between the siblings led to varying degrees of importance given to racing, it was clear that all four siblings had a natural ability. The prize money often on offer, as well as the prestige and thrill of being crowned a winner, encouraged them to keep focused on and develop their running.

As with many sibling groups, they were all rivals yet also shared advice and tips on racing and running, and how to better make use of their gifts as sprinters.

The lack of any real facilities in the area could have perhaps provided a ceiling as the two brothers began to become more and more competitive, and looked to develop as athletes. As luck would have it, however, Dorothy was allocated a new house in the Ely district of Cardiff, in the south-west of the city.

The children moved schools, from the Moreland Road primary in Splott to the Herbert Thompson Secondary Modern. The boys arrived at a school that embraced and promoted sports already having built reputations as some of the city's elite youth runners.

Head of sport Peter Griffin, not surprisingly, was a keen advocate of the rugby union code, and quickly attempted to recruit the Sullivan brothers to the school's squads. While Clive was extremely slight, his speed was such it was still felt he could be an effective weapon for the team.

According to Joe Latus, Sullivan's biographer in the 1970s, Sullivan had apparently little knowledge of rugby union. This seems hard to believe due to the popularity and near omnipotence of the code in the area. Regardless of how familiar Clive was or wasn't, he excelled almost immediately. He felt it provided a more enjoyable experience than even running, due to the variety of skills required, the mental and physical toughness and the camaraderie of a team sport.

Brian also excelled, and captained the school team, although running remained his first love. After passing his 11-Plus exams Brian moved to a nearby grammar school, leaving the captaincy vacant. Despite not even being a teenager, Clive was promoted to fill it. Already, his leadership skills were becoming apparent. While much faster than almost all his teammates and opponents, Sullivan also showed promise kicking, passing, tackling and instigating planned moves, proving to be more than just an out and out winger. His versatility and reading of a game stood out for such a young man.

His talent led to him being selected for the prestigious Cardiff's schoolboys team alongside fellow future rugby league international

Colin Dixon, although Dixon was then a fleet-footed winger rather than the back row forward he would go on to become.

Sullivan and Dixon, however, only appeared once for the team, such was the competition for places, with the rugby union hotbed of Cardiff producing a conveyor belt of talent. Clive certainly can't be criticised for his sole appearance as he was fully embracing the life of a young rugby union player, obsessively training on his strength and fitness and working on his flaws with the ball. His desire to be as good as possible was already apparent and he was putting his all into making the most of his considerable natural abilities.

As would become a regular occurrence for Clive, his promise and momentum suffered an unfortunate setback. Exactly how he did it is unknown as Sullivan was such an obsessive trainer that pinpointing one occasion proved impossible. However, apparently on a training run and then in a following game, Sullivan felt an excruciatingly painful spasm in his thigh muscle. The pain did not subside after some days and he was X-rayed at hospital, discovering that, according to Latus, his muscle system had been 'badly strained'.

While this is a little vague, the injury was so severe that his whole leg had to be placed in plaster. The cause given was apparently that due to the still developing Sullivan placing so much strain on his body, with his non-stop commitment to training and playing rugby, it had been severely damaged.

While for someone of that age who was so active the injury was devastating, the news was to become even worse. After around six months in plaster, his leg had lost much of its muscularity and flexibility, and was noticeably smaller than his other leg. He was then informed he was unlikely to ever walk again unaided, let alone play sport to his previous ability, due to a combination of the injury and the treatment.

It goes without saying that for Clive this was a crushing blow. Coming towards the end of his school days, it does not seem a ridiculous suggestion that Clive had set his sights on at least making some money from his athletic prowess. While rugby union was still staunchly an amateur code, Billy Boston, another Welshman, had made a significant impact in the paid code of rugby league and attracted Clive's attention during appearances on TV, for Wigan's Challenge Cup games were broadcast nationally.

While joining the paid ranks of rugby league from a union background in England still held some serious social stigma, Boston was the latest in a lengthy line of Welsh players to 'move north', following on from the likes of Jim Sullivan and Gus Risman in the 1920s and '30s.

Tony Collins, writing in his book, *Rugby League in Twentieth Century Britain*, points out, 'The vast majority of Welsh players went North because they wanted to earn money from their rugby skills, in the same way their soccer and cricket playing compatriots could do ... the risk of injury and subsequent hardship, given that rugby union insurance schemes were extremely tightly policed, was also a powerful incentive to take the money and go North.'

While the majority of players who moved to play rugby league weren't as talented and iconic as Risman and Boston, Wales had proven a regular source of solid players who helped to supplement the home-grown players from Yorkshire, Lancashire and Cumbria as the game grew and developed. Clubs such as St Helens, admittedly not that far from North Wales, had employed scouts on very solid wages to operate around the area. It does not seem unlikely that Sullivan would have been on a few clubs' radars after a successful schools career, considering the constant need for new stars and squad players.

Instead of being considered for deals with professional league clubs, however, Sullivan was reduced to gingerly walking around the streets with a pronounced limp, and in a great deal of pain. How someone could go from such a high to such a low, at such an early age, from a somewhat vague and unexplained injury is hard to fathom, especially when the career prospects for Clive had been significantly reduced.

Unlike Brian, who had excelled academically, Clive's sole purpose and aim was rugby for most of his childhood and teens, and the loss of that led to him finding employment at a nearby mechanics.

The injury caused Clive to completely abandon any interest in rugby and even recreational exercise. Even as a spectator, Clive greatly disliked attending or watching any rugby during this period, only reminding him of what he had lost. This carried on for almost a year, at a time when a young sportsman such as Clive should be growing physically and perfecting his ability, perhaps even landing a few professional trials.

The Sullivan family tried to rehabilitate Clive physically, and indeed, mentally, encouraging him to go on long walks to build the muscle in his leg back up. The hope also remained that the apathy that had also understandably developed could be in part eradicated. The walking slowly began to bring back some of that old confidence and love for activity.

Clive eventually began playing for the work's football team, although only as a goalkeeper due to his continued inability to run. According to Latus, Sullivan spent most of games exercising and moving his leg rather than paying a great deal of attention to the action at the other end of the pitch, although he showed some ability when he was called upon, his handling skills with a rugby ball coming into good use.

This renewed form of competitiveness, along with the walking and occasional gym sessions he'd begun to attempt had made Clive confident enough to begin running again. While these trial runs were a far cry from the displays of speed and power he had exhibited for most of his young life, it is a mark of his determination and mental strength that he persisted with his training despite being told they would do little good and get him any closer to returning to rugby.

Instead, he slowly felt the green shoots of recovery. Eventually he felt physically fit enough to try to enlist in the army, following in the footsteps of Brian, who had decided to join the Royal Air Force rather than go to university.

Unsurprisingly, Clive was also successful in his application, even being encouraged to enrol in the more prestigious position as a radio operator rather than being a driver as he originally intended. Despite that, his leg had still not been fully tested and there was some doubt both in the household and by Clive himself that it could stand up to the rigours of army training.

But, before that had even really started, he was asked to play in an inter-corps rugby union match within his first few days, it being assumed, correctly, that as he was from Cardiff he would be proficient at the game. He was stationed at Catterick, North Yorkshire, and it was felt by the higher ups that it would prove both a bonding experience as well as a means of identifying players talented enough to represent the forces on a wider scale.

The British armed forces have always had an active and prestigious sporting heritage, with rugby union being one of the jewels in its crown. Even inter-corps, boxing tournaments, rugby union and soccer are a source of huge pride for those picked to represent their unit.

The game proved to be a catalyst for not only Clive's rugby league career but his life as a whole. Latus breathlessly describes it, 'Clive saw the ball coming down to him as though it was fitted with a homing device ... It dropped into his waiting hands, he made an automatic side step ... and he was off down the touchline like a shot.'

Latus explained that Sullivan was so emotional at realising he had regained his ability to play rugby again he openly wept after scoring the try, such was his relief and joy. While Clive throughout his life was not known to be overly emotional, when it came to rugby and his own performances, they were a source of incredible anxiety and relief, so this outpouring of emotion seems plausible.

After overcoming such an injury, Sullivan threw himself back into rugby training and army life, becoming a mainstay of the regiment's team while also enrolling on elite paratrooper training, as much to improve his strength and conditioning as to progress his forces career.

Paratrooper training was, and still is, one of the most demanding physical and mental courses that the British armed forces can provide. Yet it is entirely in keeping with what would become to define Clive as both a person and as a rugby league player; the constant need and desire to test himself and to come out on top, and the need to challenge himself both physically and emotionally, and to overcome almost any obstacle put in his place.

Unsurprisingly, he was successful in his training and received the famous 'red beret', only awarded to those applicants who make it through the gruelling selection process.

The gruelling life of a serving paratrooper, however, was ultimately to be a short-lived one for Clive, who was continuing to play rugby union. Professionalism awaited.

The Airlie Bird Catches the Worm

THE exact details of Clive's transition to professional rugby league are somewhat mysterious and muddied. Perhaps this was intentional by all involved, as in the 1960s the 'crime' of playing rugby league was still punished severely by rugby union authorities. Players who signed professional deals and moved north became pariahs in the rugby union community. They would never be welcomed back into the fold; many ex-professional league players were even banned from entering rugby union clubs when they had retired.

In areas such as Wales, where union thrived, the local club could often be the hub of a community and the loss of that link could have a severe impact on an ex-player.

Scouts, of course, have always been somewhat hesitant to share the tricks of their trade. In a profession where being the most in the know and the best connected is vital, secrecy is paramount. Rugby league scouts, and the clubs they worked for, would be competing against each other as well as the rugby union authorities to secure the next Billy Boston.

Roger Mills's 1969 film, *The Game That Got Away,* goes some way to shedding some light on the practices of rugby league scouts and the practice of recruiting out of Wales. Mills describes a 'fifth column' of rugby league scouts who have 'infiltrated Welsh rugby union'.

The film involves an interview with Billy Wood and Ken Broom of Wigan, described as 'experts in invading rugby union territory'. The pair, with a mischievous glint in their eyes, describe, 'going on several pitches, ostensibly to look for autographs' but in fact to get players they wanted to sign, address and contact details, after which, it's 'pure business'.

'It's usually a working-class type of fella, that, shall I say, takes the bait or makes the right decision ... the only people we leave along are the people who have been to Oxford and Cambridge, we haven't got a chance of getting these boys,' they tell Mills.

Sullivan, according to his own and Latus's account, was approached by an unnamed scout 'accidentally on purpose' to ask if he fancied giving the 13-man code a crack, after a run of more excellent and exciting performances for the army side.

The team in question he was asked to try out for was Bradford Northern, a historic club in one of West Yorkshire's biggest cities. Despite that, Bradford Northern had largely been unsuccessful on the field for almost a decade, a trophy-laden late 1940s giving way to barren 1950s. Indeed, the on-pitch malaise had resulted in an off-pitch crisis with money issues being a continued source of worry for the club's supporters.

It had resulted in a vicious cycle of underperformance on the pitch, which resulted in further financial issues. Indeed, in the 1959/60 season, around the time when Sullivan guested for the team, they would finish the season 26th out of 30 with only Liverpool, Dewsbury, Blackpool and Doncaster beneath them. And, it must be pointed out, neither Blackpool nor Liverpool were hotbeds of rugby league at the time. They were in desperate need of some fresh blood and an injection of pace and flare.

Perhaps Sullivan, the slight Welsh teenager, could provide it?

The 'A' game took place at Odsal, which while not perhaps the most picturesque of stadiums, is a vast and intimidating environment. Even in 2017 it still holds the British record attendance for a rugby league game, 102,000 for the 1954 Challenge Cup Final. Its vast, amphitheatre-like design often leads to it developing a microclimate, with mists of fog drifting over it in winter and the sun beating down on its exposed stands in summer. It also leads to the atmosphere created by supporters to echo around it, before escaping up into the West Yorkshire air.

'A' team games at the time were, while clearly not held to be as important as first team fixtures, still of relevance. In the modern game, academy, reserve, or 'alliance' fixtures are normally watched by only a few hardcore fans, if any. Most clubs may post a fleeting match report on their website or a Twitter update. Yet for much of the 20th century, 'A' games were given extensive local newspaper match reports. If a first team were playing their next fixture away, then fans eager to catch some entertainment would instead support the 'A' team. The 'A' teams of the 1960s, and indeed '70s and '80s, tended to be a mixture of those too young or too old to feature in first-team rugby. The older players could help the youngsters, generally around 17 or 18, to learn the trade, while the next generation could help provide the stamina and running.

Fixtures also provided an opportunity for established players returning from knocks to get a run-out, away from the pressures and intensity of first-team rugby. It led to some eclectic teams and fans often got to spot an exciting new talent a year or two before a first team appearance, or to see old favourites exhibit some of the old magic. Alan Smith, the prolific Leeds and Great Britain winger whose career almost paralleled Clive's over 20 years, has some fond memories of 'A' team rugby.

'It was for players coming back from injury, a stepping-stone back into first team rugby,' he said. 'Plus, junior players, senior players. If you wanted to get into the "A" team you had to play bloody well in the "A" team.'

The 'A' team game for Clive, however, was not a success. It featured very little of Clive, who was ignored by his teammates, barely touching the ball and not having any opportunity to showcase his elusive running. Indeed, according to Rosalyn Sullivan, Clive was told at the final whistle, 'Come back when you learn to play rugby,' such was the negligible impact he had.

It looked likely that, after overcoming so much to gain an opportunity as a professional athlete, his chance would come and go. Leaving Odsal to head back to Catterick, Sullivan was resigned to not doing enough to earn a deal.

Bradford Northern would soon find themselves in dire straits as well. Odsal, which had less than a decade earlier smashed an attendance record, only had 324 people inside it as Bradford played Barrow in a first-team fixture. The gate receipts were an abysmal £30, and the club went bankrupt with most of the existing squad being released. Had Clive done enough to earn a deal after his trial, he may have found himself without a contract not long after anyway, although Northern did quickly reform after their demise.

The financial pressures on the game were not resigned for Bradford, either. The game, as it entered the 1960s, was beginning to see a significant decline in regular fixture games, its aggregate attendances halving from the '50s. This was partly blamed on the start of television coverage, which was quickly embraced by RFL chairman Bill Fallowfield, and quickly opposed by many clubs.

It was not the best environment for Clive as he continued to search out new opportunities to play rugby professionally.

* * * * *

As Clive's story develops, one thing that comes up time and again is his terrible luck. However, his second chance in rugby league was extremely good fortune. Johnny Whiteley, still one of the main men for FC in the early '60s, remembers the circumstances when Sullivan came to Hull's attention.

He said, 'It all revolved round me, how it came to be [him signing] ... I was a member of Hull's boys club. One of our players became a rugby league linesman and touch judge [Jimmy Harker]. He was promoted from junior rugby to "A" team football as a touch judge. It was at Odsal. Jimmy had told me, "I was at this game, and there was this black lad on the wing. He looked quite promising.

"Just by chance, the referees got into a taxi to go to the station, and he [Clive] happened to be stood at the bus stop in his army uniform. So, we stopped and gave him a lift. They got chatting and I asked where he was from, and Clive said he was a paratrooper. He was catching the train back to the barracks." So, Jimmy said, "What have Bradford done with you?" Clive said, "They haven't done anything, haven't said anything to me." So, Jimmy said, "I think you're all right. I'll see if I can get you at Hull."'

Exactly what happened next is somewhat of a mystery as two contradictory stories are told. In Whiteley's telling, 'Jimmy rang Hull up that week and they got him up.'

The Latus account is much more dramatic. Apparently, Roy Francis penned a letter to the young Welshman in the hopes of persuading him to attend another trial at the Boulevard, which would have been an extremely enticing offer, Hull not long removed from their glorious late '50s period. Unfortunately, Clive was away training. This meant relocating from Catterick to Farnborough, in Hampshire, almost the other end of England. With Harker having passed on Clive's former address, Francis's letter was sent and not received for some time.

By the time Sullivan did receive it, such time had elapsed that he felt the offer would have long gone, especially as he would have to travel over 200 miles to take up the opportunity. Curiously for a man so renowned for his politeness, Latus suggests Clive did not respond to the letter at all, feeling it would be a waste of both his and Hull's time.

Despite receiving no reply, however, Hull had been taken by the enthusiastic endorsement provided by Harker and wrote again, this letter finding its way to Clive in a much quicker fashion. Having a weekend of leave he was free to take up the offer and made the long trip up to Hull.

Regardless of exactly how long it took for FC to get to him and by what methods, the start of a long association was about to begin.

Hull FC for some time had relied upon the reliably fleet-footed service of Watts on one of their wings. Watts was also a Welshman, born in the Rhondda Valley in 1924, although predominantly raised in Cumberland.

A talented schoolboy soccer player who was on the verge of joining Workington, then a decent outfit on the verge of graduating from non-league football, Watts instead was persuaded to join Hull after also impressing as a rugby player. He broke into the first team almost from first signing on, making his debut in a 10-8 victory at the Boulevard against Batley in 1945, and he was a mainstay of the squad until 1959 when he was moved into a player-assistant coach role to support mentor Roy Francis.

Although predominantly a winger, Watts did make a decent centre as well and was prolific, racking up 19 tries in the 1952/53 season. By 1961, however, Watts had retired from on-pitch appearances.

This lack of depth on the wings suggests why Hull were so keen to attract Clive, as the team were lacking that outlet of pace and finishing which has always been a crucial part of rugby league. While Sullivan was expected to simply trial for the club and hopefully be good enough,

Hull were also attempting to secure the transfer of South African Wilf 'the Flying Dentist' Rosenberg from Leeds.

Only the season prior, the former rugby union international had bagged 48 tries for Leeds as they won their long-awaited first championship and his elusive running style was in great demand on the Humber. He had cost Leeds £6,000 in 1960 in a deal brokered by Rosenberg's Rabbi father. Wilf had proved an effective and dangerous centre for the South African rugby union team, making five appearances over three years. Rosenberg was part of a glut of South Africans who appeared in the British game in the late 1950s until the mid-'60s, the most famous being St Helens's clinical Tom van Vollenhoven, who scored 59 tries during the same season that Rosenberg scored his 44.

While a tremendous success in rugby league, Rosenberg was badly injured against Hunslet in 1961 when his jaw was broken. His place in the side lost, he was allowed to begin negotiating with Hull following his recovery, with FC eventually paying £5,000 for the South African. The deal took some tying up but FC completed the signing of Rosenberg as Clive was heading to Hull for his trial.

Clive was set for an initial six-month trial with the club while they assessed if he had what it took, and he was meant to make his debut in an 'A' team game against Halifax A but the match fell through, depriving Sullivan of his first run-out. It was therefore decided that he would be thrust straight into the first team.

After only one performance for Bradford's 'A' team, Clive was to make his full first-team debut before officially signing for a club, against Bramley at the Boulevard, on 9 December 1961.

He did have one opportunity to train with the side before that fateful afternoon. As Devonshire recalls, 'I was a bit nippy then. I was an off half [stand off] but I was playing particularly on the wing at that time. They told me I'd been dropped for this trialist. They were trying to show him some moves and he couldn't get it right. Roy said, "Terry, show him how to do it." So, I did it a few times without fail, and Clive would drop it. I was thinking, "He's useless, him."'

Despite the performance in training, Clive was still picked, and it was decided that Whiteley would be moved over to the left centre to support him. Although one of the best loose forwards ever, Whiteley had also been a quality centre, spending part of the 1951/52 season in that role. Whiteley still remembers Sullivan's debut well to this day.

He said, 'I'd played centre a few times so they asked me if I'd play centre to him. So, I played left centre against Bramley. Lo and behold the first time he got the ball, he went 60-odd yards, down the best stand side, with blistering pace. He absolutely looked the part. He brought the crowd to their feet. And again, 15 to 20 minutes later, he did the same thing. The crowd erupted [at] this little black boy, because he wasn't a big lad, was Clive.

'So, at half-time, we were winning quite comfortably, they swapped me with Dick Gemmell to see how he'd do without me.'

The swap worked out as Whiteley, described by reporter Mike Ackroyd for the *Hull Daily Mail* as showing 'hard running and accurate passes', also sent in Rosenberg for a try.

Gemmell, formerly a junior at Warrington amateur club Orford Tannery, had only been in the side for a season himself and was showing great promise.

'On the opposite wing was Wilf, who was a South African, when apartheid was pretty strong. But Wilf was a wonderful lad and they [he and Clive] got on very well together,' Whiteley recalls of the two new wingmen's relationship.

Appearing under the name 'A.N Other' and 'Mr X' in newspaper reports due to still being a trialist and still technically a rugby union player, Sullivan crossed again in the second half to achieve a debut hat-trick in a 29-9 victory. Rosenberg, on the other wing, also crossed for another in a 'feast of spectacular wing play' according to Ackroyd. Ackroyd even went as far as to describe Sullivan as 'in the Billy Boston mould', high praise indeed, although rather inaccurate, as Boston and Sullivan as players were almost polar opposites.

'He scored three spectacular tries that afternoon,' Devonshire remembers, his eyes lighting up thinking back to the game. 'I think that's why he took to me [his help before the match]. After the game, I went up to him and said well done and congratulated him.'

Again, conflicting reports of exactly what happened following the final whistle exist. In Latus's version, the rush was on to secure Clive to a permanent contract. Rumours had already begun as the final whistle blew that Halifax were also going to offer Sullivan a deal after such an impressive run-out. This, admits Latus, may have been simply the result of a rumour started by an overly anxious supporter. Either way, it reflects that rugby league was very much a cut-throat business when it came to new talent. Scouts were constantly in crowds to examine rival players and trialists who could be snatched away from a club at the last moment.

This story is corroborated to a certain extent by writer David Bond. Bond states that Colin Dixon, Clive's former Welsh schoolboys teammate (now at Halifax of all places), had spotted Sullivan at Halifax for the abandoned 'A' team game, and informed his club that the talented former schoolboy player was in the region. It doesn't seem far-fetched then to conclude that scouts from the West Yorkshire club may have attended Hull vs Bramley to catch glimpses of a potential recruit on Dixon's recommendation.

Latus states that concerned chairman Alf Smith sent some club officials to retrieve Clive from the hotel Hull had provided, and to move him to another, secret location to prevent any possible poachers from reaching him with an offer. Clearly wires were crossed as coach Roy Francis had already done the same thing, taking Clive back to his home. For some hours, however, it was assumed by the Hull board that their new winger had left the city and signed for a rival.

Whiteley again has a slightly different recollection of how the day panned out, 'At half-time, the chairman came up to me and said, "For goodness sake, grab hold of Clive. And don't let anybody get to him, because we want a word with him." As soon as the game ended, I did that and said "no interviews until you come and see the chairman". So, I directed him into the room, it was his first time ever at the Boulevard, [I] held his hand, so to speak, and left him there. Anyway, a long time after, after we had all begun to leave, the chairman came in and said we've signed Clive. And there was a big cheer, and we welcomed him.'

Regardless of exactly how and where the deal was eventually agreed, his permanent signing was announced the next day, 10 December 1961. While many in the game were aware the club had secured a gem following his impressive debut, it was unlikely that anyone could have predicted the immense impact Clive was to have.

It's worth pointing out, however, that Clive was still a serving paratrooper, and had some time to run on his contract. While rugby league was a 'professional' game, almost every player also had another job, a regular source of income. Clive working wasn't an issue, but being based at Catterick was. Despite that, using weekends off, he did manage to continue to make appearances as Hull's mediocre 1961/62 season played out.

'Obviously, he went straight into the first team,' remembers Whiteley. 'He was sensational. He was a natural athlete. I was captain. I took sort of responsibility for him in training, and we became friends. Really good friends. I sort of looked after him.'

He made 17 appearances in all, and still managed to bag 13 tries, a brilliant return for a relative novice in the sport. At only 19, Clive had burst on to the scene and made the most his chance to become a professional sportsman. He was helped to settle by Francis, as well as captain and club icon Whiteley, as the shy yet charming winger settled in.

Rosalyn Sullivan informed me, 'Roy took Clive under his wing. I didn't know Clive then, [but] he stayed with the Francis family. His wife was really good to Clive.'

Devonshire visited the Francis family and the Sullivan's regularly, as the two's friendship was further cemented. He said, 'Roy had Havershank in Beverley, [it was] like a pub. We used to go down on a Sunday morning. Clive lived there with Frankie Broadhurst [another young player]. I think Dick Gemmell lived there as well.'

Sullivan and Devonshire quickly gained a reputation for playing pranks on teammates and lifting morale in the camp and around the club.

Devonshire revealed, 'Nan Halafihi, he couldn't speak English very well. Roy had a pub called Cross Keys in Beverley. On the way back on the bus, Clive and me were sat with Nan. He lived down in Beverley. We tried to get him to say, "What do you want, lads?" So, we went in the pub and Roy was behind the bar. Clive said, "Roy, guess what Nan can say." And Nan said, "What do you want, lads?" And we all shouted "pint of bitter please!" He had about eight to buy! After that he'd never say it [again.]'

Nan Halafihi and his extended family also regularly socialised and partook in additional training with Sullivan, Devonshire and Francis.

Devonshire continued, 'Nan was a lovely lad. He had a brother called Johnny Halafihi who was a boxer, the commonwealth champion [Johnny

Halafihi failed twice in fights for the Commonwealth belt, a prestigious title]. They always had us as the café; Roy had a ring up there [above the café]. I saw Clive with the gloves on. Johnny sparred with us all.'

While it was a successful debut season for Clive on a personal level, the club was not doing too greatly. For the first time in 30 years, Hull KR finished above FC.

Rugby league has had a long and still largely unresolved relationship with relegation, and while it wasn't an issue for them in the 1961 season, the downward slide of results and performances was to have dire consequences in the seasons to follow.

The malaise wasn't consigned just to on pitch either. A loss of nearly £4,000 was also announced despite the sale of Jim Drake, one of the cornerstones of the success of the '50s, for £8,000 pounds to KR. Twin Bill remained at the club for the time being, but Jim had a great deal of utility value and experience, as he had the ability to slot into most of the forward positions when asked. The loss of such an experienced talent who had appeared for England, Great Britain and Cumberland was a big blow for the side, as the famous team of the '50s began to fragment.

While Clive was a high point of the season, the agreement of him being a serving soldier and pro rugby league player was unsustainable moving forward. Hull had unearthed a winger who seemed to be a natural try scorer, but also a winger with the athletic prowess and desire to involve himself with the team, on and off the field. He was able to help the team defensively and contribute to moves, and he and Rosenberg had the potential to be one of the most potent wing pairs in the league.

Similarly, Clive, in perhaps a more round-about manner than he intended, had achieved his dream of becoming a professional sportsman. He would still have to work while signed for Hull, but being based so far away in such a relatively inflexible job would only stem his development and prevent Hull from fully utilising his skills, a reliable source of frustration for an individual so driven to train and improve.

The army did help where they could, allowing whenever possible for Clive to travel to Hull on a Friday to play over the weekend. However, Clive was informed he would not be able to buy out his contract with the forces, which still had three years left to run.

The irony of rugby league is, for most of its history, while a 'professional game', it has only ever been part time. The game provided a nice supplementary income for its players, but it was unsustainable as a means of earning a living full-time. Injury, poor form, work commitments, a new signing or simply the whims of the selectors could deprive you of income.

As Terry Devonshire recalls, 'I signed for £25, 50 quid after I played six first-team games. Another 50 quid after I played another six first-team games. So, I played the first six and got my first 50 quid. Then I played another five and they dropped me for so long. I was playing well, and I was like, "What they dropped me for?" But eventually someone got injured and I was a regular then.'

Following the culmination of the season, Clive was sent to Greece along with his unit as part of a NATO exercise. While the exercise lasted only a couple of weeks, his unit stayed for almost all of Hull's off-season. Not being able to train regularly with the team had a dramatic impact on Sullivan, and he was injured badly in his first appearance of the 1962/63 season, against Workington Town. Clive had gained a considerable amount of weight while away with NATO, due to inactivity and plentiful servings at the base, and the extra weight certainly seemed to contribute to causing him to be injured.

Clive had already missed the first 12 of the team's 44 games that season, and this match was to have an even more damaging impact on his ability to contribute.

A last-ditch tackle by a Town defender in the game led to an awkward landing for Clive, who damaged ligaments in his left knee. He did still manage to cross for two tries in a 25-25 draw but eventually he was in such pain that he had to be carried from the field, a worrying sight for his growing number of admirers in the Boulevard stands.

Clive was to make a much quicker than expected recovery from the injury, which set the tone for much of the rest of his playing days. He would receive countless unlucky injuries but would recover well. Despite making 352 appearances for Hull FC over his two spells, a figure that makes him one of their most regularly capped players, he is not among the top six who have made long runs of consecutive appearances for the club.

Indeed, not long after returning from his first knee injury, it gave way again, resulting in a second operation. All told, 1962/63 was a poor season for Clive, as he only made nine appearances, although, typically, he still crossed for six tries.

Rather uniquely, his older brother, Brian, who had by then developed into an elite-level sprinter, replaced him in the team. He was signed after impressing on trial and scoring a try in an 'A' team game against Hull KR A in April 1963, and made his debut against Huddersfield.

'Reputed to be faster than his brother Clive,' according to the *Hull Daily Mail*, he was a solid addition to the squad. Unlike Clive, however, who was noted for his fearlessness both in attack and defence, Brian was more an out-and-out winger, rarely venturing infield. He would, however, help further settle Clive at the club and in the area as Brian also eventually enrolled at Hull University, putting down further roots.

The signing of Brian did, however, put Keith Barnwell's nose out of joint and he asked for a transfer. Behind both Sullivans and Rosenberg, teenager Barnwell seemed unlikely to get a solid run. A black Briton like the Sullivans, Barnwell also had supreme pace, but question marks over his handling and positional play had seen him out of favour.

Overall, the 1963 season marked a nadir for the club as they were relegated, having only picked up four wins and finished bottom. Relegation was introduced at first on a three-year 'trial' basis, the idea being that it would produce more competitive rugby across the two divisions. It would also reduce the sheer volume of fixtures, which in a winter sport with frozen pitches could create terrible logistical issues. Indeed, January of 1963 saw five weeks of fixtures scrapped due to the worst winter for 13 years, causing a fixture congestion that forced the RFL to extend the season until June.

The decline of a generation of experienced and ultra-talented players all at once proved too big an obstacle to overcome for FC. The young players breaking into the side were talented, but in the 'take no prisoners' world of rugby league, it was a big learning curve.

The side did badly need that fresh blood, ultimately, and Clive could hopefully provide that if he could stay fit and be regularly available for selection. But as a winger, he would also need a good platform to be laid on by the side's playmakers, which in turn relied on the forward pack. It would be a major reconstruction effort.

The off-season provided an opportunity to grasp that opportunity to rebuild, both personally for Clive and the club. Clive worked hard, and gained a level of fitness and sharpness that would come to define his time in the sport. Never a huge drinker either, a recreational activity still a major part of rugby league to this day, he was ready to mature into the athlete and sportsman he had shown glimpses of.

This new dedication immediately proved effective as after seven games he had crossed seven times in the new season. As usual with Clive, however, things would not go to plan.

Dicing With Death

HULL, very much a team in transition, had a least found a regular and reliable source of points on their left flank. Clive had already contributed 21 points as the 1963/64 season was in its early stages. A renewed dedication to getting fit and healthy during the off-season had evidently had wonderful results.

Clive had further good news. He was to be released from his army contract at Christmas time after the club bought it out, allowing him to move to Hull full time and find work that would blend better with the life of a professional rugby league player. '[Hull] ended up buying him out,' remembers young hooker Alan McGlone, who was soon to become one of Clive's friends and teammates. 'He was still going to the barracks when I signed on. I don't know what was involved money wise, but it went on most of that season. Eventually he came out.'

Yet Sullivan's bad luck continued. The *Hull Daily Mail* of 14 October 1963 reported, 'Clive Sullivan breaks shoulder, out for months'. The report went on to mention, 'The 20-year-old coloured boy ... was in a road accident in a blackspot in Marshfield, Gloustershire.'

Travelling with some other paratroopers, the car apparently spun off the road and hit a pub, the Lord Nelson. His injuries proved to be even worse than first reported, as he also broke three ribs and badly damaged one of his lungs. It was at first feared he might not even survive. A regular run in the side was the least of both Clive and the club's worries as he recovered in Bath hospital. After overcoming the initial shock and trauma, it then appeared likely that it would be a long road back from the injury to be able to play the game ever again.

More unwelcome news would arrive for the whole of the Hull club. Roy Francis left, taking the remaining Drake twin, Jim, with him, the pair signing for Leeds RLFC. The man who had done so much to turn Hull into a regular force in the 1950s had decided to take the opportunity presented at Headingley.

Francis also paid Hull £7,500 for Dick Gemmell in January 1964, as the young centre was increasingly showing the potential to be a talented international-calibre operator. Gemmell had been angling for a move for some time, telling the press that Hull were not 'go-ahead' enough for him. Hull had first set a price of £10,000, a huge amount of money for a talented yet still young player. A frustrated Gemmell then stated in the press, 'I thought there was a law against extortion.' Eventually, the deal was tied up.

'The reason Roy went was that side [had all but] disbanded,' remembers Whiteley. 'We all got old and got past the 30-odd mark, the Drakes, Mick Scott. Harry Markham had died. Tommy Harris [hooker] was still going well. Roy was a shrewd cookie. Leeds came and offered him, whatever they offered him, which would be lucrative. And he just packed up and left, and gave me his whistle.'

Francis was reported at the time as saying, 'It's difficult to be leaving Hull, to be making breaks with people I've known for 14 years,' but he added, 'The Leeds offer was too good to refuse and would give him great opportunities.'

Leeds were something of a sleeping giant at the time having occasionally challenged for honours but waiting 90 years for a league title, from their formation in 1870 until finally winning the prize in the 1960/61 season. That team had also begun to fragment, and needed rebuilding, just like Hull.

Yet Leeds regularly attracted big-name players, paying big money to do so. Perhaps, in Francis's eyes, he would have rather rebuilt with a bigger budget than at Hull, which while far from frugal, didn't have the money Leeds could provide to mould a new side.

Headingley was also one of the best stadiums in the league and Francis himself pointed out, '[the] facilities from top to bottom are such that everything is there for a good job to be done.' The club had even paid £10,000 to install undersoil heating in a bid to prevent any more winters from causing fixture cancellations.

Reading between the lines of reports at the time, it also seems that Leeds were eager to hand almost complete control over the Francis, who for so long had selected his team with the help of the board at Hull. Francis was, according to the press, the 'footballing power' at Leeds, taking complete control of coaching and training and working with the 'football manager' Joe Warham. Warham had also undertaken an extensive young recruitment drive that was beginning to bear fruit in Leeds's 'A' team.

Alan Smith, who was involved with Leeds at the time, can vividly remember the impact Roy had, 'Leeds had won the title in '61, in '62, lots had moved on, retired. There was a big gap. Joe Warham was the scout and kind of the coach. Roy came and revolutionised the game. The first thing that happened was, everyone was given a pair of [running spikes]. We were trained like athletes. Like track and field athletes. From that point, he brought in older players to nurture the younger players like me and John [Atkinson, another prolific winger].

'He was a very clever man [was Roy]. He was years ahead of his time. Other clubs would come watch Leeds train. It was hard work, relentless. Sprint, sprint, sprint. He brought the Yorkshire sprint champion down one day and a couple of our lads beat him. That's how fast we were. Everyone was quick, and fit. We'd win a lot of the games in the last 30 minutes.'

Devonshire, still a youngster at the time, was aware of the impact Francis had had and would continue to have throughout the game. '[He] was a coach beyond his years. Years later, coaches were doing what he was doing. He got that big pack [at Hull in the '50s.] He turned them into a well-drilled machine. He was brilliant.'

Whiteley was indeed named the new player-coach, an obvious choice considering his standing at the club. It was also a long-held ambition of Whiteley to take over the managerial reigns. Francis had long seen 'Gentleman' John, as he was nicknamed due to his clean style of play and warm and friendly personality, as his successor.

Whiteley had already been made Francis's official assistant in the months prior to Roy's exit to Leeds. It was a move in part to keep Whiteley out of the clutches of Featherstone and Oldham, who, as reported in the *Hull Daily Mail* at the time, had considered Whiteley for their head coaching roles. It highlights the esteem Whiteley was held in by his peers, that, still a player and untested as a coach, he was already in demand across the game.

To add to the ease of transition from player to coach for Whiteley, he had also suffered a bad Achilles injury the previous season, ruling him out for some time when it came to playing. At the age of 34, while still a superb player when fully fit, this was the perfect time for him to step into his mentor's shoes and begin the badly needed rebuilding job. The *Hull Daily Mail* did, however, dampen any immediate expectations of a return to the glory years, pointing out, 'Whiteley faces a task every bit as big as that which confronted Francis when he took over.'

The side's rapid transformation continued with more players coming and going. Stan Cowan, a Scottish-born winger who had featured regularly for the club in the 1950s, including in the championship final against Oldham and the Challenge Cup against Wakefield, was let go at the age of 32. Alan McGlone, a hooker from East Hull amateurs, was snapped up. Like Whiteley, he had learned the game as much on the streets as on a field, as he revealed, 'You learn your rugby in the streets. British bulldogs, from lamppost to lamppost. You learn that ability to beat people, to side step.'

Second rower Jim Neale was also signed from Whitehaven. Neale was already an established first-grade player but still had plenty of years left in the tank, vital for the back row, often described as the 'engine room' of teams.

Neale would prove to be a favourite of his teammates but he was underrated by spectators. Devonshire, as a centre, would often play alongside Neale in attack and defence.

Devonshire said, 'A player's player was Jimmy Neale. He wasn't recognised, as he should have been. A second row forward, hard as nails. You could be getting beat 30-0 at Wigan and he'd be saying, give me that ball, give me that ball! Frank Foster who played for Hull KR, he told me once, if he had to pick a combined team between Hull FC and Hull KR, he'd pick Jimmy Neale. And that's come from another tough forward. He'd take a clout rather than give you the ball.'

McGlone, who played in the pack with Neale, also spoke highly of him, 'Jimmy Neale was someone who'd be the first one on the team sheet, because of his work rate. He'd always be there for you, especially if you got into a brawl!'

Despite the new additions, Clive was still seen as one of the side's key weapons. McGlone still remembers the aura around Clive at the time he first signed on, 'The thing that impressed me was he had this big car. After training we'd all jump in that, seven or eight of us in the back. I was 18 years old when I was signing for Hull. Everyone knew us by his car.

'I got my signing-on fee and I got a Ford Prefect. I got one of the lads to go with me for it; I'd never driven before. I pulled up alongside Sully's big car in my Ford Prefect [at the training ground].'

Derek Davis, a stand off, was signed from Leeds, as were prop Brian Rowe and winger Geoff Stocks from Huddersfield. Chris Davidson, another stand off and only 17, was also quickly promoted from the club's 'A' side after some impressive displays.

Clive made a much quicker recovery than anyone could have anticipated. He was back training with the side within two months and was deemed fit enough to feature in the last three games of the season. It's testament to his dedication that yet another injury, with potential to be life-altering, was overcome so quickly with the minimum of fuss.

He was badly needed as Terry Devonshire was the team's top try-scorer with 12. Wilf Rosenberg only crossed nine times before departing the country and the game to return to South Africa, unsurprisingly to open a dental practice. Brian Sullivan managed six, and despite the injuries and disruption, Clive still finished with seven.

In comparison, players such as John Stopford at Swinton scored 45 tries alone that year, highlighting Hull's lack of strike power when Clive was absent.

Despite the lack of cutting edge, the team began to take shape as a young and vibrant group mostly hailing from around Hull. Terry Devonshire, Clive and Brian Sullivan, and David Doyle Davidson, all had skill and pace in the outside backs, and despite being young, all had first-team experience.

Hull's ability, when in the right mood, to play exhilarating rugby was highlighted by a 34-10 win over Doncaster at the Boulevard on 7 September. With Clive on the left wing and Brian on the right, the *Hull Daily Mail* loudly hailed the 'flying Sullivans'. Clive got the second hat-trick of his career, while Brian crossed for two.

Reporter Mick Ackroyd reckoned that 'the number of tries coming from the wingers is a tribute to the attractive brand of rugby Hull are serving up at the moment' and admired the 'high speed attacking'. It came in a purple patch for the Sullivans as Clive had notched nine in four games and Brian had added nine in six. Both brothers thrived on the dryer pitches found at the beginning and ends of the season.

'Sully would have been twice the player he was if he played in summer,' recalls McGlone. 'On a dry ground! Sometimes you'd ring up and say, is the game on or not? With loads of snow and a frozen ground. And they'd say yeah, we are going to put a bit of straw on it. The ground would be solid, hard. The supporters would come and help clear it. You'd have no skin on your knees or your elbows.

'With thick mud, you couldn't see how good people like Clive could be. He'd come into his own around spring. He'd have been like Jason Robinson [the rugby league and rugby union winger].'

Added to this impressive back line, Keegan was also able to act as a reliable goal kicker having fully dislodged Peter Bateson from the full back spot, offering plenty of first-team experience while chiming into the line of attack, as well as Devonshire, who aligned excellent passing to his turn of pace.

Davies and Davidson could hopefully provide some direction and playmaking in the middle of the park. Jim Neale would go on to be the under workhorse of an emerging young pack which would come together in the coming years. And McGlone would be the tough foil from hooker.

Whiteley was evidently excited to be working with a clutch of new talent, telling the press at the time that the club had a 'splendid set of youngsters ... our youth policy is correct'. Whiteley was, however, still registered as a player, and still made the odd appearance, pointing out, 'It is essential to have some experienced players in the team.'

Fully fit and with a new coach and a new side around him, the opportunity was there for Clive to finally begin to fulfil his undoubted potential.

Meeting Rosalyn

CLIVE was permanently living in Hull following his discharge from the parachute regiment. Now that Roy had left, Whiteley fully embraced and looked after the two Sullivan brothers. 'The pair of them were wonderful, they were gentlemen,' said Whiteley. 'They were wonderful lads. I don't say that silly, I don't say that because we are talking about a story. They were good kids. By this stage, Roy had left and taken over Leeds. I became player-coach, so then I was responsible.

'We used to go down to Costello, the running track, and run him on there. I was working until 1pm on New Year's Day, and I took him to the Powderhall sprinting in Scotland, as it was his desire to run. I picked him up at about 4pm. I drove him all the way to Scotland for him to race.

'But from playing rugby, the Powderhall sprints were a different dimension. It had Olympic sprinters in it. I mean he ran well, but being a rugby sprinter and a Commonwealth sprinter, it's a different field. We had a good day. And the year after, we took his brother, Brian. I'd say Brian was half a yard quicker than Clive, and bigger, but he didn't have that same certain urgency as a professional athlete.'

Newspaper reports from the time state that Clive failed to reach the final of the 120-yard handicap event, although Keith Davies, a winger for Workington, managed to finish fifth in the final.

Sullivan had also quickly bonded with Devonshire, and the pair would visit the clubs and pubs together around the city.

It was on one of these occasions that Clive would first meet Rosalyn, a young woman from the nearby village of Welton, the second eldest of seven children. Rosalyn can still remember their first meeting.

She said, 'I left school when I was 16. I went to go work at Hawker Siddeley, which became British Aerospace. All my friends used to meet at Feriberry, at a big pub called the Duke of Cumberland. I used to go to dances at Brough [another nearby village]. [That was] where the Aces played; they were *the* group. We grew up with live music, not records. When we heard they were playing at the Duke of Cumberland, the landlord knew us. I was only 17, and he let us come in. There are only so many bitter lemons you can drink [at that age], so we took sweets!

'That's how I met Clive, he reached over and pinched one. He asked to see me the next night. That was July time. Everyone knew everyone in Welton.

'You didn't see any black people. I thought everyone's going to know. We went to Bridlington [together] to see the Aces who were playing again. On the way back, he said, "I want to marry you." I thought, "This is just a big joke." I said, "Don't be daft." But we continued to see each other. And I thought, "I'll have to tell my mother."'

Rosalyn, via Clive, was introduced to a group of young black men living in the city.

She continued, 'He was living with his brother [when he met me] down Glen Cole Street. Of course, he got to know the other black people [in Hull]. Keith Barnwell [Hull FC winger]; Jack Whitehill [an amateur boxer] whose wife was white [as well]; Stuart George, he became a roadie for David Bowie, he was a fisherman. It's funny; the black people in Hull all seemed to know each other.'

It's hard in 2017 to fully understand the pressures than a young mixed race couple would feel, although it wasn't a completely unique sight in early 1960s Hull.

Rosalyn said, 'I didn't know how they'd react. Because I don't think I'd ever heard any prejudice, but it wasn't the usual state of affairs. I'm going back to 1964. I told her [Rosalyn's mother]. But living opposite us was an Indian lady who had married someone in the army. They had two boys. I said, "I've met this guy and he's coloured." She said, "How dark is he?" I said, "A bit like Warren and Keith [the neighbours]." It hadn't really registered. She said, "I think it's better we meet him."

'My sister wouldn't have been a year old, as we were really spread out. [Clive] showed up with his white shirt, suit and best tie. As it happened my parents had been called for a meeting at the local club. And my mum was saying, "We aren't going out because of you." I was flustered. My sisters were all agog. He got his jacket off, he got his tie off, and got sat down. When my parents got back he was quite comfortable and they spoke … Clive was polite and a gentleman. At the time, I don't know if my dad was that approving.

'When you go back to the '60s in America, [white and black people] they were still segregated. I think being in a small village, I didn't have a problem at all. I don't think we'd ever come across [racism], and it wasn't discussed.

'But I knew I was only a nine-day wonder. I was talking to a lady last week, who was black [about how it can feel]. You can walk into a pub or anywhere, and you can feel the disapproval kind of thing. It creeps upon you. You can feel the disapproval. But he was well accepted. I had no idea who he was in regards to rugby. He was just a nice guy. He was easy to get on with. He had shyness about him. He had a lovely winning smile. We had similar backgrounds and we got on.'

Rugby league players are not all household names even in 2017, and in the 1960s, while both Hull clubs had passionate and loyal support, the players were not well known to everyone in the area. Rosalyn herself had very little knowledge of the sport or how well Clive was doing within the game.

Rosalyn said, 'As time went on, he said he played rugby. I was just like, yeah. A couple of guys meeting on a Sunday. My dad belonged to a club and a couple of the fellas there knew. And they'd say, "She's going out with Clive Sullivan, isn't she?" I think that made it easier for my dad.'

Along with his personal life, Clive's on-pitch career truly began to take off. Typical of rugby league, the two divisions, relegation and promotion concept was already scrapped; so Hull FC were now back in the top (and only) division in English rugby league. The clubs had voted unanimously to return to one, large division, after clubs saw huge drop offs in gate receipts. It deprived the game of many of its 'marquee' games, such as Hull FC and Hull KR, which would be guaranteed to add a few extra supporters on to gates, eager to see local pride played for as much as league placings. The new merged league contained an incredible 30 teams, and 'split' into a top 16 and a bottom 14 halfway into the season.

The sport also embraced substitutions although, unlike today's rolling replacements, a team was only allowed one for injuries during the first half of a game. While they could not offer the coach a tactical option as is available now, it could at least prevent sides from being forced to play a man down if a player was badly injured.

Clive encouraged Rosalyn to attend one of the games at the Boulevard, as their relationship continued to progress. She remembered, 'I said, "I'll be okay in my jeans won't I?" He said, "Oh, no. People get all dressed up." I went, and that was when I realised it wasn't just a game in the park. People were coming up and asking for his autograph. We walked through this players' entrance, and that was kind of an awakening.'

Rosalyn continued to go to watch games at the Boulevard and understand the unique culture and flavour of the supporters, 'You knew your core supporters. I never sat in the threepenny stand. But apparently, they were the WAGs [in that stand]. They used to taunt the players. Clive used to have words with them. When he started out, he was just an out and out winger; he'd wait for the ball. He used to get bad circulation in his hands and his feet. He said he'd almost be crying when he'd get back in the changing rooms, with heat ache. The forwards, they would be heavy muddy pitches and it would be forward driven in those conditions.

'We continued going out and he got injured one time and he didn't turn up. I eventually found out, he was in hospital; he'd had an operation. What they'd do was make a special appointment and they'd go in. That was the start of realising how dangerous this sport was.'

The injury was to his shoulder and, along with another leg problem, quickly curtailed what had been an excellent season. Sullivan had run in 18 tries in 26 games, missing eight matches in total.

The shoulder injury was the result of an unlucky knock in a game but the issues with both legs were clearly ongoing and would need to be solved sooner rather than later, particularly for a player whose key attribute was raw pace.

Still, Whiteley and his young side still had immense promise, and Whiteley became a father figure for the likes of Sullivan, Devonshire and McGlone.

It was something that Whiteley completely embraced, 'Lads of that quality, and me being a boss, they were like sons to me. All them little things, like me giving him a lift home and taking [Clive] to the running track, you become a part of each other.

'As a young coach, to have someone the quality of Clive [was an asset].'

Cars were still relatively rare at the time, and Whiteley became an unofficial chauffeur for the young players both in their personal and professional lives, 'When Clive and Rosalyn started courting, I took them everywhere in the car. So, I had a little interlock with him.'

Also in 1964 came the signing of Mick Harrison, an imposing young prop who quickly became a key part of the Hull side and Clive's social circle.

'I didn't start until about [the age of] 11 or 12,' Harrison, still physically imposing even in his older age, remembers about his start in the game.

'Then I went to fish trades down the Boulevard. They had boxing and rugby. I played for them for a year then Yorkshire with people like Johnny Maloney.

Then Whiteley took me off the park, and signed me on. I got £100 in my hand to start with. Then £150 after 12 games. Then another £150 when I played for Yorkshire. £150 if you played for Great Britain. But when you got that badge, you felt like one of the team. Keegan had one. Whiteley had one.'

Earning a badge was a huge source of pride for Hull born and FC supporting lads, such as Devonshire, 'If you played 12 first-1team games, you'd get a badge. And then you had to buy the blazer to put it on. You had to earn it.'

Running out at the Boulevard was a transformative experience for the players. Harrison, like all his teammates including Clive, worked steady jobs around the training and playing.

'The jobs I got weren't very good. But the gaffers were big Hull supporters, so they'd say, "Look Mick, get off." They were crap jobs, but I had time off to play rugby, which was what I wanted. It was hard working around the rugby ... [but] with us being local kids, to play for Hull was a big deal.

'It was two lives. You worked, and then you put the jersey on. It was like a different person. You were heroes when you put that black and white jersey on.'

Clive's two lives were taking shape. He had the ability and desire to succeed in a youthful team, and he was now in a committed relationship. But rugby league in the 1960s was not for the faint-hearted and it would test him to the limit.

Beauty and Brutality

SAY 'rugby league in the 1960s' to some people and they may think of the novel and black and white film adaptation, *This Sporting Life*. The film was released in 1963 and depicts the glamour, violence and money of a star rugby league player in a West Yorkshire town. Or, as protagonist Frank Machin, played by Richard Harris says, 'We don't have stars, that's soccer ... it has people like me.'

Machin is a miner and fights, literally, to make money and get away from his humdrum life. The overarching story is a melodramatic 'love story' but Machin is portrayed as an uncouth brute who only really excels at inflicting and withstanding violence on the field. The film's scenes of fast-paced, brutal action, in the thick mud in front of huge, baying crowds, is one of the most vividly portrayed examples of sport ever seen on screen.

For some, it may have seemed that the production over-exaggerated the violence, and the uneasy mixture of bleakness and glamour. But rugby league in Clive's early career was a 'take no prisoners' game.

Mick Harrison, in the age of contested scrums, was in the heart of the brutality straight from the off. Youth and inexperience was not a reason to avoid punishment. As Harrison recalls, his first season was a baptism of fire.

He said, 'Every game was hard ... when I was a kid, I think I had a broken nose for the first season. I was thinking "this is easy", then *bang*, welcome to rugby league. But, you soon learned. You'd break their noses [back] ... Dennis Hartley, who played for Cas [Castleford]. When I first played, he stitched me a few times. But, I learned a lot off him. They used to call him "The Vicar", I think. He'd bang you, then bless you and say sorry.'

The same goes for McGlone, who was given an immediate, rude awakening to the game. He recalls, 'My first away game was at Warrington. There was this old prop Charlie Winstead, he was as wide as he was tall. I kept picking him out because I had a bit of a side step off my right leg, I could go one way and make a break. He had a flat nose, and he was saying, "You're making me look bad," and I was sticking fingers up at him.

'One time I stepped him and he stuck his arm out, and he caught me with his arm. It was like a cricket bat had hit me. I woke up in Warrington hospital 17 hours later, with the physio George Stevens. The bus had gone home without me. We got a train back the next teatime. I was saying, all I saw was black.

'Then, the next game, Bill Drake was getting changed, he was like a legend. He was putting like a hardwood bat on his forearm and bandaging it. I thought, that's what hit me! That's what hit me! It was like the shape of half a boomerang, smooth. If you caught someone in the head, even accidentally, you could break your forearm if you didn't have an arm protector. Stiff-arming was still a part of the game in those days.

'I was an apprentice boilermaker, so I went straight in the shop and got one made. That was your baptism, but it went out the game and they banned it. But it was tough to say the least.'

The Hull players gave as good as they got. Harrison quickly set his stall out as a pack leader and enforcer for the young side. For talents such as Clive to shine, one side's pack of forwards had to get on top, and in the 1960s, that was not a job for the faint-hearted.

Devonshire recalls of Harrison, 'Mike used to be a good tackler; he'd hit them across the chest, not head. We used to say after Mick hit them, "Do you think he'll get back up?"'

This aggressive style was, if not encouraged, given a wide berth by the referees of the time.

'The referees were all right,' Devonshire says. 'You could get on with them. [Referee] Eric Clay sent me off, and I'd scored a couple of tries. And he was saying, nice try Terry. Then Bob Hay hit me so I kicked him. Daft really because we were mates. I heard, "Devonshire, off!"

'On another occasion Mick got punched and said to the ref Billy Thompson, "Don't send him off; let me get him back." So, he did, and the ref said, "Okay, now 1-1."'

McGlone, at the heart of the contested scrums, also gave plenty of punishment.

He said, 'It was a war of attrition. It was brutal. The rules allowed that. Being a hooker it was six forwards against me. Throwing stiff-arms, or grabbing handfuls of mud and putting it in your eyes. It was always tit for tat. I'd drop them; let them know they couldn't get away with it.

'Off the field, I didn't have a bad bone in my body, but on the pitch, I was a different person. I had six people going to any methods to stop me getting that ball. And trying to do it without the referee seeing. I got sent off seven times in my career.'

The Boulevard, with its intimidating threepenny stand, provided a crucial weapon against opposition teams.

'You'd be playing and the threepenny stand would tell you who'd give you a clout,' remembers Devonshire, who had flourished in the left centre spot, placing him near the touchline and the stands. 'I got hit hard once and I got up, shook my head, I had to show them I could take it. And I heard them shout "number four, Terry, number four". And I looked at him and he was about 6ft 3in, and I said, "You sure it wasn't number five?"'

This chorus from the stands, while helping the home team, also caused opposition players and even officials to suffer torrents of abuse which even Harrison, in the thick of the action in the centre of the park, could pick up on. He said, 'It was very intimidating the threepenny stand. You used to see the wingers edging in nearer and nearer infield, because there wasn't much distance to the crowd. Even the linesman had to look at the stand to see if they could put the flag up.'

McGlone has similarly glowing memories of his time playing in front of the Boulevard, although its galvanising effect sometimes backfired. 'It was fantastic. On a Christmas Day, there'd be 18,000 people, for years you'd play on Christmas Day or Boxing Day. They'd sit out of the stands, right along the touchline. And some of the comments, the fishermen, the Hessle Road people.

'You think you wouldn't hear it but you do. And it was so humorous. I remember Billy Boston breaking down the wing in front of that threepenny stand. I thought, "Billy Boston, I'll knock him in that stand." And you're full of yourself, and I went across full pelt, and he dipped his shoulder, and he goes in under the sticks and I've got a dislocated shoulder. He was like a bull, people used to bounce off him.'

Despite the abuse and claustrophobic nature of the Boulevard, it was somewhere which Alan Smith, out on the wing so an easy target for abuse, enjoyed playing, 'The Boulevard was just something else; the crowd make it. So close to the ground. So close they could breathe on you.

'The highlight of the season was playing at Hull. The threepenny stand, they used to shout [at me], "You ugly, flat-faced bastard." You had to be on your toes. I always had a good game against Hull and Hull KR, because you knew. If you showed any sign of fear and apprehension, they'd soon find you out. But there was a great deal of mutual respect and we'd [the players] all have a beer afterwards.'

While the Boulevard was seen as one of the toughest grounds to visit, many of the other grounds could produce rowdy and volatile crowds.

'I remember a night game at Hunslet, it was muddy and sloppy,' remembers McGlone. 'You couldn't pass the ball. There was scrapping and scrapping. Me, Jim and Geoff Gunney [Hunslet prop] all got sent off for fighting. It was pissing it down. As we went round the stand, this brolly came down and cracked me on the head, split it open. Jimmy grabbed the person by the scruff of the neck, was about to hit them, then realised it was a woman!'

All the players quickly developed favourite, and least favourite away grounds, and McGlone continued, 'My favourite grounds were Headingley and Wakefield. I always seemed to play well there. I didn't like Dewsbury and Batley. Batley, it was uphill, and it'd get worse in the second half! I had one old woman follow me round at Dewsbury [shouting abuse]. Bramley, you had to go through a pub and get changed in a loft!'

Harrison likewise had grounds he used to hate turning out at, 'My worse was Odsal, you'd have to start at the top and walk down through the crowd. You got some right stick ... It was a long walk that.'

While this paints a picture of a game based purely on aggression on pitch and intimidation from the stands, it was also a game featuring athleticism, speed, and skill. Clive, now firmly established on the left wing, was the perfect embodiment of that, mixing both elements into an increasingly impressive whole. Devonshire was often called into action when Clive, desperate to be involved and desperate to get hold of the ball, would go looking for it.

Devonshire revealed, 'He was quick on the field. I was an off half, but in my latter years I went centre to Clive. He'd say, "I'm going Terry, cover me." That meant he was fed up on the wing and went looking for the ball. So, I'd cover if the opposition got the ball. He couldn't stay still in one position.'

Even Harrison recognised Clive's ability to carry the ball with power and aggression infield, 'He was a strong lad. When he played, he'd come in and he was like a forward, he'd bang them down.'

McGlone, at hooker, often would link up with Clive as he drifted infield, 'Sully was a workhorse. He was one of the first to come in [from the wing for the ball], as a hooker I'd invite him in. It's only come into rugby league recently, to give forwards a rest. He was doing that in the 1960s. He had a massive heart. He wasn't scared of anything. He had determination, the will, and a lot of natural ability. You can't be a superstar like he was in his day without having natural ability. Some people can push on to play internationally but people like Clive just have that extra ability.'

In Clive's day, it was much more of a rarity to see a winger willing to do a forward's job, getting stuck into the midfield rucks. Smith, making regular appearances on the wing for Leeds, remembers how the role was utilised by his team, 'You can't compare the game with the game today. Sometimes you'd come inside [from your wing], sometimes in moves. But it was always stay on your wing, and stay deep. We had a certain remit that we could roam, but if you got caught leaving your wing free and got caught out, people would have a polite word with you.

'As a young kid, I was always told that … when you play in a good team, like me, John and Clive, we all had a bit of a different style. We always played at about 12 and a half stone. That was deemed to be reasonably big for wingers then. Bigger wingers were Roy Mathias [who played for St Helens], they were 14 and a half stone. That was big then. Some would want to run through you. Some people wanted to run round you.'

Clive was almost certainly in the latter. 'Billy Boston was always about power, and strength,' remembers McGlone. 'Solid. Massive thighs, really hard to stop. Sully was like a ballerina; Billy was pure, brute strength. Sully was a weaver and had a swerve, and he'd go round someone with ease. It wasn't a side step, taking them the wrong way; it was the speed and swerve.'

Clive was rapidly gaining a good reputation across the game for punching above his weight in attack and defence. And it was not just from his teammates, according to Harrison, 'Clive was a hard tackler, he ran hard. Everything he did was hard. But he wasn't dirty. He was so well respected all over the game. And you had to earn respect them.'

Yet he was also gaining respect and admiration for his ability to cross the try line. Rosalyn, was getting to know Clive more and learn the ins and outs of a complex character in an often-complex game. She believes that the thrill of finishing tries also created Clive's tenacious style of play and desire to get hold of the ball, 'I've spoken to musicians and they say they get something back from the applause. You're a type of entertainer as well as a sportsman. And being a winger and a finisher. It's not like that now, they are a uniform size.

'You had your big forwards, your little half backs, slightly bigger centres and your streamline wingers; they were sprinters, more or less. Clive was naturally quite muscular. But there was nothing on him.'

The physicality and brutality on display at grounds across Yorkshire, Lancashire and Cumbria did, however, offer a respite from the own realities of the spectators' often-tough lives. I once spoke to the director of the national mining museum, an ex-amateur rugby league player himself, and he told me that the game offered a release from the pressures, stresses and strains of working life, especially in tough professions and mining and trawling, both for players and spectators alike.

'Sometimes we'd play Featherstone Rovers,' Devonshire told me. 'We'd play them on a Saturday afternoon. They were mostly miners. They'd have gone in, just had time to swill their faces. So, they'd have black all over themselves apart from on the eyes. They were hard as nails, big lads. It made them look more intimidating.'

In Hull, trawling was still very much a way of life, and Hull FC was still the focus of their attention while back on dry land. Writers Alec Gill and Anthony Clavane have both likened the trawler men to cowboys or frontiersmen, striking out across the lawless ocean, 'hunting' for catches, and desperate to land the hauls required to pay their bills. Indeed, many trawlermen actively embraced this comparison, dressing flamboyantly in suits with wide bell-bottomed trousers or jeans and flannel shirts while home.

The city also had a booming trade in second-hand paperbacks, telling stories of cowboys out on the open ranges of the United States. Sailors would buy a handful to take with them on the way out for a three-week trip, devour them all then sell them on to men heading out as they returned, or enterprising children who would sell them from rowing boats.

Hull FC, seen as the trawlermen's team, was also synonymous with the song 'Old Faithful', sang by the crowds at the Boulevard. The song was first sung by country star and 'cowboy' Gene Autry in the '30s, and was first sung in recognition of one of FC's earliest stars, Joe Oliver. Oliver was a long servant to the club and was a consistent and prolific try-scorer and goal-kicker.

The song stuck around with its lyrics, about a cowboy and his trusty horse riding the range, facing up to 'every kind of weather', and 'carrying me back to the one I love', understandably ringing true to men accustomed to facing extreme situations out on the unforgiving ocean. The 'love', it could be argued, was Hull FC, rather than families left behind, such was the devotion shown to the club.

'They were the big supporters [fishermen] on Hessle Road,' remembers Rosalyn, who was not from a fishing family, having come from a village more inland. 'I wasn't part of that, living in a village. They seemed very different to me. They were a tight-knit community. It's probably why they liked rugby, because it was hard. They were men ... When I lived in Welton, a lot of skippers lived out there. They wore bell-bottomed trousers and they were very superstitious. They wouldn't do washing on the day they went.'

The men, when on shore leave, were referred to as 'three-day millionaires' with a pocket full of pay and a desire to make up for lost time, which was noticed by Rosalyn, 'They were a breed apart ... They used to book a taxi when they get home, they'd go from pub to pub to pub.'

Harrison, who regularly shared a drink with the fans in pubs and clubs, remembers their generosity, both with the players and their support in the stands, 'They were good with their money. They'd buy everyone a beer then be skint. But that's the way it was ... They never had much, but the fishermen once told me they got a taxi to Workington [to watch Hull FC play Workington Town].'

The trawlermen, and indeed the other supporters around Hessle Road, regularly saw the players out and about, which further cemented the bond between player and fan. While it's hard to believe it, even the intimidating Harrison was given stick directly to his face if they felt he was underperforming, 'We had to [drink with the supporters]. You took the pats on the back and the criticisms ... We had to live with them. They'd tell you you'd played badly. That's how it was in that day.'

As the 1964/65 season also saw a resumption of regular hostilities with Hull KR, it gave an opportunity for some of the FC players to celebrate in the east of the city, which offered a terrific opportunity for the mischievous Devonshire and his accomplice, Clive.

Devonshire remembered, 'If we beat Hull KR, we'd all go drinking down the road. Rub their noses in it. They'd say, "You bastards, we knew you'd be down." Mostly it was a friendly rivalry. It was mainly banter, but some people took it really seriously.'

Despite, or perhaps because of, this intense support and familiarity with the support base, pre-match nerves were a major issue for all the players. This wasn't simply due to their youth and relative inexperience as the likes of Devonshire, Sullivan and Harrison had to contend with them for almost every game throughout their careers.

'Everyone gets nervous,' Harrison told me. 'I used to sit there and yawn all the time. Some people would wear lucky socks. Go out in the same order in a line.'

The nerves and pressures resulted in everyone on the team having a quirk or mannerism that would be a hallmark of their preparations, according to Devonshire.

'Jim Heald would always get sick. Wilf Rosenberg would pull his shorts and move his arms [in a warm up fashion].'

Regardless of the nerves in the dressing room and Clive's continued injury woes, he ultimately was still the club's top try-scorer for the first time in his career with his 18 putting him well ahead of any of his teammates.

The young side also fared well back in the enlarged First Division, finishing the season in 13th place. This meant that they could qualify for the play-offs when the division split into two and the top 16 competed to see who would be champion. Unfortunately for Hull, however, they came up short, losing 15-9 against a good Wakefield side despite a valiant effort.

A Clear Run – Finally

AFTER such impressive form in 1964/65, albeit a season interrupted by more injuries, the test was if Clive could maintain his impressive strike rate in 1965/66. All told, since his debut in 1961/62, Clive had only made 59 appearances, but with 44 tries already to his name his ability was not in question. What was in question, however, was his ability to appear consistently. His talent was worth nothing if he was sat in the stands rather than being out on the field.

The midpoint of the decade also marked some upturn for the game in Hull. Arthur Keegan, such an effective and vocal full back, still young but captaining the side well, was selected for Great Britain's Ashes tour to Australia. Although Australia won the series 2-1, Keegan was the side's main goal kicker, kicking five in two games before being replaced for the final Test. While the series did not go the way he would have intended, the experience was vital in adding an extra layer of knowledge and experience for Hull FC.

While Hull were not challenging for honours at the time, it does highlight that the international selectors would consider a player who stood out even in a mediocre side. The 1966 tourists featured players from 17 different clubs and were managed by Jack Errock of Oldham, representing an 18th club, showing the wide pool of talent the selectors had to choose from. Alongside Errock was 'co-manager' Wilf Spaven, who was the director at Hull KR.

John Maloney, a centre and an excellent goal kicker, was also added to the squad from Dewsbury, and would notch 267 points from kicks, taking over from Keegan. In Maloney, Hull had one of the best centres in the division, crucial for helping wingers gain opportunities to finish.

The partnership quickly proved effective for Clive as he was soon having the best season of his life with 23 tries in 36 appearances an excellent return. Eight of those came at home and away against Batley, where he scored every type of try imaginable; close-to-the-line efforts showing strength and poise, supporting efforts off teammates' breaks highlighting his poacher's instinct, and scores from within his own half which left Batley for dead, exhibiting his speed and natural skill. Both performances garnered glowing headlines, highlighting his 'superb' wing play.

Johnny Whiteley was also signed to a new five-year contract. Although he had taken over fully from Francis immediately, Whiteley's previous contract, which still had a year to run, designated him as the 'assistant coach'. Local press reported, as Whiteley signed his deal, that '[he] had been considering a move into the lucrative rugby league sphere in Australia and had talked over the possibility with Hull officials' but that 'most of all, he wanted to stay at the Boulevard'.

Remarkably, the contract still designated him as a 'player-coach'. Now 36, it was almost unheard of for players to still turn out at that age, although it was pointed out 'his appearances are expected to be limited'.

While FC had a solid season, across the city, Hull KR pulled off something of a masterstroke by signing the diminutive half back Roger Millward from Castleford for £6,000. Millward had been a superb junior player, well-known throughout the game as a player of immense promise. Castleford, however, had an established and talented half back pair of Keith Hepworth and Alan Hardisty.

Millward's game time was limited to filling in for the injured pair or making appearances on the wing, where the 5ft 4in Millward's vision and passing ability was wasted. So, in the summer of 1966, KR chairman Wilf Spaven brought him in, with the hope that Millward would be the final piece of a carefully assembled team. Millward scored on his debut at Craven Park against Batley in a 28-6 win and rarely looked back.

KR had also renewed their lease on the ground, giving them stability to go with a quality team. Aside from Millward, they also had such talents as full back and goal kicker Cyril Kellett, and back rower Frank Foster, a £6,000 signing from Workington.

Foster in particular proved to be a success, a player renowned for his toughness. Local legends sprang up around Frank. He had apparently knocked out a bull on an East Yorkshire farm with one punch, and would challenge all his dockworker friends to fight him en masse to see if they could knock him down.

To top it off, Hull KR also had an exciting young 6ft, 15st back rower called Phil Lowe pressing to gain first-team action. He would be well suited to the increasingly sped-up play of the balls and set moves.

While Hull FC, despite Clive and plenty more talents, only finished ninth in 1966, KR were fast becoming one of the sport's emerging forces. They won a Yorkshire Cup that year at Headingley by beating Featherstone 25-12 with Millward orchestrating from midfield. Roger Pugh, the Hull KR historian, describes the performance on that day as 'a mixture of excellent teamwork, classy football and tough defence'.

The RFL had introduced the 'four tackle rule', and KR quickly adapted to the restrictions, often spreading the ball out wide via Millward to catch out teams accustomed to a slower, more traditional brand of rugby. They also finished second to Leeds in the league table, their highest placing for a generation. They scored 178 tries, a record for the club, with wingers Chris Young and Mick Blackmore showing terrific form.

Millward and his KR team became a repeated thorn in FC's side. 'One of the best players I'd seen was Roger Millward,' recalls McGlone.

'He had everything. When we used to play derby games against them, we used to think if we can stop him, we can win. It was always my job to take him out. No chance. I could never get near him. He was too quick, too clever. A hard little bugger as well. As much as I tried, he was too good, too brilliant for me to get near him.'

Devonshire, however, felt FC could shackle the little general, due to the nature of the contests, 'He [Millward] was never brilliant against Hull as both teams seemed to block each other out.'

While Hull KR had begun to produce the goods on the field and FC were inconsistent, Clive, Whiteley and his teammates had created a great atmosphere. One of the after-training challenges Clive laid down was who could beat him in a race, even when they had a head start.

'The backs, although they had pace, Terry Devonshire thought he had a bit of speed,' McGlone told me. 'Over 50 yards, a short distance, he had. Terry was always the joker in the pack. He'd say he'd beat Sully. No friggin' chance! We used to have two bob, half-pound bets; Sully would give us a start, like, a 15-metres start. You'd think you were going to do it then he'd be past you and ten metres in front ... That was always part of training all that banter. It'd be from under sticks to the opposite sticks.'

Clive, Mick Harrison and Alan McGlone were all also picked for a Great Britain under-24 squad in November 1966, which played France in Bayonne, a port city in the south.

'I remembered it was my first time on a plane,' McGlone recalls. 'I roomed with Mick Harrison and Clive roomed with Alan Burwell [of Hull KR]. It was an experience. It was a lot of rivalry, with international teams. It was more a slogging match than a game of rugby. It was brutal. We actually got beat. I got picked to play the return game, at Oldham. This was a Wednesday night match, and Johnny Whiteley was going to take me. But we played on the Saturday and I tore my stomach muscles down one side, right from top to bottom. So, I missed that.'

Clive also didn't feature in the return, but his form in 1966 had clearly attracted the attention of the RFL. 1967 was to see the Australians head over to the UK for another Ashes series, and, after a disappointing series Down Under, Britain were desperate to pick up a win.

While Clive's 23 tries marked him out as a winger of class and poise, Len Killeen of St Helens (32), Trevor Lake of Wigan (32), Bill Burgess of Barrow (25), and Geoff Wriglesworth of Leeds (25) all scored more that season. Ron Cowan of Leeds ran in 23, although Leeds and St Helens were top-four teams – Barrow and Wigan actually finished below Hull – so it couldn't be argued that Burgess and Lake were simply in better teams who gave them better opportunities.

The pressure was on for Clive to make the selectors have little choice but to choose him. It looked likely that he might need to do it without the home comforts Brian supplied him, as his brother looked likely to move on. He had already requested a transfer midway through the season as his first-team appearances had becoming increasingly limited. Dewsbury were rumoured to be interested in the older Sullivan, the chairman Mr Bailey remarking that 'a fast winger could change us into a dangerous side'. With Hull requesting around £4,000, a significant sum in 1966, the deal never materialised.

The dynamic between the two brothers, who had pushed each other so much when growing up, must have been fascinating around this period. Brian, usually seen as quicker, was not seen as being the same standard of player as Clive. Yet Brian, while eager to leave to play regularly, would still have been around the club, willing to step into the void should Clive become injured again or lose form.

Breakthrough and Breakdown

FRANCE is seen these days as a rugby union hotbed. Yet the 13-man code has always had a stubborn, loyal following in the country. Despite being banned in the country under the Vichy government during the Second World War, the sport had quickly bounced back.

In 1951, with the charismatic and brilliant full back Puig Aubert, they toured Australia and won. They repeated the trick in 1955 and, even with that golden generation retired, injured or past their prime, they managed to draw another series Down Under. Aubert was the driving force of a team that bordered on a cliché. They were unpredictable, carefree, and often devastatingly brilliant.

The 1960s team were not quite so good, but they weren't far off. At home, particularly in the south of France, they were an extremely tough proposition for either Britain or Australia. In fact, France had scored five consecutive wins over the British, highlighting the wonderful mixture of brain and brawn in the '60s vintage.

Aubert himself was raised in Carcassonne, a large town nestled in the south, inland from the coast. Its imposing walled city dating from the time of the Romans still stands today as it did in 1967. Inside the walls is the Stade Albert Domec, a small stadium around which sits a running track.

It was Sunday, 22 January and the weather, while cold for the locals, was milder than the biting winter back in Hull. The stadium was filled to capacity, over 10,000 despite the climate, as Clive waited on the wing.

Five years of stop-start appearances after making his rugby league debut had led Clive to the point of his full Great Britain bow. The side had some familiar faces to Clive as Mick Harrison, still only 20, was also making his international debut. Arthur Keegan was starting at full back, and Brian Tyson from Hull KR was also in the side.

The French were much more experienced, Britain using the occasion to trial a few fresh faces before the Ashes series, and it had not been a great showing as they trailed by 11 with only a few minutes left.

In the 13th minute of the contest Clive had scored a walkover try. But, as the *Hull Daily Mail* reported, 'His first international appearance looked like being a flop … twice he uncharacteristically slipped up in defence.' Only the heroics of clubmate Keegan spared Clive's blushes, his rearguard action limiting the French to only one try. Despite that, full back Pierre Lacaze, who had kicked Britain to defeat the previous year, was at it again, slotting over five penalties.

A sixth successive loss seemed to be almost certain. The French were deep in Britain's half, and, to assure victory, they attempted a drop goal. The kick didn't make it but the British needed something extraordinary, so close to their own try line.

'But then,' wrote the *Hull Daily Mail*, 'Brian Tyson of Rovers and Clive Sullivan of Hull linked up in a brilliant move.

'Tyson swept forward with the ball, linking up with Terry Foggerty, who slipped a pass to Wakefield's star centre Neil Fox … Fox, in a desperate attempt to snatch victory, gave the ball to Sullivan on the halfway line.'

It's intriguing to wonder what would have happened had Clive been bundled into touch at that very moment. What would have happened if Clive's troublesome injuries suddenly returned as he attempted to accelerate? What if he had dropped the ball? It rarely happened to him, but nerves can affect players at the top levels in unusual ways.

But none of that happened.

'As he flashed down the touchline, Sullivan left three French defenders clutching at air. Turning inside, almost at right angles, he beat winger Marty, and swerved past Lacaze, and turned again to sweep under the posts for a try,' continued the newspaper.

Fox converted the ensuing goal, and Clive's two tries alongside two from captain Alan Hardisty had given the British an impressive victory. Such was the poise and pace illustrated by Clive, the almost exclusively French support gave him a standing ovation. Although a tough crowd to win over, they could recognise a special player.

Mick Harrison was also described as 'outstanding' in the pack and Keegan was lauded for his defensive discipline.

Clive's selection had come during a superb season on a personal level, during which he scored 30 tries in total. Both sides of Hull had become home to thrilling wing play as Chris Young had also crossed for 34 tries for KR. The Ashes would be decided at the back end of 1967 as the Australians would tour the UK and then France, also taking on a variety of club sides along the way.

Tragically for Clive, however, he was struck down with yet another thigh injury. During June of that year, it was reported that, although discharged from hospital, he would be given 'bed rest' for ten days.

The ongoing thigh issues were evidently more than simply just strains.

Whiteley recalls how the rare and potentially debilitating injury badly impacted on Clive's morale and ability to perform, 'We just thought it was muscle strain [at first, but] his thigh muscles were calcifying and attaching themselves to the bone. So, he was in dire trouble. For someone to be as fit as he was, to be like that ... He had to have operations. I knew it was breaking his heart, he was coming down and training, but he couldn't run as he was.'

The injuries, especially one so rare, had a profound impact on and off the field, according to Rosalyn, 'They had to operate in the end. Mr Birkin, the specialist, he wrote it up in a medical journal because it was so rare. It had [ossified]. So, he had to scoop that out of the left leg. Clive would start training again, but it'd still cause him problems. So, he had to go back in and the surgeon said he was loath to take more away. But apparently his skin was not good healing skin, [so] he had a scar like a tramline.

'Then about two years later, the same thing happened with the other leg. It was really difficult, all the time he's injured, he doesn't play, and he doesn't get paid. He's off work. The kind of jobs he did was in factories, where you didn't get sick pay. So, it did create a lot of stress and pressure. And they weren't well paid, playing rugby.'

The procedures, so invasive and now having been performed on both legs, mark something of a watershed in Clive's career.

'I just remember his first two to three seasons, the speed he had was unbelievable. From a standing start, he was like shit off a stick,' McGlone told me, clearly still in awe today.

'He was an athlete, like a sprinter. I'd say he was 10.3 over a hundred yards [in his first few seasons]. But he started to lose that with the rigours of the game.'

The sprints and games at training which had been such a good bonding experience for the team no longer had the same predictable outcome when McGlone and the others challenged him, 'So, we eventually began to take money off him [via these races]. With those extra 15 metres, he'd be on my shoulder, but you'd just make it.

'Before he lost that speed, he was unbelievable. I've never seen anyone as good as him during those first three seasons. After that, some other people could compare to him. Unbelievable speed, and awareness, and being in the right place at the right time, the ability to read a game.'

Fellow winger Smith recognises how Clive's ability to adapt was an induction of his innate understanding of the game, 'People get used to you. So, you've got to change and improve. People work it out ... Your top players have to keep working on surprises.'

Although Clive's hand was forced into making changes to his play due to the repeated injuries, Smith's point illustrates how tough it is for a player in any era, particularly wingers who are expected to make the most of sometimes limited opportunities.

Clive, despite his brilliant ability to recover and adapt, couldn't manage to do so in time to be considered for the 1967 Ashes series. It was a cruel blow after making such a brilliant impact on his first international appearance. He didn't feature for FC again until halfway through the 1967/68 season when the opportunities had already been and gone.

It was deeply unfortunate both for Clive and Great Britain. While KR winger Young was picked for every one of the tests, Britain could not call on a reliable outlet on the opposite flank. Bill Burgess of Barrow,

Bill Francis of Wigan, and Gary Johnson of Featherstone were selected for the first, second and third Tests respectively.

Aside from that wing spot, the side was largely settled. Millward, so instrumental for Rovers, partnered St Helens Tommy Bishop in every test in the halves. It's a mark of the depth of the British game at the time that such mercurial talents as Alex Murphy of Leigh and Hardisty and Hepworth of Castleford lost out to the chosen pair.

Rovers also provided prop Bill Holliday, who had joined from Whitehaven, and he captained the side for every Test. In contrast, the sole Hull FC representative was Arthur Keegan, who was hard to drop following his heroics in France earlier in the year.

To further highlight the disparity between FC and KR at the time, the latter beat the Aussies in a tour match in front of a packed Craven Park, 27-15. Described by historian Roger Pugh as one of KR's 'finest ever performances', the likes of Millward and Holliday set their stall out with some wonderful rugby league.

It was such an impressive performance from Rovers that Australian skipper, and all-time great, Johnny Rapper, was moved to comment, 'This is the best game of football I have played in my four tours of Britain ... this is the finest English club side I have played against.'

Despite plenty of optimism, and a run of injuries for Australia which saw Reg Gasnier and Johnny Rapper both feature less than expected, the tourists triumphed 2-1. Although Millward and Young both scored in the first Test at Headingley, a 16-11 victory for the home side, Australia managed to tough it out in the next two Tests.

Journalist and historian Harry Edgar wrote when looking back at the series, 'The four-tackle rule was removing the need for heavyweight, rugged forwards with specialist skills in the scrums, and replacing them with fast-moving back rowers who could play like centres. The Aussies had unearthed the prototype in Ron Coote.'

While Coote missed the Kangaroos opening fixture defeat, he scored a try in the two following games as Australia secured a famous win over their old rivals. Before the series had started, however, Rovers had also pulled off a significant derby victory, 8-7 in the 1967 Yorkshire Cup Final at Headingley.

Clive, too unfit to play for Britain, also missed out on his first appearance in a cup final after FC had upset the odds to beat Castleford,

Halifax and Leeds en route to the showpiece. FC also missed Jimmy Neale, such a crucial cog in the pack, due to injury, whereas Rovers were at full strength.

The game was a see-saw affair, played in terrible conditions, as David Doyle-Davidson crossed before Millward intercepted the ball to race over. Both sides kicked penalties before Davidson dropped a goal as the clock wore on. Finally, however, KR crossed via winger Alan Burwell, back in the game after a year out to complete his college education.

It was a bitter blow for FC and, for Clive, it must have been agonising to be left sidelined again when both club and country needed him.

Rosalyn, who recalls one of Clive's favourite grounds to play at was Headingley, spells out just how frustrating and tough it was for him when he was injured, 'If we ever went to a game when he was injured, and he'd sit with us [his family], which wasn't often, he'd shake all the time. He was on there. You go to a game and you make comments and shout. But he wouldn't speak.'

Although the Ashes series had been lost, as well as the Yorkshire Cup, the end of the season was to see the World Cup played in Australia. The race was on to see if Clive could make the tour.

Married Life

WHILE the start of the 1967/68 season had been one of absolute frustration professionally, on a personal level it saw Clive marry Rosalyn, with Terry Devonshire acting as his best man. They moved in together on Hull's Ella Street, a pleasant suburban area outside of the bustle of Hessle Road and the centre of Hull.

Combining rugby league, family life and a regular working life presented plenty of challenges for the Sullivans, as Rosalyn recalls.

She said, 'He was working in the factory at Hawker-Siddeley. What he'd do was rush home, and have his main meal for dinner. Then on a night when he was training, he'd have a light meal. He'd come in, have it. Get changed, get his bag, and out. Then after training he'd have a quick drink and then home. That was the life.

'But also, there used to be a couple of nights' overtime, where you could boost your wages. Because wages weren't good. So, he couldn't do that. But when you consider you've done a full day's work, not many guys would want to jump in their car and go train on the cold nights. Plus, you're up for work the next day as well. He started work at half seven. You accepted it because all the lads were full-time workers. Arthur Keegan, [Ken] Huxley, they lived out of town. They had to drive.

'Training started at half past six. Then away games, Saturdays, get up, go through the retching performance [due to nerves], quick breakfast. They'd be away for 11. They used to stop on the bridge at Goole. They used to have some food, although Alf Macklin [a young winger] used to take a pack-up, as he didn't trust the food. Then they'd have a walk over the bridge to stretch their legs, then on to play. Before

I ever had Anthony [Sullivan, the couple's first child] I used to go down to Pat Devonshire's [Terry's wife] house.

'I'd wait for the lads to come back, which was about 10pm. That was because they would lose someone or the bus would break down! So, me and Pat are getting wise, we said, "We'll go to the pub and wait for you." Suddenly the bus was getting back early! But you can imagine, a load of fellas. They used to go off somewhere and have a few pints. You'd get used to that. So, Saturdays were out every other week. Home games I'd go to.'

It wasn't just the disruption to daily routines that created issues. As already highlighted, pre-match nerves were a major issue for plenty of players of the time, just as they are now. It's easy for fans and journalists to forget that the players running out on to the field are human beings as well. They have families and friends who witness the pain of injuries, the drive, often bordering on obsession, to win, and the self-doubt and self-criticism.

Clive, as one of the most determined and committed players of his generation, was certainly guilty of this, according to Rosalyn, 'Before a game, he was really uptight. We'd end up going to the pictures for him to relax. Then on a Saturday morning, he'd have his routine. He'd have his breakfast and then start retching. And this was before every game. He never got out of that. But he was very determined, he wouldn't give up.

'But he wasn't the easiest of patients either. For all people saw a smiley face, friendly to everybody, he had his moments. It was difficult to keep the spirits up. That was my role really.

'I think I'd been to a wedding. It was a Challenge Cup round against Barrow. And they scored a try and it was 6-8. He came home and cried and he said if they had been fit, they wouldn't have won. I've seen him in the depths. I don't think other players would have seen him like that. Or he'd come home from internationals and say, "I wasn't good enough." When you're watching a game, you're a supporter. You don't see what goes on in the dressing room. He would never say, "Wasn't I great?"'

It wasn't just the grind of day in, day out, rugby. Clive was gaining a well-deserved reputation for his generosity with his time with fans and with local businesses in the city of Hull, who, as Rosalyn says, had 'adopted him'.

Alan McGlone was well aware of the sacrifices his teammate made, 'He never would have held his hand out and asked for a fee. Because that wasn't his character. He'd do owt for nowt. He'd go in pubs for darts and dominoes, giving trophies out. He'd turn his overtime down at work to go do stuff like that.'

Johnny Whiteley, a mentor to so many of that generation, is also renowned for his willingness to make charity and personal appearances even to this day, in his 80s. That spirit of generosity towards fans certainly seemed to have rubbed off on Clive.

Yet it led to a busy social life as well as a busy professional life, recalls Rosalyn, 'In summer, in the breaks, Clive never turned anyone down. Fetes, openings. We did so many things; we didn't have one Saturday off. And it was because, he always said, the fans pay my wages.'

With his off-field generosity and undoubted ability on the field, it was easy to see why he had so quickly become beloved by FC fans.

Yet his ability and sensational international debut were creating a growing interest in his health in the wider rugby league public. After losing the Ashes, the 1968 World Cup, held on enemy soil in Australia, could provide perfect revenge.

Whiteley, acutely aware of the attention his star winger was attracting and the pressure a perfectionist such as Clive was placing on himself, devised a strategy, 'I isolated him from training. I said, "Never mind people are beating you [in training]. We are going to get you back." The press kept ringing. So, I'd say, "Oh, he's brilliant. He's just getting stronger." But, he was only hobbling, then. But he was such an essential part of that selection. So, I told all kinds of fibs. But we got him fit and running well, and back on track.'

Although Clive only made 20 appearances that season, he was still lethal, scoring 16 tries. The re-signing of Dick Gemmell also helped, as the centre, who Devonshire recognised as a 'very good player', added more class to the backline. He re-joined for £4,000, a significant discount on the fee Leeds had paid only a few seasons previously.

While Gemmell had been a success at Leeds and was still pushing for a place in the centres for Great Britain in the upcoming World Cup series and during the Ashes, Leeds had the young pair of Syd Hynes and John Langley chomping at the bit for first team rugby. Gemmell 'was pleased to be signing for Hull, I have always wanted to return to the Boulevard' and he added, 'While I've enjoyed my time at Headingley … with a great set of lads, it's best for all if I return now.'

Rather unfortunately, Gemmell's wife fell down a flight of stairs, fracturing her ankle, which held up his move in the days following. It caused logistical issues for both club and player as he sought employment back on Humberside.

Whiteley's tactic of taking the pressure off Clive, alongside the addition of Gemmell, worked. It was no more obvious than in a 57-6 thrashing of Doncaster away to close out the season, with Clive running in seven tries in the rout. Clive crossed for three in the first half and four in the second half as Doncaster's 'awful' defence was breached time and again. Terry Devonshire, playing at stand off to allow Gemmell and Maloney to play in the centres, placed many of the tries on a plate for Sullivan. Yet Clive also scored a wonderful length-of-the-field effort early in the second half.

Seven tries remains the record for Hull FC for the number of tries scored by an individual in one game at the time of this writing.

'Clive wasn't one that sang his own praises,' Rosalyn told me 'So if I weren't at a game, he wouldn't say, "I scored this fantastic try". He'd say, "I scored a try," but it'd be what I read in the papers.' But she does remember his elation after the game at Doncaster, 'That was a big thing because he broke the record.'

The Doncaster game could have proved even more significant, however. Brian Sullivan, after being in and out of the game during his time with Hull FC, had transferred to Doncaster after a successful stint on trial during the 1968 season. He played seven times, scoring one try, but retired from the sport altogether a month prior to the famous seven-try match. It deprived the two brothers, who had always been competitive yet supportive, the chance to oppose each other on the field.

Statistically, Brian was a success for Hull FC. His 22 tries in 62 games was not bad at all for a team that could struggle with consistency, both in terms of selection and on-pitch performances. Yet, he had not appeared at all in the first team since the 1966 season. It's also far from a bad return for a player and man for whom rugby league was not a passion like that of his younger brother. Mick Harrison – who had respected Clive so immensely for his willingness to help the forwards

– recalls, 'He never had the heart like Clive … He wouldn't be like Clive, coming in, he'd just run.' Devonshire is slightly more direct, 'He never had the bottle.'

Although Clive had lost Brian from the club, his brother remained in the city. What's more, Rosalyn and Clive had their first child, a boy named Anthony, born in November 1968. Clive's roots were very firmly placed in the city, even if he was hoping to temporarily up sticks to play on the other side of the world.

It was no surprise, after such a strong finish to the season, that Clive was named in the touring party for the 1968 World Cup. Britain were the reigning world champions but that victory had come in 1960. A tournament had been scheduled for 1965 in Australia but had been pulled due to financial concerns from the Australian Rugby League after a terrible tour by the French in 1964. By 1968, none of the class of 1960 remained for Britain. Indeed, many had hung up their boots entirely.

The squad selected didn't even bear much resemblance to the side which had lost the Ashes the previous year. One thing that did remain was the half back pairing as Millward and Bishop were selected. It was hardly surprising, as Millward had spent the season scoring 38 tries, making him the top division's leading scorer. It was an unprecedented return for a non-winger and a feat not come by in living memory.

Competing with Clive for wing spots were Chris Young, who had scored 27 that season, and John Atkinson of Leeds. Atkinson was one of the bright young things emerging at Headingley during a Challenge Cup-winning season and had scored 34 tries himself.

An almost entirely new pack of forwards was selected with Ray French (Widnes), Mick Clark (Leeds), John Warlow (St Helens), Charlie Renilson (Halifax) and Arnold Morgan (Featherstone) all on tour for the first time. Peter Flannagan of Kingston Rovers was selected at hooker, with prop Cliff Watson of St Helens acting as the experienced hand, having made his Great Britain debut in 1963.

Plenty of other relatively inexperienced players were also picked. Mick Shoebottom, a gifted and immensely popular scrum half at Leeds, made the cut. His teammate Bev Risman after only two appearances for his country in warm-up games against France, was named as captain after original choice Neil Fox was ruled out with a last-minute groin injury.

Another player who missed out was McGlone, who had had a brilliant season for FC. He remembered, 'Towards the end of the season they were picking the touring side to go in 1968. I was meant to go as number two. I got my letter from the RFL, and I was so looking forward to it, me and Sully could be roommates. I got injured against Castleford; I tore some cartilage in my knee. It really caused me problems. I strapped it up and tried to keep playing but I didn't make the tour. It was my biggest regret in rugby league that I didn't tour.'

The squad had more attention than would have perhaps been anticipated as the Challenge Cup Final of that season had been one of the most dramatic in living memory, the infamous 'Water Splash Final'. In front of a near-capacity Wembley crowd and a captivated BBC audience, Don Fox, brother of Neil, had shanked a last-minute penalty wide as Leeds beat Wakefield 11-10. Fox, named the man of the match, sank to his knees as the whistle went, and commentator Eddie Waring had uttered his famous 'poor lad … that poor Don Fox … the lad's in tears' line.

The fact the final had been played on a badly waterlogged pitch, so bad that the ball regularly stood up on the turf rather than bounce and players slipped on almost every tackle, added a touch of comedy to the tragedy. Journalist and ex-cricketer Robin Marlar, describing the game, said it best, 'All the evident skills of individuals had been brought to nothing.'

With the excitement and drama of the final fresh in fans' and players' minds alike, the British squad was quickly assembled. Risman, writing in his autobiography, said, 'Following the Wembley weekend [Challenge Cup Final], the tour party gathered in Leeds … this group was better prepared than any previous national side leaving these shores … the last week included the fitting of our official uniforms, photographs and media interviews … no stone was left unturned by our management team of coach Colin Hutton, manager Bill Fallowfield and RFL chairman John Smallwood.'

Despite – or, perhaps, because of – the influx of new players, Britain set off for the World Cup in high spirits, and they were the bookies' second choice after Australia.

The squad flew out on Saturday, 18 May. Both Hutton and Fallowfield had been acutely aware that this could create significant issues, as Britain's opening fixture was due to be played the following Saturday at the imposing Sydney Cricket Ground. The arduous 36-hour flight was then followed by press obligations. Risman recalls, 'I was much in demand to give my opinion on a host of irrelevant topics, even to the extent of giving my opinion on my taste in women.'

Along with the considerable jet lag, it prevented the side from gaining anywhere near enough preparation time. Ray French, writing in his autobiography, stated that Britain '[had] insufficient time to recognise each other's faults and qualities'.

Training, from the little that could be done considering the punishing schedule and lack of spare time, was conducted in front of the 'hotel'. The squad was based in the Olympic, although according to French it was an 'old-fashioned Sydney pub with rooms' as opposed to anything too flash or opulent.

Clive, and fellow wingman John Atkinson, had quickly struck up a solid friendship, and it was the start of a long association between the pair. As two of the country's premier young wingers they had developed a level of mutual respect after opposing each other in club games. Alan Smith, who was becoming a regular on the opposite wing to Atkinson for Leeds, remembers the pair's friendship tinged with rivalry.

He said, 'For years, Clive always seemed to have the sign over John [in games]. And that kept John on his toes. Plus, the fact they [always] roomed together.' Both Atkinson and Sullivan were left wingers for their club side, and only one would likely be picked. The choice was made to go with Clive for the opening game.

Back in Hull, the excitement of seeing a local favourite turn out in a World Cup was building. Whiteley, interviewed in the local press, felt, 'It will be quite an ordeal for Clive, especially walking all the way to the centre [of Sydney Cricket Ground]. But I feel confident he will overcome his nerves and have a grand game for Britain.'

The Australian team they were set to meet was one of the greatest ever seen, both before and since. Bob Fulton, Johnny Rapper, Graeme Langlands, Ron Coote and Arthur Beetson were part of the squad, and all were subsequently named in the Australian 'team of the century' announced in 2008.

Despite the talent and skill those men possessed, however, the Australian press had lauded the likes of Millward, Bishop, Shoebottom,

Risman and Sullivan. The Australian view was that they had the superior pack, but should Britain be allowed to play quick, running rugby, the skill and speed may prove too much for the Kangaroos. Clive, as one of the quickest in either side, would be a key outlet, and would be well watched by the Australian defence.

Although the fixture had all the makings of a classic, the 62,000 in attendance saw a game that never sparked into life. The Australians won 26-10 in a drab match mostly remembered for the over-eager whistle of the referee, New Zealander John Percival. Percival, described as 'pedantic', continually penalised Britain. It was to such an absurd degree that even the local media, who had seen their side benefit from most the calls, nicknamed him 'ten-yard Jack' for marching Britain back so often.

Risman writes, 'Mr Percival … ruined the match, penalising us for a series of apparent offences that even the usually one-eyed Aussie media failed to see. In the end, we were at a loss at how to deal with the barrage of penalties.'

Despite the myriad problems Britain had to face, they had managed to head in at half-time still in the game, trailing 10-7. Ian Brook, on the opposite wing to Clive, finished off a wonderful, fast-paced move that showed glimpses of what Millward and Bishop could produce if given the opportunity. Twenty yards out, Bishop threw an outrageous dummy, went through a gap and fed his teammate, back rower Rob Haigh, who then quickly gave the ball back to Bishop, who passed to Millward. Millward then sidestepped and left the Aussie full back, Langlands, for dead, before offloading for a waiting Brook to crash over. Clive, eager as always to get in on the action and use his poacher's instinct, had also drifted infield during the build-up, should the ball be shipped out in the opposite direction.

Clive also pulled off a miraculous double tackle towards the end of the first half, highlighting to everyone that there was much more to his game than try scoring. Australia, just short of halfway, gave the ball to the rampaging Beetson. At around 16st, Beetson had at least 3st over Clive yet, executing a perfect round-the-legs tackle, Sullivan brought Beetson down with the minimum of fuss.

Beetson managed to get the ball out of the tackle to hooker Fred Jones in support, however. With the British defensive line disrupted, Jones had an opportunity to make up some serious ground. Yet Clive, having already brought down Beetson, quickly regained his feet and produced a superb ball-and-all cover tackle on Jones, exhibiting Clive's superb blend of pace and strength.

Unfortunately for Clive and Britain, as the second half wore on, Eric Simms continued to kick penalty after penalty to edge the home side ahead.

With the Kangaroos having built up a solid 20-7 lead as the game began to wind down, Simms dropped out for Australia, straight to Clive, who got it on the full. Quickly gaining pace, and taking advantage of a disjointed Australian defence line, he exhibited the trademark 'swerve' on opposite winger Johnny Rhodes, leaving Rhodes literally grasping at air as he sailed past.

The only defender left to beat was a covering Fred Jones, the roles reversed, but Clive easily went over in the corner as Jones was nowhere near quick enough to make the tackle. It was a wonderful try to score on a World Cup debut, a perfect embodiment of the 1960s Clive Sullivan.

Pace, poise, special awareness and an unwavering desire to make it over the try line were on show. Even the staunchly partisan Australian crowd gave the try a round of applause, as Clive was mobbed by his teammates in the aftermath. The Australian press, slightly less generous, described the try as 'extremely simple' and down to Australian defensive mistakes.

Simms kept kicking the Lions to death, however. The penalty count finished 18-7 in favour of the home side. It was a disappointing result, although under difficult circumstances. When the likes of Clive, Millward and Bishop had been given their opportunities they had delivered. But the constant loss of field position, and the kicking of Simms, proved too big a mountain to overcome.

But the result was not seen as a complete disaster. The Lions still had games against France, to be held in New Zealand, and then a match against New Zealand, nonsensically to be held back in Sydney. Britain were considered the favourites against both. Unfortunately, things were not to go as expected.

Down and Out

AS Britain travelled to Auckland they were due to meet a French team with the bit between their teeth. The French had pulled off an opening-round upset, beating the home side 15-10 in front of a crowd of 18,000. The Kiwis had had second row Brian Lee sent off after only 12 minutes and France's stand off Jean Capdouze ran riot, scoring a try and kicking five goals to contribute 13 of his side's points.

The travel to New Zealand again deprived Britain of any real chance to regroup and prepare. Just to add to the Lions's terrible luck, Auckland was hit with an unseasonably torrential downpour on the day of the game. Carlaw Park, the venue for the fixture on 2 June, was already notorious for the pitch's tendency to become a mudbath. For Britain, who had a side built to play fast, direct rugby, it again caused a disruption to their game plan. In theory the British players, so used to playing in awful conditions back home, should have been able to adapt. Instead, as Risman recalls, 'We got bogged down in the mud ... [which was] a leveller.'

France defended heroically, and quickly and ruthlessly adapted to the conditions. Capdouze, having a wonderful tournament, kicked early and often. With the sides locked at 2-2 with only ten minutes left in a dour game, French winger Jean-Rene Ledru collected yet another Capdouze kick and sealed a famous 7-2 win for France, knocking Great Britain out of the cup.

It was a disastrous result and one in which Clive had seen little ball. His talent required space when receiving the ball, and the conditions had hampered any attempt by the British to provide him with just that.

Clive, as well as the whole squad, was despondent as they returned to Sydney.

As the tournament was in the traditional rugby league round-robin format, Britain still had to play the fixture against New Zealand. Both teams had been eliminated as the Kiwis had been beaten 31-12 in Brisbane, leaving only pride left to play for. It also meant that Australia would have to play France in a meaningless 'league game' before the two met for real in the final two days later.

In front of one of the smallest crowds ever in attendance for an international in Sydney, 14,000, Britain, and Clive, finished well. The Lions won 38-12 with Clive bagging his first international hat-trick.

Unfortunately for Clive, the local papers were more concerned with what they felt was lacklustre effort from both sets of players. The *Sydney Sunday Telegraph* stated in its match report, 'In a season of miserable representative matches, yesterday's had the dubious distinction of being by far the worst. It was dreadful. Nobody wants to watch a game of football in which players from both sides are quite obviously just going through the motions.'

Although Britain had not finished bottom of the table, the performances had not been up to standard. Frustratingly, they then had to travel to Queensland for a 'promotional tour'. As if to highlight what could have been, they won all four games on dry pitches, the warm and sunny climate providing the perfect platform for the rugby they had hoped to provide. Clive himself produced some sensational performances; even if they were in glorified friendlies, his four tries against a Queensland select team at the famous Lang Park in Brisbane was a highlight.

Australia beat France 37-4 in the last group game and then beat the same opposition in the final two days later, 20-2, to win the World Cup.

While the tournament was a financial success and the Australians were classy and worthy winners, it was not a classic tournament by any means. Indeed, in the League Publications *History of the Rugby League World Cup*, it is described as host to 'some of the worst international displays of the post-Second World War era'.

One of the few real bright spots was indeed Clive, who did as much as he could with the little opportunities he was presented with. His displays grew admiring glances from the Australian press, who felt he was the best winger on display in the whole tournament. Although that was a magnificent personal achievement for a man like Clive – so humble regarding his own talents and yet with a desire to win and perform at all costs – it must have come off as bitter sweet. His four tries, one against Australia and the hat-trick against New Zealand, made him the tournament's top scorer, although he also shared the accolade with Ron Coote and Aussie winger Lionel Williamson.

The Lions, already away for well over a month, then had an unscheduled stopover in Hong Kong. The plane for the journey home had developed a fault that required a special part and, despite assurances that they would only need to stay for one night, they ended up languishing in the unbearably humid city for a week.

Upon his return home, Clive found that Hull FC had recruited well in the off-season with more youthful additions. Len Casey, a wiry young forward, was signed out of the amateur game. Howard Firth, a big yet raw rugby union winger, was also added to the squad. Firth, from Doncaster, had scored 34 tries for Hull RUFC the previous season. The *Hull Daily Mail* pointed out that, on the back of his signing, 'With Clive Sullivan on the opposite wing, Hull now have two of the fastest men in the game on their flanks.'

Leaving the squad was Clive's good friend, Terry Devonshire, who joined York. Although talented, loved by his teammates and popular with the Boulevard crowd, Devonshire was rarely getting a run at his preferred position at stand off. And while he was also an effective centre, Gemmell and Maloney were the first choice.

On the field, the 1968/69 season got off to a surprising start. One thing that Clive had not lost despite his time spent in Hull was pride in his Welsh roots. 'He was first and foremost Welsh. He was a really proud Welshman,' Rosalyn recalls. Rugby league had continued its regular pillaging of rugby union talent. The Welsh union team was gutted, losing 13 players to league.

David Watkins, a talented fly half and one of Welsh rugby union's top stars, had been signed for a massive £16,000 signing-on fee by Salford. Terry Price signed for Bradford and Keith Jarrett joined Barrow for £14,000. The big-name arrivals boosted gates and they added even more flair to British rugby league.

The number of quality Welsh rugby union players turning pro, along with the already established stars such as Clive and Colin Dixon,

A teenage Clive in the army

On the defensive against Wakefield in the 60s

Clive in typically rugged and uncompromising form as a defender. Terry Devonshire can be seen looking on

Clive is given a suitcase prior to his first tour by the Hull FC supporters' club

Pre-season training for Hull FC

With mentor Johnny Whiteley meeting and greeting

Clive and Mick Harrison at The Boulevard

The GB squad being shown the delights of a Sydney factory on the 1968 tour.

Clive and Mick Shoebottom on tour in 1970

Clive celebrates at the final whistle in the 1972 Rugby League World Cup Final

Chaired off the field in 1972, as a world champion

Carving open the Bradford Northern defence in 1977

Clive was as prolific for Rovers as he was for FC, seen here touching down against Dewsbury

Business partners and friends off the field, opponents on it. Clive and Sammy Lloyd

Clive with The Queen Mother before the 1980 Challenge Cup Final

Determination etched on his face during a lull in the 1980 Challenge Cup Final

A career ambition achieved for Roger and Clive

Exhausted, yet elated. Hull KR are the 1980 Challenge Cup winners

Hull KR parade the Challenge Cup

A final triumph, back where it all began

A minute's silence at Craven Park, in remembrance of one of the game's greats

Roslayn Sullivan raises money in Clive's memory for cancer research

promoted a reformation of the Welsh rugby league national side. Wales's rugby league team had been an off-and-on idea having first played in 1908 against New Zealand. They had competed regularly from that point, until 1963, when the side was mothballed for five years.

On 9 November 1968, at Salford, Wales played England in a fixture not seen since 1953. The side was captained by John Mantle, the back rower St Helens had signed from union with Newport four seasons prior. Clive lined up against friend and rival John Atkinson, with Watkins at stand off for Wales and Terry Price at full back.

Although the England side was somewhat experimental, with the likes of Millward not featured, Wales still pulled off an impressive victory. In front of 6,000 fans, Clive continued his superb run of scoring on debuts as he contributed one try in his side's 24-17 win.

Back on Humberside, Hull's young team were maturing well. They started the season in great form, particularly at the Boulevard. Firth proved an immediate success, scoring a superb 14 tries in his first 14 games. Clive, almost keeping pace with his new wingmate's strike rate, had scored 12 but, as usual, however, disaster struck.

During a frustrating 26-7 home victory over Keighley, in which reporter Mike Ackroyd claimed Hull were 'wasting Clive Sullivan's brilliance' due to 'fumbled movements', Clive's right thigh was re-injured. It was one of the last acts of the game as he was injured in crossing for his 13th try of the year after he 'fell awkwardly and did not get up'.

The injury was a serious blow both to Hull's ambitions and Clive's morale. Joe Latus claims in his account that the injury led to Clive deciding, in the days afterwards, to give up the game for good.

While one of the qualities many people who know Clive mention was his determination, the repeated injuries were exhibiting a brutal physical and emotional toll.

As McGlone explained, the wear and tear of professional rugby league was non-stop, 'If you do ten years of professional, your body will suffer … I broke that thumb; it went bang, the bone stuck out. I thought "shit", John Stims put it back in and put some tape on. Then it's an operation.

'When I hit 30 I was knackered. But you're still playing first team rugby and strapping yourself up. When I signed when I was 18, there was an old forward like Cyril Sykes, like 30, 31, he was putting that many bandages on he looked like a mummy! I didn't want to end up like that. I was hyperactive, it'd be doing backflips and running up walls. And I didn't want to get as old as that.'

While McGlone, at the heart of the forward battles and scrums, was far removed from Clive's position on the wing, Alan Smith tells a similar story of injuries, 'I broke my tibia, fibula, cruciate ligament, broke my shoulder, injured my hand. Clive and John [Atkinson] will have [had] a list of them. You were pulled down at speed in those days.'

Despite only being 26, Clive had started in the game as a teenager and, physically, had been through the ringer. The financial implications of rugby also impacting on 'day jobs' were also still a very real pressure.

Eventually, after the disappointment had worn off, Clive decided against hanging up his boots. It was reported he was to undergo 'heat treatment'. Whiteley, interviewed in the press, stated that, while Clive's leg was sore and he was walking with a limp, 'it does not seem as serious as first feared', but he felt that it was impossible 'at the moment to say how long it will be until Clive plays again'.

Great Britain had another midweek test due against France in St Helens in the coming weeks. After his performances at the World Cup, and early-season form, Clive was considered an automatic pick for the side, but, after failing a late fitness test, was replaced by clubmate Gemmell.

Clive's misfortune was Gemmell's gain as he produced a man-of-the-match performance in a 34-10 win.

Clive featured little for the rest of the season, not adding any more tries, as his recovery took place. He was sorely missed as Hull, after such a strong start, finished 13th, although only a point behind KR.

The frustration of another season written off due to injury, plus Hull's continued underperformance, boiled over in January of 1969, when Clive asked for a transfer away from FC.

'If the request is granted, it could bring one of the biggest fees in rugby league's history, for Sullivan is widely regarded as rugby league's most devastating winger,' the *Hull Daily Mail* reported.

Clive himself gave his views on why he wanted to move, 'We are all in the game to better ourselves and I feel that the time has come for me to change clubs. A change of clubs may give me a change of luck, as well.'

Ever since the World Cup, rumours had swirled that Clive was growing unhappy in Hull. Wigan, with Billy Boston in his last season, seemed the likely destination. Indeed, Rosalyn told me that Wigan had come with 'an open chequebook' and asked Hull to name a price.

Britain were also due to tour Australia again in a bid to regain the Ashes. Another disappointing, injury-hit season could have profound consequences for Clive's chance of touring and avenging the World Cup losses.

Rumours in the press and the stands also suggested that Hull were not in a great financial position, although they did post a slight profit of over £1,000 for the financial year. The feeling was, however, that a move for a big fee could help both Clive and Hull, although FC made the right noises at persuading him to stay, noting that the request had only been granted 'very reluctantly'.

'Clive, as he pointed out to us, has not been fortunate enough to gain financially the full amount that his talent should have earned him,' chairman Reg Lee was quoted as saying.

Any transfer would be put on hold for the time being as fitness concerns still lingered over Clive. He made an appearance in a pre-season warm-up game and then scored a hat-trick in an 'A' team game against Huddersfield A, although he received another bad knock on the thigh.

Eventually he was transfer-listed for £15,000, a record amount for a winger. Although Clive had said he would appeal should the fee top £10,000, he accepted the figure. It was likely that FC, and indeed Clive, knew that the price was beyond the means of the clear majority of clubs, and whoever did come in with an offer would most likely offer cash plus a player.

The re-aggravation of the thigh injury in the 'A' team game, however, required another period of inactivity and rest.

Ironically, as the 1969/70 season began, Bradford also showed an interest. Despite an afternoon of face-to-face negotiations between representatives of both clubs, an agreement was never reached, leaving Clive a Hull FC player for the time being.

Although he had had more minor surgery in the off-season while his future was sorted out, Clive quickly regained his place in the first team when fit and played some wonderful rugby. The Yorkshire Cup, played early in the season, highlighted the rugby Hull and Clive could play when at full fitness. They knocked out Castleford, 30-4 at the Boulevard in a wonderful performance. Then followed wins away at York (22-15) and, most impressively in the semi-final, a nail biting 20-17 victory over reigning champions Leeds at Headingley. Across the city, Hull KR had also reached the semi-final but were knocked out.

Terry Devonshire, in the York team for that game, recalls coming up against his friend and ex-teammate, 'I got the ball, I'll always remember it. He hit me so hard, a right bad tackle, shook me off. Bang. He said, mates off the field, but not mates on the field.'

Hull FC's last Yorkshire Cup win had come 46 years previously. Although KR had been undoubtedly the best Hull side for most of the '60s, they had still only won a Yorkshire Cup despite the obvious talent they possessed. If FC could beat Featherstone as the decade played out, it could restore some bragging rights back to West Hull and make up for the defeat in the previous year's final.

Featherstone were not to be underestimated, however. Steve Nash, a young scrum half, was to go on to play for Great Britain. Cyril Kellet had also left Rovers for the West Yorkshire side and was as deadly a goal kicker as ever.

Triumph, at Last

AGAINST the backdrop of the cup final, the relationship between Johnny Whiteley and the Hull board was becoming increasingly strained. Whiteley had been given full power to make team selections the previous season as the traditional style of selection by committee was being challenged by coaches who felt they were being made fall-guys for board members who played favourites.

One of the key plot points of *This Sporting Life* is Frank Machin being caught in the middle of the two warring directors of the club, Maurice Braithwaite and Charles Slomer. Machin's failure to stay on the right side of one leads to favouritism from the other. While Machin's story has much more added intrigue, it's an interesting example of how a player's ability and form could be discounted when teams were selected by vote.

For the current season, however, there was to be a return to the status quo. Whiteley's plight was quickly surmised in a quick quote provided to the local press by a spokesman for the board, 'Johnny will submit a list of players available and his suggestions. Then the directors will pick the team.'

Whiteley still remembers the debates that took place to this day, 'The unfortunate thing about those days was, no coach in England picked the team, it was all committees. When I first started, I never saw it in a different light. You are paid by the club to do a job. But then you think, hang on a minute. I'm with these kids every day. I know their qualities, I know what I tell them, I know what feedback I get. They [the board] don't.

'Take Clive Sullivan, I could say, do this, do that, then they drop him. And he'd think, he's got me dropped. So, I thought the system was jeopardising my professional ability.'

Although Whiteley remained, the speculation surrounding such a long-standing stalwart was far from ideal. Further to disrupt the team, another long servant, Arthur Keegan, was injured prior to the cup final and was said to be 'unable to lift his arm higher than his shoulder'. Keegan was in his testimonial season and it was a dire shame that a player who had been so consistent for FC, making 306 appearances since finally winning the battle for the full back spot seven years prior, missed out.

Into his place stepped Martin Oxbridge, a 24-year-old who had played almost entirely for the 'A' team, only making seven prior appearances for the first team. It was decided that Dick Gemmell, who was also not 100 per cent fit in the build-up, would play and also act as captain.

Some 11,000 spectators were at Headingley on Saturday, 20 September to watch the game. The strains of 'Old Faithful', sang with passion and commitment by the majority Hull crowd, met both sets of players as they entered the field for what proved to be a tense and dramatic 80 minutes. Hull, rather than the distinctive hooped black and white shirts, wore predominantly white shirts with a black V, whereas Featherstone were in the traditional dark blue and white kit.

Hull started nervously, despite, or perhaps because of, the overwhelming support. They regularly blew promising opportunities or simply failed to complete their sets of tackles. Featherstone, not showing the same urgency to attack but making fewer mistakes, slowly began to wear down Hull. Hull's nerves were not helped when Kellet, so deadly a goal kicker, had slotted over a penalty after only three minutes.

Joe Brown, the Hull loose forward who had debuted in 1964, then levelled it up with a drop goal. Brown, who was a talented and intelligent footballer, was unfortunate to have followed in the footsteps of Whiteley, a player few could live up to, yet he was in the process of having the game of his career.

The edgy first half came to a close when Kellet notched another penalty, this time a more difficult kick from further out, leaving Featherstone 4-2 ahead.

In the second half, Hull again squandered chance after chance. Brown made a break but attempted to score himself rather than look for support. Brian Hancock, stand off for the day and in the embryonic stages of a long association with the club, also bombed a try opportunity.

Finally, the pressure told. Brown, again, finding himself in space, grubber kicked ahead. He regathered the ball himself then sent Clive away down the touchline, where he used his pace to go in at the corner.

After Maloney converted, Hull were 7-2 and although they had one hand on the cup as the second half ticked on, another try would be crucial.

Clive seemed as likely as anyone to add to his tally and help bring the cup back to Humberside but things did not quite work out as planned.

'Sully went through a gap with about a quarter of an hour to go,' remembers McGlone, 'and he was going that fast he put the ball down over the dead ball line. He got a bit of ribbing in the dressing room about that, people saying he needed to get some glasses.'

Clive, interviewed following the game, revealed his anguish at blowing such a brilliant opportunity, 'I tried to turn inside to go in under the posts, and my feet just shot from under me and I was out of play. I felt like crying.'

If Featherstone had managed to claw their way back into the match, Clive may never have lived it down. Instead, the result was confirmed as Dick Gemmell's reverse pass found Brown again, who sent Jim Macklin over with Maloney adding the goal.

Featherstone didn't make it a comfortable end, however, as Nash, well shackled for most of the 80 minutes, managed to squeeze over in the dying seconds, Kellet adding the conversion. But it was too little, too late and the scoreline was 12-9, with Joe Brown being named man of the match, to few people's surprise.

It was to be the high point of Brown's career at Hull, as the local paper succinctly put it, 'Rarely can any player have had such an uneven time. Hailed as a great star after commanding performances in Hull's Yorkshire Cup run, he has been a comparative disappointment in his last few matches for Hull in which he has found his knee a handicap.' The troublesome knee eventually required major surgery that further disrupted the forward's career.

The win was a huge boost for both the club and its fan base. The team paraded the trophy along the Hessle Road, a wonderful event for the tight-knit community. Noticeably, the bus also snaked along some roads in East Hull, in theory enemy territory. Yet they received a 'warm reception' according to the newspaper coverage.

After what seemed like a coming-of-age performance for the team, Clive had a change of heart regards leaving, and said, 'I'm thinking of asking to come off the [transfer] list. I want to talk to the directors.'

He was honest about his own performances, stating, 'I know I am not playing all that well, but it is just a question of regaining confidence. It is slowly coming back to me.' Typically, however, he refused to make the excuse of the thigh injury for what he felt were performances below his standard, 'It feels very well. I have no pain in it at all.'

Although there was good news for the Hull board when it came to Clive, the respite of the cup win proved short lived. Speculation in the press again suggested that Whiteley was set to leave at the end of the season due to frustrations with the board. To make matters even worse, there was growing player unrest. The board, eager not to fan the flames, claimed that any rumours of unrest 'were a complete fabrication'.

The fact that Joe Brown, alongside fellow first-teamers Shaun O'Brien, Nick Trotter, Ken Huxley, Eric Broom, David-Doyle Davidson and 'A'-teamer Ken Foulkes, all had asked for transfers as the season wore on suggested the board were not being entirely truthful. Chris Davidson was also being looked at by Wigan and McGlone was then dropped from the first team, with 'allegations from other players he was being victimised because he had complained about payments for away mid-week matches'.

Fifteen first-teamers, not named in the press coverage but not including captain Arthur Keegan and Clive Sullivan, met with the supporters' trust. The players' spokesman stated, 'There's one man running the club and, as far as we are concerned, he is not making a success of the job ... it is no secret that some of the directors owe their place on the board to the fact they have secured proxy votes, so he is the one who cracks the whip.'

Against this increasingly chaotic and disjointed backdrop, Clive went about his rugby quietly, and quickly got back up to speed. While it was far from his most prolific season (although he still scored 21 tries), it was his most consistent to date as he made 38 appearances. The most dramatic moment of the season, aside from the cup final, was Wales's game against France in Perpignan. Since the team had reformed and pulled off the win over England, a 'European championship tournament' had been created, featuring the Welsh, English and French. In the first such tournament since the '50s, Wales were heavily beaten 40-23 at Headingley against England, although Clive took his tally to two in two with another try. They then lost at 'home', in Salford, 8-2 to the French, when the familiar sight of Jean Capdouze's kicking dominated. With simple pride to play for, Wales travelled to the south of France. Clive said, 'This was the best game I have played since coming back [from injury].'

He scored two tries and another from Terry Price helped set up a 15-11 win. Following the final whistle, however, referee Dicky Thomas, who had disallowed a French try, was knocked out by pitch invaders.

'When the whistle went,' Clive told reporters, 'people crowded on to the pitch ... I was punched in the back as I made my way off.' The fans had already pelted the Welsh players, particularly the wingers Clive, and Frank Wilson, with beer cans as the game wore on.

In the modern game, the issue would have created major controversy. Remarkably, however, Rugby Football League secretary Bill Fallowfield was rather more flippant about the ugly scenes when asked for a comment. He replied, 'If you a 6ft, 15 stone forward, it is pretty easy to make sure you get through the crowd.'

When asked if the England vs France game to be played in the coming weeks should still go ahead, Fallowfield drew a rather bizarre comparison, stating no fixtures would be abandoned, 'In America, all the protection in the world could not prevent John F. Kennedy and Martin Luther King [Jr.] from being assassinated. In the same way, the French RL cannot really be blamed.' As it happened, France won 14-9, although England took the championship due to points difference.

Hull also managed to complete the season in 11th place, a slight improvement on the previous year. They finished behind Hull KR again, however, and 18 points behind Leeds, who were top. It was the fourth consecutive year they had achieved the feat, although due to the nature of league they only won the championship proper once.

By this stage, Francis had moved on to coach the North Sydney Bears, although Joe Warham had offered some continuity. Yet the ability and talent of Francis had been evident throughout his time with the club, as they had become one of the games premier forces.

Although Johnny Whiteley's Hull side had never finished particularly high in the league table, they had gained a reputation for exciting rugby. Furthermore, Whiteley himself was held in such high esteem due to his playing career that he proved to be a popular choice as Great Britain coach for the 1970 Ashes tour, being picked over the other contender, Joe Warham.

Whiteley's appointment had come via a somewhat convoluted manner, however, and he was described as applying for the post via a 'scribbled note'.

'Some time ago Hull asked me if I was interested in the position. I said I was and the club sent an application off on my behalf,' Whiteley told the day's press.

'But I was informed later that the application was not acceptable and had to be made by me personally. At the time I was laid flat on my back with this injury and I thought it was a waste of time, so I forgot about it for a few days.

'Then on the spur of the moment I decided to write a proper application, because of my predicament I could not do it very well and it was nothing more than a scribbled note.'

With Whiteley in post, he had some choices to make. The World Cup performances had opened doors for plenty of other players and British rugby league at the time had a serious amount of talent to pick from.

Harrison, who was in the running to be selected, recalls, 'There was that many good players in that day. The ones that could have gone on the Lions tours were unreal. People think we were all big fat players. You only got the odd kid that was fat. They were all big, well-built lads.'

Clive, despite not being prolific that year, was to be selected, along with John Atkinson, who had been the league's top scorer with 38 tries, and his Leeds teammate Alan Smith.

Smith, well-known for his modesty, remembers the set-up, 'Clive Sullivan, '60, '70 and beyond, was Great Britain's first choice right winger. On the 1970 tour, they didn't take four wingers, they took three. I was back-up boy. And I was okay with that. Getting on tour to me was beyond my wildest dreams. What was I doing on tour with them?'

Leeds and Castleford players dominated the team on paper, the latter having finished second in the table to Leeds and won the Challenge Cup. It was one of Whiteley's key tasks to blend the squad into a team capable of facing an imposing Australian side.

'The build-up for games like Leeds and Hull, Leeds and Cas, there was lots of aggression in them,' remembers Smith. 'When we all got on the plane, you could feel it in the air, we were all warriors. [Keith] Hepworth, [Alan] Hardisty, Malcolm Riley [who were all Castleford players], Phil Lowe [of Hull KR]. The anger! But we became great mates.'

Thankfully for the British, Whiteley was up to the task, according to Smith, 'His ability to keep everyone together, his ability to juggle with a heavy schedule with lads who wanted to play. We'd do anything for him. Johnny got a lot of the psychology from Roy [Francis] and a lot of his training ideas from Roy.'

One of Whiteley's key rules was banning the players from sharing rooms with clubmates, to discourage any already existing divisions in camp from growing. Clive roomed with John Atkinson, who had remained a good friend after their time touring two years previously. Atkinson, speaking to writer Phil Caplan for his biography of Mick Shoebottom published some years later, said that Clive was 'brilliant' to room with. That was 'because he'd been a paratrooper and he could get up early and make you toast and press your trousers'.

Although Whiteley had created a settled and cohesive unit quickly, testament to his abilities as both a coach and motivator, he had left the UK under a cloud. Whiteley's five-year deal as player-coach at Hull had expired and he was officially a free agent, able to negotiate with clubs both in Australia and back in the UK. He told reporters that he had 'an entirely open mind on the situation', and Whiteley would indeed have to at least return to the city at the culmination of the tour to tie up personal commitments.

Yet it was hard to see how he could come back to the only club he had ever known. Aside from the selection issues, the ugly boardroom feuding had continued almost all year.

Joe Latus, who wrote his own account of Clive's career in the 1970s, publicly blamed his fellow board members' selections for Hull's Challenge Cup first-round exit against Castleford. The sniping in the press continued as Latus, the man the players had insinuated was behind the 'proxy votes' selection policy, was asked to resign by the newly-elected chairman, Charles Watson.

'I am sorry to hear that Watson has been appointed chairman,' Latus told the press, and he added, 'Lots of matters need airing.' In response, an angered Watson informed the public, 'Latus does not run the club ... but that does not alter the fact that he tries to.'

It must have been a relief for both Whiteley and Clive to arrive in Australia, away from the press and speculation. However, Ashes series in Australia are headline news so it may have been a case of out of the frying pan and into the fire.

Unlike the World Cup of the previous year, the tourists arrived in plenty of time, and played a variety of warm-up and friendly matches. Britain won them with ease, the only real talking point being the wild and aggressive tactics employed by some of the Aussie sides, desperate to make a name for themselves against 'the Poms'.

The first Test was to take place at Lang Park in Brisbane. Hopes were high in the whole rugby league community that the games would live up to their billing, rather than being a repeat of the damp squibs that 1967 and '68 had produced.

A last-minute problem was created when Malcolm Reilly, the talented 21-year-old loose forward, allegedly headbutted a local businessman at a party.

The businessman had allegedly goaded Reilly by calling him a 'pommy bastard' and saying, 'Wait until Beetson gets you.' It created a farcical element to the tour as legal representatives attempted to issue Reilly with a writ, even when he was preparing to run out on to the field. Later in the tour, Reilly then hospitalised South Sydney Rabbitohs full back Ray Longbottom after a street altercation outside of South Sydney's supporters' club.

Although peculiar footnotes on such a heavily hyped tour, these incidents illustrate how hard the home nation was gunning for the tourists. Highlighting the spirit to be then found in the camp, however, Reilly's teammates all contributed sums to help pay his legal fees.

Reilly was still picked at loose forward for the opening game despite the controversy, as was Clive on the left wing alongside the captain, St Helens's Frank Myler. Atkinson was on the opposite wing, with Mick Shoebottom inside him. Terry Price was at full back.

One of the biggest surprises was the absence of Roger Millward, who was dropped in favour of Hardisty. Similarly, Dennis Hartley was left out in a bold choice, David Chisnall of Leigh stepping into the breech alongside Cliff Watson in the front row.

The 42,000 people in attendance that day saw one of the most heated and brutal international matches of the 1970s. Smith, watching from the sidelines, saw the drama unfold, 'The first test in Brisbane Clive was picked on the right. Johnny Whiteley picked all the recognised wings and half backs. Unfortunately, they lost it. They lost the match but they didn't lose the war. It was a vicious match. It turned nasty at the end.'

Australia prevailed 37-15, with two tries coming via Johnny King down Clive's wing. Clive, rightfully so proud of his ability to defend his wing, had been caught out.

The animosity and tension between both camps had also boiled over in the second half. Chisnall attempted to kick opposition prop Jimmy Morgan. The two began to brawl, and Cliff Watson joined the fray. Morgan butted Watson, who returned the favour, shattering the Aussie's nose. Watson was sent off for his efforts.

The ferocity of the violence and the image of a bloodied Morgan made headlines across Australia. The tourists were described as 'leaving a sick taste in the mouth' by Aussie rugby league bible *Rugby League Week*. To add to Morgan's shattered nose, the Australians left the Test having been brutalised en masse. Beetson and full back Langlands had sustained broken noses, stand off Phil Hawthorne had damaged both legs, and second row Ron Lynch had a fractured cheekbone.

Trailing 1-0 in the series and with even more anger directed towards them after being vilified in the press, Britain had it all to do.

In response, Whiteley rang the changes and Millward was recalled for the second Test. There were changes in the front row, back row and centres, along with a switch on the wings. Clive was to be dropped for Alan Smith.

Whiteley explained to me his rationale, 'I was fortunate enough in 1970 to be the coach of the Great Britain side, which toured Australia. [Clive] was a great tourist. At that time, we had three magnificent wingmen. John Atkinson, Alan Smith and Clive. Because they'd played together [Smith and Atkinson], he missed out.'

Despite the good news, Smith was apprehensive about replacing his friend, 'The second Test came up, but Clive, after the first Test, he wasn't having his best tour. All that does is give opportunities for people like Roger Millward and me. So, Johnny Whiteley fantastically manipulated a great group with a great team spirit. I thought Clive might not talk to me after I took his place.

'But it didn't work like that. Everyone rotated. We'd play a Test match at the weekend then a tour match midweek. I felt quite honoured that I played in the second Test. But what a support [Clive] was to me. He said, don't worry about it; it's your time. But then his time came again anyway.'

Smith had grown to greatly admire his fellow winger on the tour, 'We got on really well ... The memory I have of Clive, aside from thinking he was the best winger of the time and idolising him, was the operations he had on his legs. The quads he had in his legs were removed, he could still run! That staggered me. The character of the man [to come back from that].'

It was typical of Clive's character to seek to offer his advice and support to the less experienced Smith, especially in the now close-knit squad. Yet, for a perfectionist such as Clive, it must have been a crushing blow to have lost the first Test and have been dropped.

Families were not taken on tour at the time, and, as Smith points out, communication back home was greatly restricted, which would have further increased any feelings of isolation Clive or any of the other players would have felt.

Yet the closed-off nature of the side, away from home comforts and in a hostile country, led to more bonding, especially on a mid-tour visit to New Zealand before the second Test.

According to Smith, Clive revealed a penchant for the Everly Brothers, 'I remember in New Zealand, me and Clive got closer, loads of [other players] had gone to play Greymouth [in Auckland]. They left all those that weren't playing in the hotel. [Those playing had] gone on the train, took a day, played, then took a train home. My memory of Clive, he'd put on "Ebony Eyes" on the jukebox. He knew all the words, all the way through.'

In front of 60,000 at the Sydney Cricket Ground, Britain levelled the series. The game was just as intense at the first encounter and Leeds centre Syd Hynes was sent off after kicking Artie Beetson. Disaster also struck as British full back Derek Edwards was injured in tackle, Smith remembering, 'John Whiteley carrying him off the pitch.'

Yet despite being a man down, and with Mick Shoebottom playing as a replacement full back, the Lions secured one of the greatest victories in their history, 28-7. Millward was at the fore, scoring two of his side's tries and kicking all six goals, his 20 points matching the record set decades previously by Lewis Jones. Perhaps disappointed at seeing their side lose, or perhaps enjoying the festivities too much, the Australian crowd then descended into brawling among themselves, on the terraces, in further ugly scenes.

Smith describes the rivalry with the Australians as 'fierce', and adds,'The first 20 minutes were a battle, physical, mental. It was a show of determination, which side's going to come out on top. Test matches now seem to be the same for 80 minutes. Ours was a war for the first 20. But with a lot of skill. Roger, he survived in a cauldron of fire [that day].

'But people like that. It's why people watch boxing and wrestling. People watch motorbike racing and car racing to see if there's going to be a crash ... You had to have the agility, strength and courage of a boxer [out on the field]. Nobody who played the game was soft.'

Unsurprisingly, Whiteley decided to stick with the same side for the last Test, although Derek Edwards was in no position to play after being injured in the previous outing.

Then a mini crisis followed as Terry Price was also ruled out with a fever and Ray Dutton, the last specialist full back on tour, had also been injured.

Although Clive had never played full back, nor would he, it may have presented an opportunity if Whiteley had moved other members of his team around.

Clive's last appearance of the tour, however, came against a Newcastle outfit. In front of 20,000 fans, his tour ended with him leaving the pitch injured. Although it looked another serious setback, it turned out to be a relatively straightforward hamstring issue.

Shoebottom was therefore drafted in at full back, with Whiteley pleading with his side to 'play football not fisticuffs'.

With locals queuing overnight to gain a ticket, an additional 2,000 more than the first Test crammed into the Sydney Cricket Ground to see the decider. The rowdy crowd then threw beer cans and fruit at the Lions as the game got under way.

To nobody's surprise, it was another brutal game. This time it was the Kangaroos who went a man down after Beetson punched Cliff Watson on the hour mark after a running battle between the pair. Australian full back Allan McKean kicked repeated penalties and the home side also scored a try, but Britain blew them off the park, running in five tries in a 21-17 victory.

In a reverse of the World Cup two years previously, Britain had performed wonderfully yet Clive had been a peripheral part. Yet, while he didn't feature in the last two Tests, his generosity with teammates was an important part. The whole squad had been vital in creating a siege mentality that had fostered an overwhelming momentum and spirit.

Ultimately, he was part of the last side to win an Ashes series Down Under. Whiteley also secured the unique feat of winning the Ashes away as a player, in 1958, and as a coach.

However, the question about which of them would be at Hull in the coming season was still up in the air as they headed back.

Upheaval

IN retrospect, the outcome of the Johnny Whiteley 'free agent' saga seems obvious. Board disruption, with disgruntled players, did not present the most enticing of environments for Whiteley to return to. Added to that was the fact he was an Ashes-winning coach, who had won the series in the cauldron of Brisbane and Sydney, and he was a man in demand.

Yet there was a hope that Whiteley would return to the Boulevard, such was the bond he had with the club and the community that surrounded it. On a more practical level, Joe Latus, allegedly the source of much discontent, had left the board while Whiteley was Down Under.

But one week after returning from the tour, Whiteley confirmed that he would not be returning to the club with which he had had a 20-year association. Speaking to the press at the time, Whiteley felt that it was 'time for a change' and wished to concentrate on his businesses outside of the game.

Speaking to me, and looking back, however, Whiteley is much more candid, both about why he left and if he indeed was a 'free agent'.

He recalled, 'I started beating the drum, as much for the players' sake [to oversee team selections]. And I lost. I lost. People left the Hull football club, in that era, the late '60s; they were drifting from the club that they loved due to mismanagement. I was one of those. I never had a contract, and I've never had a contract in my life.'

Whiteley's last playing appearance for Hull had come on 6 February 1965, in a defeat at Warrington. While the side he coached picked up only the Yorkshire Cup and were staunchly mid-table, it was one that attracted lots of praise for the clean and attractive style of rugby it played. Roy Francis had been praised for his 'total rugby' employed at Leeds and it's clear to see that Whiteley was attempting to mould a similar style, but with less financial resources and more behind-the-scenes issues.

It's sad to reflect on how that era ended as Hull had a side which had grown together and, following the Yorkshire Cup victory, perhaps they had the potential to push on. To keep with some sense of continuity, Ivor Watts, the great winger from the 1950s, who had been Whiteley's assistant, was appointed as his successor.

Sadness at Whiteley's departure soon turned to a sense of shock when he did the unthinkable to those located in West Hull. He was unveiled as the coach of Hull KR, with Colin Hutton moving 'upstairs' to become the football manager, a partnership described by the *Hull Daily Mail* as 'perhaps the strongest behind-the-scenes directive in the game'.

'I look on this post as a challenge, and I am open to any challenge', Whiteley informed the press after his appointment. 'It may be difficult after so many years at Hull [FC] but I am sure the players and supporters will accept me.'

Whiteley's job immediately gave him more headaches, however, as Roger Millward, now revered in Australia for his masterly Ashes performances, began agitating for a transfer out of the club. Although he was denied a move, the problem did not seem likely to go away any time soon.

Back in the west of the city, Watts had a tough task after such a blow to morale, but at least the boardroom drama had been nipped in the bud. The 1970/71 season saw Clive make a move into the centre positions, inside Howard Firth, who had proved to be a shrewd signing. It's indicative of Clive's ability that he was a more than competent centre.

While in the modern game a second row would be considered a possible stop-gap centre, in Clive's era the centre spots were often filled by players who could also play at stand off. Like the ability of rugby union fly halves to play at outside centre, the elusive running, game management and passing skills of a stand off and centre in rugby league were similar enough for one to deputise for another.

Clive, who had burst on to the scene as a fleet-footed winger, was always more than a player who relied solely on speed. But in deputising for Dick Gemmell, who had been injured in the off-season, he showed just how deep his understanding of the game was. Clive, while still seen as a winger, would regularly fill in at centre while Mick Crane, a young, local 'A'-teamer, was introduced into the first team.

In the first competitive meeting between KR, under Whiteley's stewardship, and Watts's Hull FC, Rovers picked up an 18-8 victory in the BBC Floodlit Trophy. Despite the loss, Clive, in his new role at centre, crossed for a try and picked up plaudits for his committed display.

Despite the subplot to the game, it only attracted a disappointing 4,000 fans to Craven Park. Then, after barely more than 2,000 fans had seen Hull's home fixture against Salford, board member Frank Giblin was moved to comment, 'Saturday afternoon football is dead.'

The attendance was illustrative of an alarming trend of decreased figures across the sport. While both cricket and soccer had seen attendances fall in the 1960s, they had stabilised somewhat by the start of the '70s, although they were still below the figures seen in the pre-television days.

Tony Collins, writing in his seminal *Rugby League in Twentieth-Century Britain* points out that 'spectator sport became, in economist's terms, an inferior good'. Although many sports saw their traditional support base growing in affluence, rugby league began to see the traditional cornerstones of its communities break up, never to be reformed. Yorkshire's mining community was still strong as the '70s began but Lancashire's was beginning the slow process of winding down. Textile production was declining much more rapidly, almost ceasing to exist in less than a generation. For Hull, the vital shipping industry was also beginning to show worrying signs.

According to Brian Lavery, 'The decline of the fishing industry, in a way it was kind of inbuilt. The main cause would be the Cod Wars between the Icelanders and the British fleet ... And it started to decline really rapidly in the early 1970s. And the reason for that, ironically, was the success of the female protestors.'

The female protestors were the so-called 'Headscarf Revolutionaries', led by Lillian Bilocca, who had pushed for safety reforms following the loss of three trawlers in 1968.

'It's arguable that the changes to all these maritime laws, while they saved countless lives, it ironically added to the cost,' Lavery told me.

'They had to have mother ships. And a radio operator. Believe it or not you could sail without a radio operator ... by the late '60s and early '70s they started to invest in stern trawlers, where you fish from the back of the ship. They were a lot bigger, like three or four times bigger.

'Plus they had freezers, on sideliners you would catch the fish, people would gut them and process them on the deck as the waves were crashing in. On stern trawlers, they could be dropped into a factory below deck and frozen. You could fast-freeze fish; fill up a hold, a catch more than ever before. Because you could do that, the stern trawler could be out for three of four months.'

By 1971, a third less people worked in the industry than 20 years previously, when Hull FC had produced that great team of the 1950s. The rise of more choices of leisure activities for some, and a reduction of disposable income for others, was a terrible one-two punch for rugby league.

The final, telling blow, was the so-called 'slum clearances', the further fragmentation of communities. The Bransholme council estate, found just to the east of the river, was developed as the '60s came to an end. A mixture of high-rise flats, terrace housing and bungalows, some of terrible quality, sprang up as the often equally poor housing on Hessle Road was pulled down.

Rosalyn recalls, 'As they knocked down Hessle Road and moved them to Bransholme, that community was lost.'

Although this was happening across the north and across rugby league communities, the lifeblood of Hull FC was that Hessle Road community.

To the RFL's credit, they did recognise the slide quickly and employed a consultancy firm to attempt to deal with their 'image problem'. One of the solutions was that promotion and relegation was to be reintroduced, although not immediately. It was an attempt to stamp out dull, pointless fixtures between teams with nothing to play for, or huge blowout victories for the best teams against the worst.

The report was, however, damning in many other areas, such as the game's overall financial administration and engagement with the national media. Solutions were either never implemented or done so slowly and poorly, which caused lasting issues for the sport.

On the pitch, and specifically for Clive, it was good news. Largely injury-free, aside from one or two knocks to his vulnerable thighs, he produced a consistent and impressive season in his new role of one of the side's most senior and experienced heads. Alongside him in the roles were Mick Harrison and Alan McGlone as well as Terry Devonshire, who had re-joined mid-season.

The return of Clive's 'bosom pal' Devonshire had a galvanising effect. Clive made the joint highest number of appearances for Hull that year, 41, and was destructive, scoring 33 tries as the side finished a respectable eighth, their best in some time, and four places above KR.

Clive's best performance arguably came in a home win over Featherstone where he scored two tries, one of which saw him run for 60 yards with the ball. Another, when he went 75 yards away at Bradford, suggested his pace was nowhere near as eroded as some had speculated. It allowed Clive to equal the scoring record of Keith Bowman set in 1953/54, a wonderful return considering he filled in at centre on 15 occasions.

Despite such a wonderful season, Clive was surprisingly omitted from the 1970 World Cup squad. The tournament, held in the UK, had been heavily hyped mainly for a repeat of hostilities between Australia and the Lions. Perhaps it was a hangover from his previous displays, but the Leeds pair of Smith and Atkinson were first choice, with Welsh rugby union convert Keri Jones, who had had a great season for Wigan with 40 tries as the league's top scorer, acting as back-up.

Smith told me, 'Then you could pick three Great Britain teams. There'd be loads of wingers, centres, and half backs. [Don't get me wrong] they are talented lads and hard lads [but] now, you can just get a team together.'

It was a bitter disappointment, but at least the blow was softened somewhat by a campaign where Clive had rehabilitated his reputation as a player of real quality and proved he could play the majority of a season. He also missed out on more ugly and brutal scenes of violence between the warring British and Australians, particularly in the final, when Australia won. Alan Smith told me, 'The rugby league won't let young kids watch it [due to the fighting]. Ron Coote told me it was the hardest game he ever played in.'

Watts was tied down to a three-year deal following the end of the season. Alluding to the recent strife, chairman Watson was quick to highlight that FC had become 'a big, happy family' which could 're-establish itself as one of the elites of the game'.

With his feet firmly under the table, Watts began his restructure. Arthur Keegan, such a great servant to the side, left for Bramley as player-coach. The end of the Whiteley era, and indeed, the '60s generation, was highlighted even further when Dick Gemmell retired for good.

Repeated injuries and the wear and tear of professional rugby league, as well as the emergence of Mick Crane and Clive in the centres, led to Gemmell moving into the hotel business. The role of a hotelier seemed to be a popular one for those associated with rugby league in Hull as Roy Francis left the North Sydney Bears to take up a post in North Yorkshire. John Maloney was also transfer listed.

As was typical of Hull FC at the time, however, the good times were fleeting. The players 'retained by the club' protested the financial terms they had been offered. Theirs fees remained smaller than those of Hull KR, despite the league placings, and the 'broken time payments', specifically for midweek away games in which FC lost, were so low that the players 'would lose money'. It was another ugly public spat as the players, none of whom had renegotiated terms, pledged to train on their own, away from the club, to keep fit.

The anger was understandable as around the same time Hull also announced their biggest post-war profit. In the club's defence, they had lost money consistently during the '60s and with crowd figures showing no signs of recovery across the game, it required a tightening of purse strings to ensure financial viability.

The dispute was eventually resolved, away from the press, although Joe Latus sought re-election to the board.

On a personal level, after such a positive 1970/71 season, the key test for Clive would be if his leg could hold up for another full campaign. He also had the added pressure of being named captain of the side due to Keegan's departure. Clive was indeed an experienced player, approaching 30, although his long spells of enforced inactivity had had the small bonus of giving him a freshness rarely seen in players of that age.

He started extremely well, picking up six tries as the season had barely begun, while Hull collected eight points from the first ten available. Their good start came despite a terrible injury to McGlone, such a crucial presence in the scrum and at the play of the ball.

He recalled, 'It was in the Eve Hardaker Cup [pre-season 'friendly' against Hull KR]. I used to have this thing with Sully. I'd give him one of these [a look]. He'd know I was off from acting half, and he was always there, and he'd get the pass. I did it, broke through, beat one person, looked over my shoulder and the grass hadn't been cut. My stud got caught in the grass and I got hit, the pain was unreal.'

McGlone had damaged his cruciate ligament, a severe injury even today. It would sideline him from the game completely for almost 18 months.

Despite the injury to McGlone, the good start was just what Clive needed. An early-season tour by New Zealand to Great Britain had been arranged, both for Britain to keep the triumphant Ashes-winning side active and New Zealand to gain touring experience the year before a World Cup.

Although early indications were that Alan Smith and John Atkinson would edge out Clive again, Smith broke his thumb in a game against Salford the week before. Atkinson himself also picked up a slight injury, clearing the way for both Clive and Les Jones. Jones was a wonderfully talented St Helens winger who was unlucky to have been around in the era of such brilliant British wingers, yet he was handed his chance.

'I had hoped I would get selected, but the news still came as a marvellous surprise,' Clive told reporters about his recall. 'I have been quite pleased with my game this season.'

New Zealand at the time were considered underdogs but they had defeated Australia prior to their arrival, highlighting their quality when in the right mood. To add to their determination, they were the first touring Kiwi side since the mythical 'All Golds' of 1908, the tour that helped solidify rugby league in both Australia and New Zealand. Then, as now, a rugby union-playing nation, rugby league still retained a major interest for the New Zealanders, even if it did not have the extra needle and edge to be found with Britain and Australia.

Unfortunately for both Britain and the Kiwis, the games were met with the complete apathy of the rugby league public in the UK. For Clive's return to the side in the first Test, only around 4,000 fans attended The Willows in Salford.

They missed something of a thriller as both sides jockeyed for the lead until New Zealand pulled away to win 18-13, nilling the British during a tense second half. Although Clive did not get on the scoresheet, his defensive efforts were back to their usual high standard as most of the scores came down the opposite wing.

A major loss for the British was Mal Riley, who had decided to head to the New South Wales Rugby League Premiership, the precursor to today's NRL. His move deprived him of selection for the national side, although Riley, feared and admired in equal measure, quickly won the league with Manly. While logistically it would have been near impossible to select him anyway, it was hard not to feel that the British team were the ones that missed out, deprived of his skill, aura and aggression.

Roger Millward's earlier agitation for a move Down Under, along with Manly paying £15,000 pounds for Reilly, marked the growing momentum and confidence in the Australian game.

The British league had been losing the odd player to Australia since the 1960s with Brits emigrating as the famous 'Ten Pound Poms'. Alan McGlone was one such player to be tempted in those days.

He said, 'I was playing for Hull, there was no way you could get a transfer. Once you signed on with a club, you were there for life, unless you retired or emigrated. I was 20 and had one daughter who was about 18 months. We didn't have much, a little council house and a sofa. I booked the six-week boat from Southampton [to Sydney], it was £10, and the government paid for it anyway. I was off. And I tore a cartilage in my leg against Castleford in the last game of the season. They had offered me a fantastic offer; the average at Hull was £12 a week. But that was your wage as well as a journeyman. But they'd [Canterbury-Bankstown] offered me £2,000 and a job as a carpet salesman for one of the directors.'

Yet as the 1970s progressed, Australian clubs wanted to pay big fees for British internationals. Tony Collins writes, 'In the 1970s ... an even greater number of British internationals [made the move], attracted by better wages, the Australian lifestyle and the star treatment accorded them by being high profile names in Sydney's biggest sport. Ironically Britain's 1970s Ashes series victory accelerated the exodus Down Under.'

At 30, and with injury issues, Clive would not have been a player looked at, especially with a young family as well. Had he been a decade younger, however, he undoubtedly would have been in demand. The upshot, however, was that his star began to shine even brighter as one of the country's top players remained in the UK to ply his trade, as others moved on and headed to the Sydney clubs.

Ultimately, however, Reilly or not, Britain were 1-0 down in the series against New Zealand. Clive was picked for the second Test, at Wheldon Road in Castleford. The crowd was still extremely poor, with only around 4,000 attending again, as Britain blew an 11-5 half-time lead to lose 17-14. Although Clive did score, Britain had fallen a long way from the heady heights of the Ashes in 1970.

It was a dire result in all regards. New Zealand were a better outfit than given credit prior to the tour, or indeed after it. But to lose a series after being in commanding positions in both games, in front of sparse crowds, was disastrous for British rugby league.

Bizarrely, the last game, held at Headingley, attracted the biggest crowd of the series, although at scarcely over 5,000 people it was still an awful turn-out. Clive retained his place and helped the British to a face-saving 12-3 win, the Leeds pair of John Atkinson and young stand off John Holmes bagging all the points scored.

An aggregate attendance of 13,330 watched the three fixtures. The game's shrinkage was accelerating alarmingly, leading Hull KR director Ron Chester to ominously state, 'Rugby league isn't dying, it is dead.'

Despite the almost overwhelming gloom, Clive continued to excel for Hull as well as in the Test series. Still predominantly a winger with the odd spell at centre, he managed to make another 41 appearances for Hull FC in the league. He couldn't quite match the previous season's try tally but he still finished with 31 to his name. It was another brilliant return from a player acting as his side's captain and focal point.

Aside from Clive, however, it was a terrible season for Hull, as they dropped down to 19th place. Although Ivor Watts's side played well at home, they were regularly beaten badly on their travels, with the likes of St Helens, Rochdale and Wigan racking up 30-plus points wins in the era of the three-point try. Hull KR also did not pull up any trees, finishing a disappointing 14th.

It was clear that Hull, rugby league and indeed Clive needed a boost. Perhaps the 1972 World Cup, to be held in France, could provide just that.

French Flair

ASIDE from the World Cup to be played mid-season in 1972, rugby league in the UK would be shaken up with the reintroduction of the Second Division. Of the 30 teams, the bottom 14 would be relegated and the rest would remain in the First Division. The convoluted manner of naming a league champion, whereby the team that finished top after the regular season would be named 'league leaders' but the champions would be decided via play-offs, was also scrapped.

While the modern Super League employs such a method for crowning a champion come the season's end, in the 1960s and '70s part-time athletes played the game rather than today's full-timers. The sport also had an abundance of cups at the time. The Yorkshire/Lancashire cups, the Challenge Cup, the recently added League Cup (Halifax winning the inaugural one in 1971) and the BBC Floodlit Trophy were all on top of regular-season fixtures.

The fatigue on players caused by so many matches, training and playing after long days at work, was probably only matched by the supporters who had so much rugby league to watch. The overabundance of rugby was yet another reason given for the continued stagnation of crowd figures. It was expensive, and not always enjoyable; players would began to psychically break down due to the hard slog of games.

To prevent dour, defence-orientated rugby, six tackles were also set to be introduced, as opposed to four tackles. The hope was that with an extra two tackles to use, sides would try and play expansive rugby rather than simply hammer the other side with forwards before kicking for territory.

For both Hull FC and Hull KR, relegation was a real concern now that it was reintroduced. Both had slid the previous season, although in Whiteley's defence, he regularly lost key players, such as Millward and Phil Lowe, to bad injuries.

For Watts, who was attempting to take over from one of the most iconic figures Hull FC had ever seen, and do so as established players such as Clive, Alan McGlone and Chris Davidson began to age, it was a big ask. Hull, perhaps sensing that the campaign would be a tough one, opted to re-hire Roy Francis, back in the country and available. In a rather convoluted structure, Watts would remain as coach while Francis would act as manager.

The deal had been in the pipeline for some time as chairman Charles Watson had spoken to Francis as far back as the 1970 World Cup Final at Headingley about a return to the Boulevard.

Francis would have 'complete control of team selections'.

Francis, having had such success with his style of rugby at Leeds and North Sydney, was desperate to bring that brand back to Hull, exclaiming, 'My aim is to plan attractive football, but also winning football.'

Despite what appeared to be a demotion on the face of it, Watson was adamant that Watts still had a role to play. Watts himself even admitted, 'Something had to be done and I believe that Roy is just the man to put Hull back on their feet.'

One thing that Watts and Francis had in their favour was the continued emergence of Clive as a leader and figurehead. Not only had Clive proven an effective captain of Hull FC, he had also stepped up to captain Great Britain, although under tragic circumstances.

Mick Shoebottom, Clive's friend and international teammate, had received a grievous injury caused by, of all people, Colin Dixon in a championship semi-final at Headingley at the back-end of the previous season. Dixon, who had many years previously appeared in the same Wales schoolboys team as Clive, had steamed into the effervescent Shoebottom as he scored a crucial try. Shoebottom, at the age of 26, fractured his jaw but also received what at first was believed to be a serious concussion. It was soon discovered it was much more serious, a brain haemorrhage, as the sight of a stricken Shoebottom in the Headingley changing rooms left his teammates in shock.

After overcoming that life-threatening injury having been rushed to hospital, Shoebottom then suffered a stroke in the following weeks causing speech and memory issues and the loss of any feeling down his right-hand side. It was a tragic end to the thrilling career of the player nicknamed 'The Lionheart' for his energy and commitment. Showing typical determination, however, he managed to recover enough to lead as full a life as he was able, surpassing many of the initially limited expectations.

Although it would be a stretch to call him a victim, the shadow of the incident hung over Dixon as well, who always maintained that the contact was accidental. For the rest of his career, even when appearing for Great Britain on a few occasions in the years following, he was widely heckled and booed by fans, especially at Headingley.

It illustrated the continued brutality and danger inherent in the game, yet the response also showed the camaraderie, mutual respect and 'family feel' when tragedy faces rugby league. In a quickly-arranged fixture, Great Britain played Leeds at Headingley on 11 January 1972 with the profits to be donated to a fund set up for Shoebottom, who would struggle to work again, let alone play rugby league. With Roger Millward not deemed fit enough to continue his role as captain, Clive was named as his replacement. Mick Harrison and Phil Lowe were also in the squad.

Although arriving via a method nobody would have wished for, the choice of Clive to captain the side in such an emotionally sensitive fixture was telling. Aside from his abilities as a player, Clive the man was widely respected for his fair play and approachability.

The match was no more than a friendly, allowing the British selectors to try out a few fresh players. But it did produce a decent amount of money for the Shoebottom family. Fittingly, for a man who had given so much to both Leeds and Great Britain, the game ended 12-12.

A bigger test for both Clive and the team was to come against France. The original replacement for Millward as skipper was centre Syd Hynes of Leeds, but he had turned out for his club side as opposed to the British team. Against France, he was to retain the mantle. The only new debutant was St Helens's Ken Kelley. Unfortunately the luckless Hynes, who had injury problems off and on over his career, had to pull out at the last minute, allowing Clive to regain the captaincy with St Helens's Billy Benyon stepping into the centres in Hynes's place.

The game further illustrated Clive's ability as a motivator and captain. In front of a large crowd, the French went in at half-time 8-5 up despite Benyon's try, the boot of old enemy Jean Capdouze pegging the British back. Despite the deficit, and the absence of the likes of Millward, the British pulled off an impressive 10-9 win with Clive's second-half try proving key.

It was described in the *Hull Daily Mail*, understandably proud that one of the city's club captains was leading the national side, as 'one of the most satisfying victories in [France, misspelled as 'Franch'] for several years'.

Regardless if one counts the Leeds encounter or the match against France, Clive had made history as being the first black Briton to captain a British sports team. The occasion caused little discussion either in the rugby league world or further afield, which, in retrospect, was both refreshing and frustrating.

On the one hand it reflects the rugby league attitude of caring little for background provided someone could do the job. It highlights Clive's acceptance as a player and as a person, rather than being defined by his ethnicity. As Rosalyn said, 'You don't see yourself as a colour.'

On the flip-side, however, the lack of acknowledgment of this watershed moment deprived rugby league of the recognition it deserved for its open-mindedness. Although he would no doubt have been uncomfortable with it, Clive himself should have been recognised for such a significant feat.

As Rosalyn pointed out, despite the ethnic diversity found in Clive's home of Cardiff, the Welsh rugby union side would have offered him no such opportunities, 'I think in sport, it was accepted. He never played union, or never got involved. If you go back to that time [the '60s and '70s.] You never saw a black person in the Welsh rugby union side. [But] until I went down to Wales, I'd never seen so many mixed-race couples.'

It is worth pointing out that Clive's hero, Muhammad Ali, had only been back in boxing for two years after his 'exile' from the sport at the time Clive took the captaincy. Ali's political views regarding the war in Vietnam and the treatment of African-Americans in the United States made him both a pariah to Middle America and a hero to the raging civil rights movement, depriving him of some of his prime years as an athlete.

While it would be overstating the case to argue that Clive was a British equivalent to Ali, who was so different in personality and stature, this illustrated the resistance still shown towards minorities who dared to challenge the social order. Clive, so humble, gracious and approachable, quietly did just that when stepping on to the field as a captain of a side representing the whole country. The fact that he did it so impressively only added to its potency.

Although race and racism in rugby league has never been as blatant as that seen in football for many years, or as covert and insidious as found in rugby union, it did exist.

'Clive has had racial abuse from supporters,' Rosalyn told me.

'He'd either bow. He had a way of dealing with it that wasn't confrontational. He'd think, "Yeah. Well I'll show you what I can do." He'd say, "It's done me a favour, because I stood out." It wasn't an impediment. There was never any issue with our group [of friends], and I wouldn't want to make colour an issue. But it did exist. I'm not brushing it under the carpet. It was there.'

His performance allowed him to retain the captaincy in the following Test against the French at Odsal, of all places. This time, instead of a gruelling game with conservative rugby being the key to success, Clive and the team produced a thrilling display to blow the French off the park, 45-10. It was the biggest win over the French since 1959 and the tries were shared out almost equally. Nine different players, including Clive, got one each with only second rower Bill Ashurst getting two.

Clive had a style of captaincy which gelled well with the squad, according to Rosalyn, 'He was over the moon [to be captain]. Clive always went out to win, to do his best. I think he was his own worst critic. If they won and he hadn't played well, inside he hadn't won. He was an out and out professional. He played very cleanly. Over the time, the players that became that team, they knew that. And they respected him. His attitude of "you go out there and you do your best", that'll have gone through the team.'

Just to add to a brilliant week personally for Clive, his daughter Lisa was born in the aftermath of the win.

Although Britain were flying, it was not under the stewardship of Johnny Whiteley, who had resigned his post due to personal reasons. His replacement was Jim Challinor of St Helens.

Although Whiteley had left the role, he still recognises today the impact Clive had captaining Great Britain, 'Being black as well, it shows you the heart of the man. You don't see colour, you never look at that. You're all a part of the system. And that's what Clive was.

'In my young days, people like Clive would have stuck out like a sore thumb. You'd never see a black lad. By Clive's era that stigma was starting to lift a bit. And Clive was a wonderful advocate for that. Aligned to being a wonderful rugby player, he was doing a wonderful service in that era.

'Because he was a gentle man really. People who look at rugby players as bullies and tough cookies, [and] while he was a tough kid, he had such a gentle nature. He was warm; he'd go into schools. It was his presence; he had an aura about him. Words can't describe that. He'd walk into a pub with you, and everyone's eyes would shine. Clive Sullivan!'

Despite Whiteley's joy for his friend, his resignation from the national side had some unintended consequences for the game back in Humberside. Hull KR, who had been doing well up until mid-season, parted ways with Whiteley after he left the post with Britain. According to KR historian Roger Pugh, 'The board was unhappy about it as they believed there was prestige in having the current Great Britain coach at the club ... There was always those in the club's hierarchy who did not like Whiteley's strong Hull FC background.'

Whiteley, speaking to me in 2017, was upfront about why he parted ways with Kingston Rovers, 'Hull KR promised me I'd have some input on selection, which I felt would give me a start of what I was after. I did have a say, as virtually ten of every team pick themselves. And at Hull, you just sat there and the board would pick the side.

'At Hull KR, Colin became a director. We'd all pick the selection on a Tuesday. We'd sit round after training. The chairman would say, right, any nominees for the full back on Saturday. You'd nominate your lad, and the directors would nominate theirs. I'd say Smith, they'd say Brown. But of course, they'd have had a meeting beforehand. So, Smith's got no chance. I'd get outvoted. But I saw through that. I blew my top and said I'm not having this.'

With Whiteley available, the opportunity presented itself to bring him back 'home' to the Boulevard. He was quickly unveiled as part of a 'dream team' with Ivor Watts as his co-coach, and Francis still overseeing the whole operation. 'I cannot see why a three-man coaching team should not be able to work together,' Watts told the press. 'The club's prospects must be a lot brighter than for some time.'

Despite the brains trust now operating at Hull FC, the season was a disaster. Francis, using his Australian connections, brought in a plethora of Aussies to help bolster the playing ranks. Signed from such clubs as Lakes United and Macquarie in the Newcastle Rugby League competition, the players were largely unheard of and struggled to settle.

'It was hard for the kids coming over,' Terry Devonshire told me. 'They'd never seen snow before.'

The only real successful imports were Mervin Hicks, a former St Helens prop who had emigrated to Australia but returned to play for Hull, and Len Dittmar. Dittmar, a back rower, had appeared for Queensland. 'Len Dittmar was good, a nice guy,' Devonshire said about his former teammate.

Although they struggled to fit in, the Australians were badly needed. Alan McGlone was suffering from injuries and Mick Harrison was heartbreakingly denied a place with the World Cup squad as he badly damaged his knee cartilage, also depriving Hull FC of his services. Chris Davidson was also unsettled, on and off the transfer list as Wigan attempted to sign him.

Defending his transfer policy, Francis told fans, 'I know there are fans on Humberside who are wondering whether I have been wise in bringing all these Australians to the Boulevard, but I have had to play for time and let's not forget I hardly had an A team when I took over … now we are getting into our stride at the Boulevard, but it all takes time and has meant a lot of work behind the scenes.'

Despite the effort put in, Hull suffered such indignities as five consecutive defeats. 'Injuries and loss of form have left Hull in a bad state,' Francis conceded, 'but we cannot expect to climb out of the cellar with this frail ladder … We have the basis of a good side. What we need are the cornerstones.'

In an attempt to find the right solution, Ron Cowan, the younger brother of 1950s Hull FC player Stan, was signed for £1,000 from Leeds, and John Maloney was re-signed from York for £1,500. They also attempted to sign a 21-year-old goal-kicking winger from Castleford, Sammy Lloyd, for £2,500. The Lloyd move ultimately didn't come off but he was to play an important part of the story of Clive Sullivan in the coming years.

Despite the new blood, the side were often edged out in winnable games against fellow strugglers such as Huddersfield and Bradford. The fact that Clive, by far the team's most reliable player for converting chances, seemed guaranteed to be missing for a few weeks due to international commitments only added to the growing sense that the season was heading downhill.

In late October, Francis dropped the bombshell that he was unable to carry on with the club due to 'business and personal commitments'. Watts and Whiteley were then given sole charge, with the suggestion being that Francis would return once his commitments had been fulfilled.

The club truly began to spiral out of control when boardroom politics again came to a head. Chairman Charles Watson lost out after coming bottom of a poll for a new board of directors. As the result was revealed, inside the Central Library theatre in the city, shareholders were heard to shout 'vendetta' and 'rigged'. Watson apparently 'lost his seat because the holder of a number of proxy votes had thrown them behind every director except the chairman'.

Joe Latus was also re-elected, although Latus himself admitted that the situation was 'chaotic' and was against the use of proxy votes. Watson had been criticised for numerous issues, such as the return of Roy Francis, and falling attendances. The club was struggling on the pitch and disjointed off it.

The only bright spot for Hull FC – and the city as a whole – was the hope that Clive could lead a successful British side in France.

World Cup and Coach Clive

ALTHOUGH rugby league had been ahead of the curve with establishing its World Cup, setting it up in 1954 as opposed to rugby union creating its own version in 1987, the tournament was not preceded with huge hype.

The fact that the British side was lacking many of its key players also did not particularly generate excitement. Millward, still injured, was out. Reilly was out. Alan Smith was also out after injuries continued to disrupt his season, alongside Syd Hynes. Alan Hardisty had joined Leeds as his career wound down, with Keith Hepworth not far behind. It goes without saying that Shoebottom was also out after his serious injury.

To no great surprise, Clive was named captain, with both his club and international teammates respecting the choice. While it could be argued he had been given the job in the first instance by default, he had grasped the opportunity with both hands.

McGlone told me about Clive's captaincy, '[He was a captain] because of what he achieved and how he was looked upon. He wasn't one for telling you on a field where you should go and what you should be doing. That came between all of us, voicing things. He wouldn't run a game on a field. He'd play his own game. He was captain because of who he was.'

That style of leadership wasn't always well suited to club fixtures, especially for a struggling team, but it was perfect for international rugby. Clive's era saw the game played in a much less structured way. Players needed to 'play what was in front of them'. Today's competitors, while superb athletes, are often much more rigid in their ability to produce a piece of magic or unexpected flair.

Clive's ability to lead by example and play off-the-cuff, along with the admiration he received off the field from fans, made him a natural fit for the role. An added bonus was his standing with the Australians, who still held him in extremely high regard.

His last club appearance before the World Cup was a try-scoring one as Hull showed what a good side they could be, beating Halifax 29-13. The British side then played two friendly games before heading to France, against York and Oldham. Both matches were more incident-packed than Jim Challinor and Clive would have liked. Firstly, Clive himself had to have a late fitness test to decide if he was fit to take part at all. In the same game that Mick Harrison had been badly injured in against Bradford, Clive had damaged his hip. Thankfully he passed the fitness test.

In the first match, against York, hooker Mike 'Stevo' Stephenson was sent off after the game had barely begun for his attempts to disrupt York's scrums. Then, the day before the squad was due to fly out, Ken Kelley broke his arm against Oldham. David Topliss, the 20-year-old Wakefield stand off, was called up at the last minute, literally meeting the squad at the airport and being given Kelley's tour blazer. Kelley's injury would rule him out for some time, and why exactly the game was played the day before the team jetted off was never really explained. Rugby league being such a physical sport, 'friendly' or not, it seemed like asking for trouble.

The team travelled alongside the British media sent to cover the event, with the journalists themselves helping to part-finance the trip. The majority of the major national newspapers sent along a reporter or two with *The Guardian*, *Sunday People* and *Daily Mirror* all having eyes in France.

The squad and journalists got on well, the consensus being that Australia would be much too strong for France, Britain and New Zealand. Although the British were determined to prove the doubters wrong, they were still realistic about their chances of coming out on top in the whole tournament. Indeed, in years following the tournament, players would often speak of how 'annoyed' they were that journalists from their own country wrote them off so completely.

One group that wasn't brought along for the trip was the wives, girlfriends and families of the players.

'The arrangements weren't made for the wives [to go to the World Cup],' Rosalyn told me. 'There wasn't the money [to go]. They didn't even get paid well for internationals. By the time he'd [Clive] had his time off work and had his subsistence, he probably broke even.'

After arriving in Perpignan four days prior to the first group game against Australia, Challinor allowed his players to go out for the night, although he imposed a strict midnight curfew.

According to the biography of John Holmes, written by his brother and nephew, the team all missed the deadline. John Walsh, the St Helens centre, was the first man spotted by Bill Fallowfield, still the RFL secretary. Fallowfield then explained that Walsh would be sent home the next morning.

Clive, showing his leadership and maturity, managed to talk Fallowfield down from the choice. He encouraged the whole squad to apologise en masse, and pointed out the damage to morale and prestige if one player returned home after only one day due to a group indiscretion, so Walsh remained on tour.

There was a caveat, however. Fallowfield allegedly told the group that failure to win the whole tournament would result in 'sanctions' being implemented on all the players. Intentional or not, it was an extra motivation for the side.

The incident, as throwaway and silly as it seems, helped to cement the team's bond and further entrench Clive's standing in the camp as a motivator and leader. 'Clive never allowed somebody to just sit and read a book … He was fair, but he demanded the best,' Mike Stephenson told me for a 2013 issue of *Rugby League World* magazine when reflecting on the tournament.

'At six in the morning, we'd all be off for a run. Clive was adamant that we trained even harder. It wasn't going to be a situation where we go to France and drink lots of wine and eat lots of food. But he also had a great sense of humour.'

Challinor also implemented only basic game plans, set moves and structures, conscious that the partially thrown together team did not need to be overburdened. Despite the presence of journalists from the national papers and games being broadcast on TV, the progress Britain made did not garner the attention one would have hoped. Perhaps this reflected the decline in popularity of the code, or the fact that the World Cup was played while the club season was still under way. While all rugby league fans want to see Britain do well, sometimes the trials and tribulations of local sides take priority.

With the French showing less and less interest as well, as it became apparent they were not going to reach the final, the apathy shown at home was spreading. The occasionally farcical nature of the tournament was also highlighted when Britain's Dennis O'Neill, the team's first-choice stand off, was injured after falling off a 'tower' of stacked chairs one evening. His injury put him out of the rest of Britain's games, although allowed the mercurial John Holmes to step in.

Holmes, and the whole British squad, rode roughshod over the New Zealanders in the tournament's next match. Afterwards, the two squads went for some drinks, the Kiwis even breaking out a guitar for an impromptu sing-song.

With Britain in the final, the squad was allowed to return home to the UK for a week before the last game took place. On the face of it this was a dangerous move considering the squad's tendency for not holding back when it came to team bonding, but it proved a very astute approach. It allowed the players time away from the tour, which can often be much more boring and lonely than it would appear on the surface. It also relieved some of the mounting pressure associated with the build-up.

It was an opportunity for Clive to return home to Rosalyn, Anthony and Lisa. Clive doted on his young daughter and being able to spend time with his family away from the building pressure of the final allowed him to reflect on the magnitude of the final with a clear head.

The fixture, when it came, was a classic when it comes to rugby finals; tense and tough. It had controversy with a ruled-out try and, particularly with Clive's score, plenty of memorable moments of skill. Yet, even immediately following the game, the British were deprived the recognition their achievement deserved.

'The French were so confident that they would win it, that when it was Australia and Great Britain in the final, the French refused to hand out medals,' Stephenson informed me.

The RFL also did little to celebrate the achievement. 'The game wasn't televised [live], it wasn't as well publicised,' Rosalyn explained.

'I don't think the game has capitalised on how good it is and the great characters they've had. When he got home [from the World Cup] off the plane there was nothing. We put up a banner. But there was nothing. It was pathetic. He just walked in with the trophy. Why didn't the rugby league arrange for them to come back during the daytime and get it televised and make a big deal of it?'

The missing medals also caused some headaches for the successful British players, according to Stephenson, 'Bill Fallowfield said, "Don't worry, we are going to strike a wooden plaque for everyone on the tour." When we received our cheque, which I think was about £50 for winning the World Cup, they'd taken off both tax and the cost of the wooden plaque.'

To say that such a momentous occasion was met with a damp squib is an understatement. Great Britain held both the World Cup and the Ashes concurrently. Not only has that not happened in British rugby league since, no British national team, or any alternative version such as England, has won the Ashes or a World Cup since 1972. It was the last squad that won any type of international tournament.

Aside from the odd series win against New Zealand, and despite good performances against Australia, no side has managed to win when it mattered most. World Cup finals and semi-finals, crunch Ashes Tests and Four Nations finals have all caused Britain/England to come up short.

Perhaps the lack of recognition from the RFL at the time was simply a matter of complacency, the belief that Great Britain would remain a side which regularly won when it mattered. Regardless of exactly why, it was a huge missed opportunity.

The British media did take more interest than normal in the game, with Clive appearing on *This is Your Life* in 1973. But in retrospect the repeated missed opportunities are hard to ignore.

Instead, it was back to the chaos engulfing Hull FC for Clive rather than basking in the glow of victory.

With the dust barely settled from the win, Clive was thrust back into a domestic relegation battle. He scored on his return to the side, in a home league loss against Oldham, carrying on his form from the World Cup. He then scored 'the try of the season' as Hull pulled off an impressive 18-18 draw at Leeds. It was described as 'a sensational try, which only captain Clive Sullivan could score ... [he] Intercepted on his own line and raced fully 90 yards to score under the posts.'

Perhaps due to bad luck, or the volume of fixtures he had played, Clive then injured an ankle and was out for at least six weeks, ending his season. His wonderful form for both club and country prior to the injury had prompted speculation that he may be set for a move away, but he was adamant that would not be happening. 'It is true that I have been fed up with being injured,' Clive told an anxious local press. 'While the recent bad results do not help, I have no intention of leaving Hull. Not after 11 years.'

Instead of leaving the club, Clive was quickly given an unexpected promotion. Firstly, Francis confirmed he would not make any return in any capacity.

'It was not fair to the players, directors, or fans to keep them waiting for a final decision ... I firmly believe I and the rest of the staff could have put Hull back on the map,' Francis informed the press and fans.

The strain of seeing his beloved Hull FC struggle so badly had evidently been affecting the Welshman, as he was suffering from ill health, 'The way everything has been going, I could not possibly return to the Boulevard this season.'

It was a sad end to a glorious association between Hull FC and Roy Francis. While Francis is lauded for the 'total football' style of attacking he brought to Leeds, and the revolutionary way he was handed the reins of power in terms of team selections, he was moulded on Humberside. It is interesting to ponder what he or his protégée Whiteley could have achieved had the Hull board handed them the control they craved when they had that exciting young team in the 1960s.

Whiteley also departed, leaving Watts alone again. Yet he also resigned, a matter of weeks after the others, following a 'humiliating affair' in which the side lost 24-2 at home to Oldham in the Challenge Cup.

'I have always had the club's best interest at heart,' Watts told the press. 'With the club in its present position, I felt the only door left open to me was to resign and create a vacancy for a completely new face.'

Watts hoped his successor would be 'a younger man, with the enthusiasm, determination, ambition, plus the time to lift the club back where they belong, at the top'.

With Hull, all but certain to be in the Second Division for the following season, a clean sweep was indeed needed. Clive certainly fit that bill and his captaincy skills suggested he would make a solid enough coach when given the opportunity. His mental strength, determination, will to win and attitude towards physical fitness also gave the impression he would make the grade as a motivator.

Admirably, Watts did offer to assist Clive for the rest of the season, perhaps to not let a man who had played so well for him bear the brunt of bad results at the end of a bad campaign. Yet, showing his character, Clive was eager to take the challenge on alone. In a direct and ambitious mission statement, he informed supporters, 'I am looking forward to the job and I will do it to the best of my ability, but I want to do it on my own and then only I will be blamed if things go wrong ... I am hoping to get some response from the players. Some discipline has to be brought into the club and we must restore lost confidence. I feel we have the players to do better.'

It was made clear, however, that when it came to the thorny issue of team selection, the board would hold power. Clive would be on a 'selection panel' alongside Joe Latus, and fellow directors Charlie Clegg and Brian Atkinson.

With rebuilding and consolidation being the name of the game, Clive presided over two wins in his first two games. First came a 16-10 victory over York with Hull displaying some pleasing rugby and Clive returning to play, and then a 26-4 home success over Doncaster in which they 'cruised' to victory.

The satisfactory results didn't last and Hull lost to Leeds, were thrashed 42-15 by a Steve Nash-inspired Featherstone, and then were beaten at home to Keighley. A win over Hunslet was a nice reprieve before a controversial loss to Castleford prompted calls in the local press for the need to 'find big forwards by next season'.

When Clive and his other backs got hold of the ball they could do damage, but the Mick Harrison-deprived pack was indeed sorely lacking direction. Clive himself scored another wonderful try, out of the centre positions, in a nail-biting 22-21 win over Huddersfield. 'Seven minutes from the end, Sullivan – who had moved into the centres – ... raced fully 40 yards for a magnificent try under the posts,' read one media report.

Alongside the stresses and strains of being a player-coach, Clive had also taken over a position at a local pub. Taking after his mentor, literally, Clive had taken over the Hawthorn Hotel in the city, where Roy Francis had previously managed. Alan McGlone, who already owned a pub, proved an excellent man to learn from.

'I was one of the first [players] to take a pub, at 28,' McGlone told me.

'They all came through me and learned [players who wanted to take pubs]. I had one just off Hessle Road, and it was only 18 months old. You used to have 20 landings a day then. I'd have all the players in, and the entire fishermen, and they'd have a couple of hundred quid and only a few days to spend it. And I used to take three and a half grand a week.

'In the early '70s. I used to do 33 big barrels a week. A good tenant house today will to six to eight a week. I used to do 37 cases of spirits. I used to do 380 cases of beer, with a dozen in a case. If they had two or three hundred quid they'd just blow it all. Salt of the earth those lads [sailors].'

Pubs filled with professional rugby players and sailors could produce some combustible elements, however.

McGlone continued, 'This kid had been sick on the carpet. He was drunk. I said to the lads [Hull FC team], just get him out. This lad, he dropped one of the forwards, hit another, then just flattened the rest of the team. Sully was there, his nose was pouring with blood. It took about eight of us to stop him, to get him out the fire escape. I started rubbing his head on the pebbledash wall, saying, "Are you going to stop?" Eventually, we let go. And he said, "I'm coming back for you!"

'Then someone said he was in the army and the British ABA [boxing] champion, he was little and stocky. We were all sat after we closed, all having a beer, with black eyes, bust noses.'

McGlone did have a unique method for cutting down on any underlying tension found in his pub, 'I used to get a big pair of boxing gloves, 16oz. I had a big back yard with a wall around it. I used to say, outside, we don't need an audience. Then I'd put the gloves on them [the lads fighting] and do three two-minute rounds, and I'd say who'd won. They'd bang each other. They'd go on and on, hammer and tong. I don't think I ever saw any of them finish the rounds.'

The demands of roles as a player-coach, hotel manager, and father was a tough one to strike a good balance between, however.

'I spent just as much time off the field with Clive as on the field,' McGlone told me.

'Going for beers, or Anthony and Lisa, I knew them as much as I knew my own kids. You had the family side of it as well as playing. You help each other. Around seven or eight players got pubs, Sully one of them. But he always had a lot on with rugby league. And he spent more time away than in his pub.'

The demands were even highlighted in the local press as Clive could only travel to a crucial away game at Dewsbury at the last moment. A 'business meeting' meant that vice-chairman Ted Danby had to pick Clive up, drive him across the county to West Yorkshire, and hope they could make it on time for kick off. If they were late, then another player, Ken Huxley, had travelled along as well to step in.

It's hard to imagine a modern-day star player or team coach potentially missing a vital game. Clive ultimately didn't make it, not playing as the side lost 23-9.

Of the remaining fixtures for that season, the only one to put a smile on the faces of the FC fans was a 17-13 win over KR, with new forward Colin Cooper playing well for Hull against his former club.

The game also featured a bizarre epilogue. Clive was 'outpaced' by KR winger Ged Dunn, who went almost the length of the pitch, Dunn even 'beckoning Sullivan to catch him'.

The press reaction and the on-field mocking clearly got to Clive, such a competitive individual. He declared himself willing to meet a challenge a mischievous rugby league journalist had set in *The Rugby Leaguer* of a straight race between the pair.

'I feel that nothing has been proved either way and I am prepared to challenge Dunn to a race, off level, in rugby kit or spikes,' he said.

Dunn, however, didn't rise to the bait, telling reporters, 'I won't do it. I think it is rather silly. Clashes between myself and Clive are an added attraction of derby games ... I will not be exploited like this.'

The humorous exchanges were much needed, as Hull's dire season fizzled out in 52-0 and 51-18 losses at Wakefield and Bradford respectively. By this stage, the team had been completely decimated by injuries, with Hull forced to field trialists and untested 'A'-teamers just to field a first team. Indeed, Bob Hemingway, a 19-year-old, signed on for the club and a matter of days later was running out at Odsal.

The club had used 48 players during the 1972 season, six of whom only made one appearance with another 20 not making it to double figures. Clive, with 18 tries from 29 appearances, was one of the side's most consistent performers during a season in which he had played in a World Cup and had a long injury.

It was clear that the following season was to present a huge challenge for Clive to be able to produce a side good enough to gain instant promotion. The fact that the club also reported losses of almost £10,000 didn't exactly suggest a huge war chest either. But when had Clive and Hull ever done anything easy?

The Second Division

ON paper, Hull were more than capable of making a quick return to the First Division. The new second tier was made up of 14 teams, with the top four being promoted. Likewise, four sides from the top flight would be relegated.

The division had some tough, established names, such as Halifax, Bradford and Workington, but also traditional whipping boys such as Blackpool and Doncaster.

Hull's side had not been bolstered massively in the off-season with many more players departing than arriving. But with Clive, Terry Devonshire, John Maloney, Alan McGlone and Mick Harrison, the squad possessed plenty of experience and skill. The likes of Keith Boxall, Mick Crane, Colin Cooper and Tony Geraghty also added plenty of youth and skill.

The Eve Hardaker Cup curtain-raiser proved a positive start to the season as FC beat KR 19-13, with Clive scoring. He 'sold a dummy and wiggled through' in a game which suggested Hull would be at the right end of the table.

The good times weren't to last. In a humiliating defeat, FC's first league fixture saw them beaten 15-13 at Blackpool. Reporter Richard Tingle described the result as 'grim' and the performance as 'not only surprising, it was disgraceful'. Clive, frustrated on the wing as the ball rarely found its way out to him, scored a wonderful individual try late on as he came inside to look for possession. It was little more than a consolation. Just to top off a terrible start, Colin Cooper was sent off. Hull were then dumped out of the Floodlit Trophy by Leeds, although the 31-2 loss was more excusable considering the division's gap between the two teams.

Hull finally showed the form they needed as they beat Barrow 33-5, with Clive scoring and Devonshire getting two. For Devonshire, who had signed on at the tail end of the 1950s, the season would prove to be a glorious Indian summer.

'Me and Mick [Harrison] were his senior players,' Devonshire told me about the season. The dynamic of friends off the field, teammates on it and coach/player on the training field was an odd one, however.

'The club took us to Bridlington for the night. [Clive] said, "Look, I can't keep you in. But if you go out, stay out the pubs. Just go for a walk." Mick said, "Let's have one [drink]." And I said, "Aye, go on." We went in a pub and Clive was sat there. I said, "I'm only having a shandy, Clive!"'

Hull then thrashed Doncaster away 36-2; Copper bagging a hat-trick from the back row.

A pattern of inconsistency for the season quickly began to form as Hull then lost to Huddersfield in the Yorkshire Cup, a tie that Clive missed due to a hamstring injury. For a perfectionist such as Clive, the result was unacceptable.

'This was disgusting,' he commented after the game. 'How a team can play so well one week then come up with something like this the next week is beyond me ... We were just as bad against Blackpool. I would not have minded if we had gone down fighting, but we did not, and changes will have to be made.'

Sullivan even threatened to drop mate Harrison, who was struggling for form and fitness following the previous season's injury. A further cup loss to First Division Bramley, in the Players No 6 Cup, led Tingle to remark, 'Hull are becoming the most unpredictable team in the rugby league, for one week they play with no idea, then the next it is a completely different story.'

Eager to get the team back on track, Clive set ambitious standards for his side, especially against the division's supposedly lesser outfits. He 'demanded' 30 points against lowly Huyton, remarking, 'We certainly can't afford to lose or just sneak home, we have got to win via a convincing margin.' Producing a captain's knock, he himself scored in a 25-7 win which put Hull top of the table, the loss against Blackpool the only blemish so far in terms of league results.

Clive had an added pressure aside from his side's results. Still the captain of Great Britain, and with an Ashes series set to be played at home in 1973, he needed to keep up his own good form as well. He did just that, scoring twice as Keighley were defeated at home. For one of the tries, it was reported that Clive 'with little room to work, outpaced the Keighley defence', highlighting his step and speed were still very much intact.

The idea of the captain of the Great Britain national team also being the player-coach of a Second Division side seems hard to believe in 2017. It would be hard to picture the likes of Kevin Sinfield, Sean O'Loughlin or Sam Burgess, all recent captains of the national side, attempting to wear so many hats.

Yet it was a task which Clive seemed to relish. His still frightening pace and ability was played up for the return game against Huyton, with the pre-match preview believing, 'Sullivan's pace can destroy Huyton's defence ... He will be the key tomorrow, for his speed should be too much for the cumbersome Huyton defence.'

With it being the last game before Great Britain were due to meet Australia, Clive had an even greater incentive than normal. While the rest of the Hull side were described as 'drab', Clive got two tries in an 18-7 away win in a wonderful personal performance.

At the age of 30, it was a reasonable assumption by those in the game that the 1973 Ashes could be Clive's last major international series. It was rare for a player, especially a winger, to stay at the top level much beyond that. While Johnny Whiteley had carried on well into his 30s, he was the exception to the rule rather than the norm.

The first Ashes Test also had an interesting twist. For the first time since 1963, the game would be played at Wembley, away from the heartland areas. The choice of Wembley, made late on after Australians refused to play at Wigan's Central Park, proved a disaster in terms of attracting supporters.

Just fewer than 10,000 were inside a ground that regularly attracted around 80,000 people to Challenge Cup finals.

While all rugby league clubs were seeing a significant downturn in support at games, showpiece occasions such as finals or Ashes series had generally held up. Wembley, only filled to a tenth of its capacity as Britain began its defence as Ashes holders, was a depressing sight.

The fact it was the first game 'back' after the World Cup win also highlights how much that brilliant achievement had slipped from the public consciousness.

It was yet another missed opportunity to build hype and attention around the national side and Clive as its captain and figurehead. The fact that a fair amount of the Australian side from the previous year's World Cup made the tour only added to the intrigue as they looked to right the wrong from Lyon.

While it was a dire turnout off the field, on the field Britain got off to a brilliant start in the series, beating Australia 21-12. This was despite the loss of yet more players to the Australian league as World Cup winning try-scorer Mike Stephenson had left Dewsbury for Penrith. Despite that, Phil Lowe cemented his standing as arguably the most destructive second rower in the world with two tries while Terry Clawson continued his lethal kicking form.

But, again, the challenges of juggling so many different roles created an issue for a club game.

Clive would be forced to miss a key match against York, who themselves were having a great season. It appeared that, with Bradford as runaway league leaders, the battle for second spot may come down to Hull and York.

With Clive captaining Britain to a crucial first win, things did not go quite as well over in North Yorkshire. Hull, with new Australian signing Ralph Michaels taking Clive's place, crashed to an 18-9 loss.

Aside from the poor result, the game also descended into ugly scenes as Terry Devonshire, Colin Cooper and scrum half Kenny Foulkes were all sent off. 'There was an appalling last seven minutes, which made a farce of rugby league and the image it should portray,' was a media report's summation of a chaotic and wild brawl as the game closed out.

Australia's next tour match was against Hull Kingston Rovers, but Clive had another headache on the home front. John Maloney, who had become Hull FC's regular goal kicker once again and had started the season well, was sold to Dewsbury after reportedly missing training sessions.

Clive returned to the FC team as they beat Huddersfield 25-16, again illustrating what a major difference he had on the side when he was in it, captaining it, and coaching it.

Another win for Great Britain in the second Test would wrap up the Ashes. With Australian captain and full back Graeme Langlands absent with a broken thumb, confidence among the British was high.

Yet they were left frustrated and disappointed. Australia, in front of a decent crowd of 16,000 at Headingley, levelled the series with a 14-6 win. Manly full back Graham Eadie, at the age of only 19, made his debut for the tourists to deputise for Langlands.

Eadie, nicknamed 'Wombat', kicked five goals in a game that saw try-scoring opportunities kept to a minimum. The British half back pairing of David Topliss and Steve Nash for the first two Tests had failed to truly click and the British only scored via the boot of Clawson.

Clive made a scoring return to Hull as they beat Batley, although they then fell to a costly loss at Keighley before a Terry Devonshire double helped put 'New' Hunslet to the sword 18-8 at Elland Road. 'New' Hunslet had replaced the historic original Hunslet after they had gone bankrupt prior to the season, a sign of the times for rugby league clubs.

By this stage of the campaign, Mick Harrison had regained his form and was not only one of the best props in the Second Division but in the whole of British rugby league. His destructive form led to a recall for the crucial third Test at Warrington, along with Roger Millward.

The match, played on 1 December, went ahead despite the pitch being frozen solid and 'arctic' conditions greeting the players.

The hard pitch, however, actually helped the Australians, who were used to playing on the bone-dry pitches found back home as opposed to the mudbaths found in the British game.

The British started awfully, as Bob Fulton intercepted a Terry Clawson offload within the first three minutes to race away under the sticks. Fulton, who commented afterwards that the conditions were the worst he had ever played in, had a wonderful game as the Kangaroos kept up the pressure. They moved and offloaded the ball regularly and repeatedly, and despite a typical poacher's try from Roger Millward, the Australians won 15-5.

It was a disappointing result and, in the post-match debrief, Clive was forthright about the side's performance, 'It was rutted with ice in parts [the ground] and I don't think our boys relished playing on it.'

While the series was a let-down in terms of losing the Ashes, the quality of the Australian touring side can't be underestimated. The likes of Beetson, Fulton, Eadie, Ken Madison and Bob O'Reilly were all-time greats of the Australian game. To go toe to toe with them over a test series showed the quality of the Brits themselves.

The bigger disappointment was that such a quality touring outfit, and quality home nation, had been so roundly ignored by the paying public. The 1970s was a time of some of the most intense, brutal and skilful battles ever seen between the two great rivals. While when Britain toured Australia, the grounds were packed out and the press coverage was wall-to-wall, it would take another decade for interest to revive to a respectable level in the UK. By that stage, Australia, with rugby league as its national obsession, had created a stranglehold on the game at international level.

Back with Hull FC, the results continued to be up and down. They lost to Halifax, admittedly a good team, before completing a home and away double over Doncaster. The second encounter, played at home on Boxing Day, a rugby league tradition, saw Clive score a hat-trick in a 40-8 win. Hull, showing their superiority all over the park, played at 'half pace', Clive himself 'showing his class to curve through the defence' for the first of his three.

A loss to Workington was followed by a crucial win over York at the Boulevard. Again, Clive showed his ability to score the tries that truly mattered as he went over for his 14th of the season in a tight 7-2 win which left Hull six points behind unbeaten Bradford, but with a game in hand. But they then fell further behind with another loss to Workington, falling to a 12-10 defeat.

Mick Harrison, completely revitalised and back on the international scene, was beginning to attract envious glances from other clubs. Harrison, described by journalist and author Phil Caplan as 'the hardest player I've ever seen', was a wonderful mixture of throwback prop from the '60s mixed with the athleticism needed in the '70s.

That mixture of toughness, skill and physicality was highly prized, and with Hull's financial plight, clubs began to make enquiries. Yet Hull knew they had a major commodity on their hands in Harrison. 'It is no secret that other clubs have been after Harrison and we have put a figure on him which they have considered too high,' chairman Charles Clegg told the press, with speculation suggesting the price was set at £10,000.

With any deals seemingly ruled out, Harrison, along with a near full-strength Hull side, produced the most stunning result of the Second Division season. Bradford, on a 19-game winning streak, were beaten 11-2 at the Boulevard with Chris Davidson scoring a try and kicking a goal.

While, barring a catastrophic collapse, Bradford couldn't be caught at the top of the Second Division, the result must have given Clive some source of enjoyment that his side had turned over the club that had passed on him so many years previously. For a fledgling coach at a club wracked with problems, it highlighted Clive's refusal to allow excuses to impact on expectations.

Although it seemed as if the result could be a turning point, instead it marked a high point as Hull FC prepared for a Challenge Cup tie against Hull KR.

KR themselves had been having a terrible season in the First Division. They too had financial worries and both Phil Lowe and Roger Millward, after impressing so many times against the Kangaroos in Tests, were being coveted by the Sydney clubs.

Based on form alone, the one competitive fixture that season, in the Challenge Cup, should have seen FC, with all the momentum, come out on top. Instead, KR enjoyed one of their few bright spots as they won 13-2 at the Boulevard. Things didn't get much better for FC when they lost 27-10 away to Bradford, and fault lines in the relationship between the club and Clive Sullivan began to show.

Hull had moved to sign Barry Kear, a raw-boned forward from Salford who had been transfer listed. Following his signing he appeared straight away in the first team in that loss at Odsal.

Clive, a major believer in training and rewarding those who impressed with selection, had little say in either the transfer itself or Kear's selection in such a crucial encounter.

The board criticised Clive's attitude, with Clive criticising the board's choices in turn. After a few days, both sides 'made up' with a board spokesman remarking, 'We agreed that in future Clive would be consulted when the club moved in the transfer market … we have full confidence in Clive and would not want him to think otherwise.'

It seems absurd that, after it had been shown how successful a coach given full reign and control could be at other clubs, Hull were reluctant to do the same. Granted, the Francis experiment had failed, but that was as much a symptom of a club at war with itself and a case of too many cooks with Whiteley and Watts also involved. Clive clearly had potential as a coach, and was an already proven talent as a leader.

Hull bounced back from the disruption with a 40-8 thrashing of Blackpool, Clive running in another hat-trick and Devonshire also adding two, and they then picked up a crucial 24-22 win over Halifax, although Clive sustained a leg injury in that encounter.

His loss was crucial as a 'weak tackling' Hull slipped further in the pursuit of a top-four finish with an 11-6 loss to Huddersfield. A win over New Hunslet kept some faint hopes alive but all hope was extinguished when Workington beat Hull 8-4 at the Boulevard. Hull, in the words of the city's *Daily Mail*, 'flopped', and would be in the Second Division the following year. Clive scored in the last league game, a 12-3 win over Swinton.

It was a disappointing campaign overall, but it is worth noting some mitigating circumstances. Bradford only lost once more all season and finished the season on 48 points, which was a brilliant achievement and one that couldn't be legislated for. The mass relegation of teams the previous year had placed some teams, such as Bradford and York, in a false position, as they weren't truly Second Division outfits.

Hull, finishing sixth out of 14, had an excellent points for and against tally but had often been caught out in tight games. When the side lacked Clive due to injury or international commitments, they tended to struggle to replicate the form they showed when he was available.

The only positive was that the next season would see a return of Hull derbies as KR were relegated from the First Division.

The major talking point for both sets of fans either side of the river following the relegation was, predictably, what the clubs were going to do to attempt to stop the rot. Rather more unpredictable, however, was the question of which team Clive himself would turn out for.

Making the Switch

RATHER cruelly for many clubs following the culmination of the league season proper, a 'club championship' took place. It involved all teams in the league system. Hull, putting their failed promotion bid behind them, showed great form. They beat Swinton and York before being knocked out by Warrington, who went on to win the whole thing.

Those results only tell half the story of a tumultuous few weeks, however. Clive announced in the press that he was 'finished with Hull FC'. The last straw appeared to be a poorly organised benefit year for him as a player, 'When the benefit started, I was promised a bumper pay-out, but it has fallen way short, and that has played a part in my decision to ask for a move.'

To add to his annoyance, he had been excluded for the British Lions team set to tour Down Under in search of the Ashes, although he refused to blame Hull's Second Division status on the loss of his place and captaincy, 'I was disappointed at not being selected for the Australia tour, but one thing I do want to stress is – for the many people who feel it may be the cause of the decision – that I am not asking for a transfer because the club failed to gain promotion … Obviously, I am upset we did not go up. But, even if we had, I doubt whether it would have changed anything, as my grievance is with Hull FC and not having to play second division football.'

The desire was serious, with Clive laying down an ultimatum to the FC board, 'After this off-season, I want to move. If not, then I am prepared to retire rather than play another game for the club.'

Despite that, Clive still played against Swinton and York but with David Doyle-Dickinson as acting head coach, stepping up from the 'A' team. Clive was then out of the side against Warrington with newspapers reporting that he had gone on holiday to Jersey.

In total, he had scored 244 tries in 332 appearances for Hull FC, jointly holding the post-war season-best tally with his 33 in 1970/71. While with the club he had also made 16 appearances for Great Britain and five for Wales.

Despite that, he only had a Yorkshire Cup to show for his immense talent and performances. It is of course a team sport, and Clive's successes and failures should be considered collectively.

Yet, it is hard to argue against the belief that Clive did as much as anyone to bring honour and silverware to Hull FC. Clive became FC's top try scorer, to this day, in a side that often did not present him with easy and plentiful opportunities.

It was clear that that relationship had come to a sad end. The question was not if Clive would move on but where he would move on to.

Immediately, it was suggested that KR were interested and Clive was open to the move. Yet FC had set an £8,000 fee for Clive, a figure which apparently 'incensed' him, as he commented, 'I could just not believe the club would put such a ridiculous figure on me. I am 31 in a fortnight's time, and who on earth is going to pay that kind of money for me.'

A bid of £2,000 and transfer-listed winger Mike Stephenson from KR was rejected. Eventually, the fee was upped by £500 with Stephenson still involved in the package. 'I have agreed to join Rovers,' Clive told the press. 'But, first, I have a couple of personal problems to sort out with Hull. Before I leave, I want everything settled with no loose strings … as far as I am concerned, I am happy to join Rovers.'

As these negotiations were on going alongside the games in the 'club championship', it meant that if the deal went ahead, Stephenson would likely step straight into the team into Clive's place, and vice versa. It wasn't to happen, however, as a contract couldn't be reached with Stephenson. Reporter John Sexton suggested the deal had collapsed as 'there is still a wide gap between the terms Stephenson wanted and the terms offered to him'.

Clive's transfer was not the only thing causing the Hull FC board major problems as the team threatened en masse to strike over pay.

The two-legged nature of the club championship games meant that the players felt they would lose out with the board having offered a £40 winning bonus in total, but the players wanted to be paid on a per-match basis as with regular season games, at £20 for a win at home and £25 for an away win.

Eventually, with the second leg of the game against York in jeopardy, the board accepted the demands. Fortunately for the board, but unfortunately for the players, Hull FC lost the second game against York, meaning the players only got paid £8 rather than a winning bonus.

On the Sullivan front, Bradford, attempting to strengthen after their superb promotion season, stated an interest. They offered £3,000 plus a player, centre Jack Marston, a 24-year-old who had failed to appear regularly for the West Yorkshire club. KR also returned to the table with a straight £3,000 offer, but without any player involved.

Aside from a return to the First Division, Bradford could also offer Clive the chance to play outside centre to Dave Redfearn, who had toured with Clive previously. Redfearn was a classy centre, a prolific try scorer in his own right and one who could provide ample opportunities for a skilful winger like Clive.

KR would be playing Second Division rugby league in the coming season, of course, but they had an air of a club much more focused and well organised about how they would reclaim past glories when compared to Hull FC.

The club had recruited plenty of experience as they pursued Clive. Neil Fox ended his prolific association with Wakefield to head to East Yorkshire. Bernard Watson, who had been a great centre for Leeds and Bradford, also joined. KR had also retained the irrepressible Roger Millward, recently-capped Great Britain international forward Paul Rose and Clive's former nemesis Ged Dunn. To further highlight the strength of the squad, they had a solid production line of young players such as stand off Steve Hartley ready to make the step up.

Aside from sporting considerations, it can't be emphasised enough just how much of an upheaval a move to Bradford would have created for Clive. Players in the mid-1970s still needed to earn a base income and Bradford would have deprived him of that ability to run his pub successfully.

In the modern era, I sometimes feel we are too quick to blast players for seeking moves to rival clubs, forgetting that they have lives outside of the game. They have family, friends, perhaps even businesses to run. But when Clive was deciding on his next move, he most certainly did have a business to run, as he was still in effect part time. He pointed this out as it became time to make a choice.

Hull KR also had an established managerial structure with ex-player Arthur Bunting acting as coach, and former Hull FC man Colin Hutton acting as a go-between for Bunting and the board. Overall, the board was marshalled wonderfully by chairman Wilf Spaven. Spaven had been chairman since the 1950s, overseeing the club's resurgence during the 1960s. It was in stark contrast to the boardroom dramas to be found at Hull FC.

Spaven was a former bookmaker who was renowned for shrewdness in the transfer market, exemplified by the capture of Roger Millward for comparative peanuts. His willingness to pay for players, but only when the price was right, was just one of his many talents.

He was widely respected for his ability to balance the demands and egos of players, coaches, and fellow board members in an era when the chairman and the board were much more prominent. His knowledge and standing in the game had seen him also be part of the rugby league council, and he regularly worked as a selector and team manager for Great Britain touring sides.

'Bradford officials got in touch with me last night,' Clive commented as the saga wore on. 'They explained everything to me, but, after considering the offer, I have decided to turn them down … with my business commitments in Hull, the travelling for training and matches would mean too much time away from work.'

With the Bradford move seemingly dead in the water, it was clear that the only move which Clive wanted was to KR.

'Rovers came in for him,' Rosalyn remembers. 'They were building a side then that was older. Then, we had The Hawthorn. Colin Hutton came to speak to him. Clive wouldn't have gone to Bradford anyway, [after] they'd said, "Come back when you come to play rugby." It was [the] travelling to Bradford [as well].'

To FC's credit, despite the breakdown in relationship between Clive and the club, they did still organise him some benefit events in the hope of generating him some income. But, inevitably, Clive signed for Kingston Rovers for £3,250. 'I am pleased it is all over, I am pleased to be joining Rovers,' he stated as the deal was formally announced.

'What Colin [Hutton] had to say, [about] the team they were building [helped convince him to sign]' Rosalyn told me about Clive making the move official.

'Okay, Clive had had his benefit [at Hull FC]. He ended up with about £1,000. Like he said, "You are loyal to the side you play in", and we had some lovely memories ... He hadn't won much. He'd been a really, really good servant.

'In a way it was a job, and it was moving a job. We lived in the west of Hull when we came out of the pub. I wasn't very happy there at all. After living in a village and having lots of open spaces, I wanted the children to have a garden. He loved it [at the pub]. But we did move out. I think we had two years there.'

Friend McGlone also recalls the move, and the feeling around the Hull FC club as such a legendary figure moved on, 'Hull more or less wrote him off as finished and he went to Rovers ... Once you're past 30 and you've had a lot of rugby, it takes a lot out of you. Signing for Rovers was like a new lease of life for him.'

Hartley, a new teammate at Rovers, also recalls that there was a belief that Clive did not have much 'left in him' in a sporting sense, at least from people on the stands, 'Many people thought he had maybe gone past his best when he left Hull, but he proved that theory completely wrong ... If he was any faster at Hull, it can't have been by that much.'

Moving between the two Hull clubs even in the modern era is not that unheard of, so, while the FC fans were sad to see such an iconic figure move to a rival and neighbour, the Sullivans were for the most part spared any abuse.

Well, for the most part, as Rosalyn told me, 'We had a silver car. One night, I said, "I can hear something Clive." I looked out of the window and shouted, "They're painting your car, Clive!" And they'd put Hull FC in red on his car. So, he jumped out of his car and chased them while I was on the phone to the police. Clive caught one of them. But he was that angry. When the police looked at what paint they'd used it was tomato ketchup! So, there was a bit of calling him a turncoat, but it settled down.'

Clive wasn't the only Hull rugby league great to be on the move. Mick Harrison, after his return to international form, was still in demand and eventually Leeds paid £10,000 to secure his signature, with rumours of interest from KR and Wigan. It was a record amount received by FC for a player and, as chairman Charles Clegg candidly put it, 'We did very much want to build a side around Mick Harrison, but how can you when you have no cash?'

The cashflow had become so dire that FC were even struggling to afford signing-on fees for amateurs, turning out for the likes of Hull Dockers, who they felt had potential.

'This could be the beginning of new things for us at the Boulevard,' chairman Clegg stated, attempting to put a positive spin on the loss of two key players. Just to add further salt in FC wounds, the man who signed Harrison for Leeds was Roy Francis, who had returned to Headingley in triumphant fashion.

Clive's new club hadn't had it all their own way in the transfer market either. Phil Lowe, as was becoming the trend for players who had played well in Tests against Australia, had completed a protracted move to Manly. Kingston Rovers had first asked for £25,000, and the move became increasingly messy and ill-tempered as Lowe arrived in Sydney before any fee was agreed.

Manly then felt that they could sign Lowe for 'free' under the rather bizarre rationale that Lowe had only signed a three-year contract. A fee therefore wouldn't reflect the supposedly short amount of time Lowe would play for the club, so, in their opinion, one didn't need to be paid. It goes without saying that this was a rather flawed argument as three years in a rugby league player's career is a sizeable chunk, especially when Lowe was hitting his prime years.

KR, Lowe and Manly, by accident more than design, ultimately became an acid test for international transfers between British and Sydney-based clubs. Court appearances from both clubs seemed the only solution with the British press pointing out that the door would be 'wide open' for Australian outfits to raid the best of the British game. Even the RFL's Bill Fallowfield, who became involved in the negotiations, was moved to point out, 'What Australian clubs have to bear in mind is how long can the rugby league game exist without co-operation at international level.'

Eventually, the matter was resolved, with Manly paying £15,000 for Lowe for three years, after which he would return to KR. If he remained in Manly, the North Sydney club would pay a further £10,000. Rather ominously for KR, despite the victory of securing a fee, Paul Rose was also vocal about making a similar type of move.

The movement of players around Hull wasn't the only major change as the 1974/75 season got under way. Fallowfield left his post at the RFL, replaced by Hull-born David Oxley, and the value of drop goals was reduced to one point.

KR were also rightfully favourites for promotion from the Second Division.

Clive's reunion with Ged Dunn proved to be an excellent bonding experience in his new side, as opposed to a source of any tension and drama, as Dunn told me, 'At the very first training session when we had [running] spikes on, because we were quite an advanced club in those days, Arthur Bunting was the coach. Our methods were advanced, all down to Colin Hutton, who was behind the scenes.

'Part of the training was sprinting on the track. When Sully signed for us the press came down for the first session. Wingers and centres sprinted together, second rowers sprinted together, props sprinted together, 50 metres or 80 metres to see who the quickest was. Me and Sully kind of agreed we'd got at a third pace at the back, which annoyed the press a bit!

'I got on really well with him and Ros. He had a young family and I had a young family. We used to go to functions together, to openings of shops. As soon as he signed, there was no problem at all.'

Clive continued his wonderful tradition of scoring on debuts with two in the Yorkshire Cup against Batley, a 16-0 win. His first try occurred with his 'first touch of the ball'. The win proved an excellent omen for the rest of the season as KR began to play some irresistible football.

Although the loss of both his Great Britain place and captaincy was a bitter blow, the removal of the pressure of being Hull FC's captain, coach and best player must have been liberating. For Rovers, he was part of a well-oiled machine rather than one of the main focal points. Ged Dunn was in devastating form on the opposite wing, and Millward and scrum half Mike Stephenson were a wonderful combination.

Proving that, if recruited correctly, Australians could also prove excellent additions to the British game, English-born but Sydney-raised Robert Smithies was also a revelation at full back.

Rovers followed up the cup victory over Batley with a convincing win over Bramley in the quarter-final before meeting Bradford in the semi-finals. Bradford had taken to the First Division well yet the game proved a tight affair, resulting in a tense 16-16 draw played out in front of a tragically small crowd at Odsal.

Back at Craven Park, George Kirkpatrick, a centre and winger who was not always first choice but was always reliable when called upon, scored a try and produced a last-minute try-saving tackle as Rovers won the replay 5-3, giving Clive an almost instant opportunity to win silverware with his new club.

Rovers, in the final at Headingley, had a tough task against Wakefield, a solid First Division side in the midst of a long trophy drought. Although Rovers had had something of a stranglehold over the Yorkshire Cup from the late 1960s, winning four of the previous eight tournaments, it's hard to underestimate the desire of Wakefield to gain some honours.

They also had captain David Topliss in wonderful form. Topliss had fully matured into the stand off he had long shown glimpses of becoming. Wakefield also had a young, talented Leeds-born forward, Trevor Skerrett, in the back row, athletic and tough tackling enough to disrupt Rovers's fast-paced style.

Clive was named in the side, with the level of quality in the Rovers backline emphasised by the fact that Ged Dunn found himself on the bench and Neil Fox, playing against the club he was synonymous with, at loose forward rather than at centre.

The game proved to be a classic, although the attendance was disappointingly low at just under 6,000, not helped by a bus strike around Leeds limiting people's ability to travel. Wakefield went ahead early via an interception try from centre John Hegarty and a penalty by Terry Cook. Yet Rovers hit back, Kirkpatrick continuing his superb form by completing a nice move involving both Rovers centres to go over in the corner.

With replacements an accepted part of the game, Clive was withdrawn and replaced by Dunn as the second half got under way. The second period became even more enthralling than the first. Fox levelled the scores at 7-7 with a penalty before Dunn and Bernard Watson went over, Millward contributing to both in a man-of-the-match performance. Yet Wakefield were not willing to roll over and die; loose forward Mick Morgan breaking in centrefield before finding winger David Smith to romp over.

With the game ticking down, Watson scored again to settle Rovers's nerves before Wakefield prop Roy Bratt kept the result in doubt right until the final whistle. Yet Rovers, as solid in defence as they were thrilling in attack, held out for a 16-13 win in a wonderful game.

Although Clive had not played for the full match, it was a wonderful way to start his career with his new side. The cup win also provided a galvanising effect on a somewhat faltering league campaign which had seen Rovers pick up three early losses. They settled down into a rhythm following the victory and scarcely looked back. Dunn's devastating form continued all season as he went on to score 42 tries in 45 games, setting a new club record. He almost equalled Clive's feat of record tries in a game as well as he went over for six against New Hunslet.

Clive did have a recurrence of his niggling injury problems over the season but still provided an effective one-two punch with Dunn. Over a span of 14 consecutive games he scored 19 tries as Rovers and a resurgent Huddersfield battled it out for top spot. Although Rovers turned the West Yorkshire outfit over in both league meetings, Huddersfield ultimately held on to take the title, Rovers coming a close second.

With a promotion and a Yorkshire Cup to show for the season, it was undoubtedly a success, and thoughts soon turned to consolidation back in the First Division.

Smithies, who had finished his season and a bit at Rovers to return home with 22 tries from 55 games, was replaced by Richard Wallace, signed from York. The pack was reinforced most significantly, with John Cunningham from Barrow and Alan Ackroyd of Castleford recruited.

The most eye-catching capture was that of Len Casey, signed from FC for £6,000. Casey had been angling for a move for some time, having been on the transfer list, and had rather bluntly stated, 'I have been as determined as ever to get away … the club has not solved its immediate problems.' Casey was a wonderful forward; athletic, robust, tough-tackling but with plenty of skill. Paul Rose also returned after a brief stint in Australia.

Again, the Yorkshire Cup provided a source of early-season success for Rovers. They beat Wakefield in the first round and then knocked out New Hunslet and Featherstone before meeting Leeds in the final. With Headingley already decided as the venue, it was a uniquely familiar 'neutral' venue for Leeds as they triumphed in a game that did not reach the thrilling heights of the previous year's showpiece.

Clive, on a personal level, had a great game, scoring early on. With Neil Fox also scoring and adding two goals, Rovers went into the final five minutes holding an 11-9 lead, yet Les Dyl went over after Fox of all people missed a crucial tackle. When John Holmes slotted over a drop goal in the final moments, Leeds had taken the cup from Rovers by a 15-11 scoreline. Fox, showing the influence he had had in the game before that fateful missed tackle, was named man of the match.

The cup defeat wasn't helped by the sudden departure of coach Arthur Bunting, who had been involved with the club since 1959 in almost every role imaginable.

'On the eve of the final, for reasons he never fully disclosed, Bunting suddenly resigned,' Roger Pugh told me in 2017. 'He said it was personal matters, and he wasn't getting the full support of the directors.'

The late upheaval had forced Spaven and the board to place Millward in charge on a temporary basis. If Rovers had held on in the final, it would have been one of the most spectacular starts to a coaching career in rugby league history; one game played, one major trophy won. Yet, ultimately, it had proved to big an ask.

After the final, Harry Poole was installed as the full-time coach and heralded a major change in how rugby league was run on Humberside, according to Pugh, 'We brought in Harry Poole, who was the first coach to get full power over team selection. That was how rugby league was in those days. Coaches coached what was in front of them. Colin Hutton was of the same mind [that coaches should be given final say over selection] and he helped to get the situation resolved where Harry Poole was given sole charge. One of the downsides was that Poole thought Neil Fox's days were coming to an end, so Fox was rather unceremoniously dumped.'

Fox was indeed let go, joining York. Despite his brief stay he had been a colossal success, kicking 210 goals and scoring 16 tries in just 59 games for a return of 470 points.

The exit of Fox was a sign of things to come as Poole began to blood the 'A' team's promising youngsters. Mike Smith, a local-born centre, and Hartley, both of whom had been around the first team squad began to establish themselves much more. Prop Roy Holdstock also began to make more appearances in the front row.

For Smith, it was a surreal experience, 'I used to go with my father to watch Hull FC. I was an East Hull lad but we used to go across to the Boulevard and watch [Clive]. I was in my early teens. I used to think, what an athlete. Then I came to know him as a good friend. I first met Clive when I was starting with the club. He had a great impact on my early years in the club. He really helped me get established in the first team. I used to get changed next to Clive.

'I got invited into the first team changing room. We were all numbered off, all the backs together and then all the forwards. Harry Poole had said, "Get next to Clive." I was really impressed by him. His physique, how he kept himself in peak fitness. His approach to the game. He was respected in that way. He was fantastic for me as a young kid. All the encouragement he gave me. He was a great defending winger, he was always coming across and reading a game. That's something I picked up, his technique.'

'There was a change of direction under Harry Poole,' Pugh told me.

'He believed in bringing younger players through. It was a testament to both [Cliff] Watson and Sullivan that they survived, and indeed prospered, under Harry Poole's direction.'

Clive, Roger Millward and Cliff Watson were some of the elder statesman of a vibrant young side beginning to form. Just like the exciting young Hull FC team Clive had been a part of a decade earlier, the foundations were laid on players raised in the city who had intense pride in the shirt. Like Keegan and Whiteley had been visible icons of Hull FCs 1950s glories, for the '60s generation, the likes of Clive and Millward were walking, talking icons of the sport for this new generation of Rovers players.

Another, alternative view of this period is provided by Tony Cope, who was a Hull Dockers amateur. While the likes of Sullivan and Millward, and eventually Smith and Hartley, were similar to generals in Napoleon's army, Cope gives more of a foot solider's perspective, 'I got to know Clive in the late '70s. A mate and me we were in our late teens. Harry Poole was the coach, a lovely chap, and we used to go down training now and then. Maybe once a week. We were doing a run round the pitch, and we used to set out the cones and the flags. After we'd finished that, sometimes we'd be invited into the dressing room for a cup of hot Bovril. Even at that stage, that dressing room was full of international players, but even then Clive, you could tell he was a family man because he'd say, "Come over 'ere and sit with me, son." He became my hero.

'He was lightning fast, he was quick ... I was working next door but one with Clive in Holderness Road. I used to go and have my lunch with him. He was so welcoming with people. I had just signed for Hull Dockers amateur club. After a game there, I got approached by Hull KR Colts ['A' team]. I signed on a contract, which meant I couldn't sign for another professional club without Hull KR's permission.

'There were a few of us like that. You'd train with the first team as well as the 'A' team. Clive would always invite you over and have time for you, even [pointing out] bits from training, "If you run this line, or you did that." He was knowledgeable of the game as well.'

Yet Clive did rope in the youngsters for help both on and off the field, as Smith told me, 'I was an apprentice joiner at the time, I was 17. Clive had just got out of the pub trade and Len Casey had got him a job at a joinery, where they'd make window frames and everything.

'I was putting in a floor for Len Casey in an evening after training. Clive got to know. He said, "Can you put me a window in?" I said, "Of course, Clive." When I got to his house, he had four bits of wood he'd got. Instead of being there an hour or two I was there all week making a window frame up!'

Smith also served as a useful friend to have at Craven Park, providing a cheaper and more reliable childcare service than many others!

'I remember when I was injured, and I was sat in the stands, and I had Tony [Anthony] sat on my knee. I was looking after the kids for them. I was about 17 or 18 and looking after Tony and Lisa.'

On the field, the league campaign was one of consolidation as Rovers finished a solid eighth place with Clive thriving.

Major tragedy struck, however, as Wilf Spaven died suddenly of a heart attack, at the age of 65. Spaven had been chairman for 848 games, and overseen the rise of Rovers to becoming Humberside's best club for the best part of a decade. His loss could have been a huge one in a sporting sense, but the loosening of restrictions on manager Harry Poole had reduced the managerial input of the board, so the club's resurgence continued. His death, however, was a deeply upsetting and shocking one for the Rovers family. When one looks back over the greatest people to be associated with the club, Spaven deserves to feature in that conversation.

Clive's great season as Rovers consolidated was well timed as the World Cup was undergoing a major restructure. Concurrent with the domestic competition, the Rugby League World Series was organised. A World Cup in all but name, it saw five nations play in a round-robin table, but all sides would face each other home and away.

New Zealand, France and Australia were the familiar names but Great Britain was split and from it rose an English and Welsh team. The choice to give Wales a spot was in part influenced by a wildly successful fixture played in Swansea; the first time a Welsh rugby league side had played on home soil in 24 years. Some 23,000 people, a massive attendance when compared to the rest of rugby league at the time, saw a Welsh team, sans Clive, pull off a famous 21-8 victory over the French.

'The World Cup in 1975 was a fantastic arrangement for the players,' Dunn, who was selected on the wing for England, told me. 'The countries that were in it, you played them home and away. Brilliant! So, we played in Australia and New Zealand. And they made the Welsh game in Brisbane ... I went with England in 1975 for the World Cup in Australia. Sully was one of the stars for Wales and I was selected for England as was Roger Millward. Leading up to that World Cup, there was a lot of interest in who out of the Hull KR squad was going to be selected.'

Clive, despite his star status, was not always first choice for his beloved Wales. This was partly down to continued injury concerns on his part but also reflected the continued poaching of Welsh rugby union's best players. Roy Matthias, a Llanelli product signed by St Helens, and Warrington's John Bevan, a Welsh and British international in the 15-man code, were competing for the wing spots with Clive.

Clive did make the team to travel to Brisbane, a fitting and final trip Down Under as an international player. Exactly why it was decided Wales and England should meet in Brisbane for Wales's 'home' game is a mystery, especially when one considers the passionate and, most importantly, large amount of support that had been shown to the Welsh side in Swansea.

The game had some hype, although this was mostly fuelled by a vocal rivalry between the coaching teams, as Dunn recalls, 'When we were in Brisbane, the two respective coaches, Alex Murphy [England] and Les Pearce [Wales] didn't like each other; there was a lot of backbiting in the press. So, they put a ban on us seeing the Welsh boys, Alex did. And Les put a ban on the Welsh boys. I remember me and Roger sneaked out a few nights before the game, and met up with Sully and a lad called Glyn Turner [who had a season at Hull KR] and a few others, just to catch up with them. We sneaked out the back [of the hotel] and they did the same. We were pretty sharp at knowing where people were [to spot us].'

Despite the friendliness displayed between the two sets of players off the field, the resulting fixture quickly descended into a glorified punch-up. Clive, and indeed Dunn and Millward, were largely afterthoughts as both sets of forwards engaged in 80 minutes of trench warfare in the rain-soaked Lang Park. Referee Don Lancashire was heard to say following the game that if he had sent every player off it would have been completely justifiable.

To nobody's surprise either, considering it took place on the other side of the planet, the game was played out in front of 6,000 people inside the huge Lang Park, more accustomed to holding 30,000 to 40,000 Queenslanders for State of Origin fixtures.

The matches and indeed the occasions themselves were far from classics but the tournament proved to be one final flourish for Clive in an international jersey. He and his Welsh teammates beat England 12-7 and it was Clive who scored the crucial second-half try. Aside from the fact that the score helped beat England in a one-off encounter, it also caused England to fail to win the World Cup as they finished one point behind Australia in the final table. Clive, in a bizarre occurrence which could only happen in rugby league, made sure he remained the last British captain to win a major honour by preventing England from picking up the trophy.

'We drew with Australia in Australia and beat them at home,' Dunn told me. 'But we lost the World Cup by one point because we lost against Wales. We lost by a bloody point. It wouldn't have been the 1972 gang showing off [about winning a World Cup], it'd be us lot.'

Away from the pitch, the Sullivans had settled into a pleasant family routine. It helped empathise the more organised nature of Clive's career on the pitch.

His appearances for Wales were also a reminder that he was, after all, Welsh, with a growing and extended family back home in and around Cardiff.

Being able to concentrate on just his rugby, rather than the added pressures of captain and coach, allowed him to spend more time with family both near and far.

Family Man

AS TOUCHED upon earlier in the book, Clive's very early life was spent with his mother, Dorothy (Doris), father Charles Sullivan, and his siblings – who were nicknamed 'the flying Sullivan's'. His parents were married for several years. However, his mother Dorothy later remarried. Clive, therefore, had two half-sisters, Sharon and Sarah, and a half-brother, Mark. Clive was 15 years older than Sharon, the first of the three Esien siblings.

The family had remained close, Sharon acting as a bridesmaid for Rosalyn and Clive's wedding. In 1975, when Sharon married, it was Clive who gave her away at the church in the Ely area of Cardiff.

'I remember the family travelling to Hull from Wales, I was filled with joy and anticipation at being my big brother's bridesmaid,' Sharon told me, '[We had] our family get-togethers at Barry Island during the summer where we would all meet up. Lots and lots of us having a picnic of sandwiches and homemade welshcakes and ginger beer, made by our mother Doris. Playing games. Rounders, family and ball games, [it was] always fun as we were a competitive lot.

'He ([Clive] was such a joy to be around. One thing I do remember is that he was always the same and always on an even keel so loving and extremely charismatic.'

The competitive streak Sharon mentioned had always been prevalent in Clive and was a key component of his success as a player. Yet it was becoming a key part of the Sullivan household as a whole back in Hull.

'Playing games at home, Clive was very competitive,' Rosalyn recalls.

'He'd say you have to fight to win. Whereas I'd say you've got to let them win to encourage them. So, Anthony, or maybe it was part of him, he became very competitive. Lisa wasn't as much. Even playing games, Anthony would knock the board over. I can see in his training he'd have gone all out, he had to be the best. I think that was because of Clive.

'When Anthony was born people said, "Is he going to be another rugby player?" And I said "No! He's going to be a ballet dancer." I couldn't imagine my little boy going out there and being bashed about ... Clive always seemed strong and he could look after himself. Little did I know.

'Clive never pushed him [Anthony] towards it. Anthony was always athletic. They used to go out behind our house and Clive would say, "He has more talent in his little finger than I ever had." I've seen Clive with a rugby ball; his handling at the start wasn't great at the start, against a wall practising. It was the things that you didn't see. He knew what his weaknesses were and he worked on them.'

The very few weaknesses that may have remained in Clive's game were dealt with via a change in routine as he settled in with the East Hull side. 'When he went to Rovers ... they were getting more professional, they were training three nights a week. With a game on a Sunday, they'd have the sauna on a Saturday,' said Rosalyn.

The demands of rugby league created a love-hate relationship with the sport for his daughter Lisa due to the work-life balance it created.

She said, 'I think when I was young; it was more of a hindrance [rugby league]. And I was only a young girl in all of the years that we had. For me, it sort of took my dad away. Now I understand ... Your weekend, that was it [going to rugby]. You didn't really have a choice. Sometimes we went to Grandma's. Sometimes you didn't want to go because it was wet and cold.'

The competitive streak found within the Sullivan family led to offers from both clubs, according to Mark, 'I spent quite a few holidays up with Clive when I was a kid [in Hull]. I'll always remember going to a game and they tried to get me to play in the Colts ['A' team]. But, being from Wales, I was a rugby union boy, and I didn't quite get it. Plus, I was only a kid at the time.'

The life of rugby league players then, and to a certain extent now, is a peculiar one. They are well known in their local communities yet aren't sporting celebrities in the vein of modern-day footballers. Their poor pay, at least compared to most other sports, was a leveller which prevented an individual from having a life much different from the supporters in the stands at Craven Park. Yet to a certain extent they were still public property.

For Lisa, who was still a young girl, it was an odd dynamic, 'If you went shopping with him, because he was so friendly and approachable, he'd be stopping all the time. I used to get in front of him, so I had him to myself. But he was a public person, shared with everyone. I always think about really famous people. It must feel very intrusive. You aren't who you are. You're Clive Sullivan's daughter. Lots of things change due to what your last name is. Hull is very insular as well.'

For Mark, much younger than Clive, it was also a surreal experience seeing his brother prosper on TV and in the media, especially after his international successes, 'I was 11 at the time of his *This is your Life* appearance.

It was one of these top-secret situations, the whole family knew but you couldn't tell Clive. It was an amazing experience. We got to meet Eamonn Andrews, who was a lovely fella. The day they recorded the show, it was my Mum's birthday, and they gave her a really special night. That was a great memory.

'I was a bit of a tearaway at the time [in my youth]. When he was in the World Cup, I can remember him scoring that famous try. And I was just thinking, "Oh my God, that's my brother doing that." That's something to remember.'

Despite the tough aspect of having to share one's dad with the general public, it also granted those associated with Clive unique memories and opportunities, as Lisa told me, 'Growing up at Rovers, it was a really good time ... At Rovers, they had cushions on the seats, it felt posh. We used to stack them up and hit each other with them.'

Clive's enjoyment of coaching and passing on his knowledge of the game wasn't restricted just to his two children, however, as Rosalyn recalls, 'He coached some seven-, eight-year-olds when we were in Brough. He was good with kids. He got a load of lads together. They all respected him.'

It wasn't just rugby league he turned his hand too either, according to Lisa, highlighting her father's selflessness but also the demands for attention, 'My dad would always play sport, in summer, round the back. Rounders or cricket. All the kids from the street.'

Clive's leadership qualities, in evidence so often out on the rugby field, were also very much on show in his role as 'leader' of the whole Sullivan family, aside from his role at Sharon's wedding. However, that often saw him having to deal with some bizarre requests, as Lisa revealed, 'We had a budgie called Dinky and a cat called Snoopy. My dad hated cats, but I was daddy's little girl and got what I wanted. My dad worked at Bradford and Bingley in East Hull. We lived in the West. Dinky ended up in Snoopy's mouth. So, my mum, in her wisdom, called my dad! "Clive, what should I do! Snoopy has the budgie in his mouth!"'

'My dad said, "What the bloody hell am I going to do, I'm in East Hull!" Then Dinky got an abscess on its bum and my dad took it to the vet. Nobody really liked this budgie. I don't know why we even had it. And they came back like a funeral march, with the shoebox. Dinky had died!'

Mark also remembers an occasion when his big brother took control of a situation, living up to his role as 'captain' of the family, 'I was staying in Sharon's pub/restaurant out in the country and Clive was as well. Sharon was away with her husband so I was running the pub. Clive was upstairs chilling with Rosalyn. I was in a band. When the pub would close, the bandmates would have a jam downstairs. A few of them turned up and Clive was like, "No! No! Nobody is coming in, you're not having a party now." It was so funny, they'd been coming round for years and Clive just wouldn't let them in.'

Indian Summer

THE following few seasons for Clive saw him produce some of his very best displays on a rugby league field. The mid-1970s Hull KR vintage was an extremely well-balanced one and it began to really show its potential in the 1976 season. The convoluted return of Phil Lowe certainly helped.

As was clearly agreed when he first went Down Under, the move was for a set three years with the option of two further years. Lowe had decided to return after three and had done so, signing for Rovers on a free transfer. Yet Manly, in a repeat of the bad blood of previous years, insisted that Lowe had no such clearance to play and their chairman Ken Arthurson threatened via the press to have Lowe 'banned'.

It was a peculiar threat, as the RFL had made clear that any such ban would not be upheld in the British game, but it again highlighted the faultiness and lack of coherence between rugby league authorities across continents. Lowe eventually made his return to Craven Park in a 21-8 win over Workington Town, scoring in 'vintage style', twisting and turning around the Cumbrian side's defence.

Clive benefitted enormously from the youthful verve of the likes of Mike Smith and full back Dave Hall and 'produced one of the finest performances of his career' that season in a 16-16 draw away at high-flying Salford. Showing that when the opportunity presented itself he could certainly still shift, he went the length of the field in one stunning solo effort after being put in the clear by Hall.

For his second, he showed that his poacher's instincts were still very much intact, supporting a 50-yard Smith break to add the finishing touches. Indeed, while Clive was still one of the stars of the show, his performances, to quote reporter John Sexton, came 'in the context of superb team effort'.

Showing that the spirit of shrewd purchases had not left the club with the passing of Spaven, Rovers also snapped up Allan Agar midway through the 1976 season after the team had made a solid start.

Agar, capable of playing at either stand off or scrum half, was secured for a bargain £3,000 fee from New Hunslet and went straight into the side, partnering Millward. He played a game against Castleford at Wheldon Road on 12 December 1976 which marked 15 years to the day that Clive had first burst on to the scene.

Although Clive did not score, it was a wonderful team performance that resulted in a 23-12 win. Agar in particular came in for praise for his 'outstanding' play, the press highlighting that his 'greatest quality is to be able to read a game'.

Clive's excellent form continued, including in a 12-9 Challenge Cup second-round against Hull FC when he produced a crucial try-saving tackle late on . It earned him a recall for the Welsh side to meet France, although an injury to Salford's Maurice Richards also helped present the opening.

The win over FC allowed Rovers to progress further into the cup and they then produced a stunning 25-15 away success at Castleford to reach the semi-finals of the famous old competition for the first time in seven years. Clive crossed for two of the scores, putting 'the finishing touches on the best move of the match' for his second when the ball went via Hartley, Dunn and Hall from 40 yards to him. He 'really had no right to be there' to collect the ball and go in under the posts.

The performance of Rovers, as Sexton reported, 'tore Castleford to ribbons with their fast and solid play' in a game which 'encapsulated rugby league at its best'. Only Widnes stood in the way of a Wembley appearance, which would have been the first for Clive and also for Roger Millward.

Then, as the semi-final approached, tragedy struck. Harry Poole, doing so well with such a wonderful side poised for glory, suddenly died at the age of only 41. 'The greatest tragedy is that he has died with the team on the verge of producing all that he had promised,' was how the local press described the shocking announcement.

'I am deeply saddened and shocked as everyone must be,' chairman Bill Land was moved to say. 'He was ... a perfect gentleman. Everybody liked him because he was such a wonderful man.' Saddest of all, Poole, who died of a heart attack, left behind two young daughters and a widow, Marlene.

Sport is rarely sentimental, however, and Rovers had to act quickly as the semi-final was literally days away, and Millward was named as the new player-coach. 'I have had a word with the lads and have asked for their help. This is all new to me and I am bound to make some mistakes,' Millward said, showing his humility despite his success over the years.

It was a huge ask to overcome a talented Widnes side and, at Headingley, Rovers went down 14-5. It was a gutsy performance from a team still reeling from the shock of Poole's death, and Clive, showing his capacity for stepping up when it mattered most, scored KR's sole try, going over from 40 yards supporting a Lowe break. Agonisingly for Rovers, Millward also managed to strike the post twice from place-kick attempts and an early second-half blitz from Widnes won them the tie.

Just to add to a painful conclusion to the season, it was revealed that the RFL had 'mislaid [a] vital letter' which apparently revealed Lowe had in fact signed on for two more seasons at Manly. Lowe was banned and the farcical situation became messier by the day with Rovers threatening to take the RFL to court in order to have the ban lifted in time for the season-concluding Premiership tournament. With no real clarification made public, Lowe played in Rovers's 18-13 win over Warrington during which Steve Hartley scored a sensational last-minute try.

It proved to be for nothing as the RFL threw Rovers out of the competition as punishment for Lowe's selection. Rovers, understandably irate, vented via Land that 'it seems to me that the rugby league are more interested in placating the Australians than they are in seeing justice done for one of their member clubs'.

In an extraordinary rugby league council meeting at Leeds, made up of all member clubs, Colin Hutton implored the other representatives to back Rovers rather than the RFL. The plea fell on deaf ears, leaving the club with little choice but to accept the ruling.

It was an unfortunate end to a fine season in which Rovers had finished fourth in the league, reached a Challenge Cup semi-final and shown class and quality in the Premiership tournament. It was also a personal triumph for Clive, who was one of the side's best strike-weapons on the flank.

Clive was given a brief scare in the build-up to the new season as he was stretchered off in a friendly against Great Britain, of all teams. Rovers lost 59-24 and Clive, who was hit by a stray boot, was stretchered off attempting a tackle. It did somewhat dampen the game's unique conclusion in which Millward, playing for Britain against his own team, was carried off the field by members of both teams to a standing ovation.

Clive candidly admitted, 'After I was carried off, I thought that would be it. Even though there was no break, it gave me quite a scare. But my wife has been marvellous and convinced me it is all part of the game.'

As such, he was quickly back in the side as the season got under way. Rovers started well, even topping the table for a spell, but they lost the first derby against an FC side 'ravaged by injuries'.

Clive himself broke one of his own records, although not a welcome one. He was sent off for the first time in his career for a high tackle in a 25-24 loss at Featherstone, although such was the performance of the referee that John Sexton in his match report was moved to write, 'The match was reduced to a pantomime, the likes of which I have never seen on rugby league field before.'

The fact that Steve Hartley was also sent off for the first time in his career, and Featherstone prop Vince Farrar received his marching orders too, does suggest some rather over-zealous officiating. Papers at the time were not above reporting overly foul or aggressive play, yet this display of officiating was so poor it was 'the day rugby league almost died of shame'. Indeed, the disciplinary panel overturned Clive's ban, allowing him to make an immediate return.

The defeat came in a run of patchy form and results. The light at the end of the tunnel proved to be the BBC Floodlit Trophy, which saw Rovers pick up a 22-14 win over Wakefield at their Belle Vue stadium. Clive bagged two of the tries, showing excellent ability and instincts to support breaks from the likes of Smith, with Rovers also defending superbly as a unit to regularly snuff out any chance of a comeback. The result provided a much-needed boost as Rovers went on to produce some 'breathtaking' league performances in the build-up to a semi-final showdown with Castleford, the cup holders.

'In a brilliant display of controlled, tactical football, Kingston Rovers swept aside the holders ... and marched proudly into the club's first ever Floodlit Final,' the match report triumphantly announced.

With Clive on the wing, Rovers fulfilled the promise they had so regularly shown over the previous few seasons with a 23-5 win at Wheldon Road. With the side as a whole defending superbly, they ruthlessly took advantage of any opportunity presented to them, Millward and Hartley pulling the strings wonderfully in midfield.

It set up a showdown with St Helens in arguably the biggest club game of Clive's career up to that stage. The final was to be held, luckily enough, at Craven Park, an added incentive for the side to win a trophy dubbed 'the second richest in rugby league'.

Aside from the prestige and financial incentives, it would also allow Rovers to get a 52-year-old monkey off their backs. They had not won a rugby league competition involving Lancashire and Cumbria sides since the 1924/25 championship, and a Challenge Cup win or a league triumph would need the belief that any team could be bested, not just those found in the Yorkshire Cup.

'We have the important advantage of being at home, and if the crowd gets behind us as they have been doing, I am sure they will lift us to success,' Millward told the press ahead of the final, in which Rovers were considered favourites.

In front of a raucous Craven Park crowd, hungry for success, Rovers delivered. With local-born prop John Millington in imperious form, as well as Casey, Lowe and Rose all helping to lay the foundations, they regularly cut St Helens to shreds. The pace of the likes of Sullivan and Dunn and the ingenuity of Millward took full advantage of the repeated platforms presented to them. Mike Smith opened the scoring on five minutes, although Saints hit back with a 'superb solo try' from scrum half Peter Glynn.

The parity barely lasted, however, as a 'delighted' Clive was put through a gap by Len Casey to go over. Casey, showing his power and poise, made a half-break before 'flicking' the ball out of the cover tackle to create a chance that Clive 'took in his stride' to give control back to the Robins. In a grainy, damaged photo snapped just after Clive had crashed over, his face is visibly a study in elation as Millward stoops to congratulate his friend and teammate.

The try opened the floodgates as Rose, Hartley and Dunn also then scored. The performance of Clive and Dunn was described as showing 'pace off the mark, deadly finishing and an eagerness to be involved so typical of this whole display', as Rovers won the game and the cup, 26-11.

Dunn scored the best try of the game, one regularly featured in compilations of the greatest the game has seen. He remembers about the game, 'I got two tries in the 1977 cup final. The first was a 100m try, Roger made the break and got it to Steve Hartley who got it to me. All started by Roger. He'd pull two people in and you'd know, somewhere along the line, there'd be a player missing, because he'd brought them in.

'The other try was more or less a walk in try from ten yards; it was a ball Roger threw out. Fortunately, because it was Roger, I was ready for it. I'm not saying, how great I was. It was that, when you played with Roger, you had to expect the unexpected. Who else would ping a ball out 20m, missing two players out. I think Bernard Watson was the centre, it completely missed Bernard, and even he was a bit surprised. When you put it down, you think, yeah, what a ball that was. Such a talented, gifted player.'

Although it is said with the benefit of hindsight, the Floodlit Trophy win would prove to be catalyst for Rovers over the new few seasons.

'I think it did [do that],' Hartley reflected in 2017. 'That particular season, and that particularly side, was the foundation of the side for the next ten years. And Clive was part of that. The backbone of it was still there in the middle '80s, and nearly to the end of it. That was the first of the major trophies.'

Mike Smith still remembers the celebrations that took place after the win, 'Rovers hadn't been in a final for a while, and the atmosphere was buzzing. There were 14,000 people there. St Helens were coming towards the back end of their time as a successful side, and it was a big challenge for us. I remember someone just putting me through a gap, I think one of the forwards. I remember being in the back at the end, in the bath after the game. Some of the supporters wanted to get in the bath with us. The changing rooms kind of backed on to the stand and the fans were coming in!'

The celebrations for Clive continued as he again was selected for Wales against France in January 1978. Injury had prevented him from playing when called up the season before, and it was his first game for his beloved Wales since 1975. It's worth noting that, such was the love and admiration for Clive, his re-selection was given significant local press attention despite the fact it was technically for a rival to England. Even players selected for Great Britain or England were not always handed such treatment.

Rovers's league form remained patchy for the rest of the season as they flirted briefly with a title challenge before falling behind the likes of Widnes, Bradford and St Helens. Their challenge, and indeed their pack, was made all the more formidable with the signing of Clive's former Great Britain running-mate Brian Lockwood, another shrewd purchase from Wakefield.

Lockwood had actually coached Wakefield, and done a fine job, and was another experienced head in a dressing room with plenty of big-match experience. His arrival did soften the blow of Len Casey's departure to Bradford, Casey revealing he was unhappy with the somewhat inconsistent nature of Rovers's performances preventing a league or Challenge Cup run. 'The spirit has gone out of the team and it as affecting my game,' he told the press, although Rovers still finished in the top four.

The 'A' team also went the whole season unbeaten and won the Yorkshire Senior competition with young winger Steve Hubbard being in prolific form both in terms of try scoring and goal kicking. The first team put up a valiant effort in the season-ending Premiership, losing 35-31 on aggregate to league champions Widnes, although Rovers actually beat Widnes 19-13 away to top off a fine season.

The collective effort of the Rovers side was highlighted by the fact six players all got into double figures for tries scored. With 15, Clive scored the third highest amount, behind Ged Dunn (16) and Steve Hartley (17).

The stage was set with Millward's feet firmly under the table as player-coach for Rovers to mount serious challenges for the biggest prizes rugby league had to offer come the 1978/79 season.

They made a perfect start by going four games unbeaten, including a first victory over Leeds at Headingley since 1966, 20-5 with Clive in typically menacing form in attack and defence out wide. They then knocked over Wigan, the only other undefeated side, in a 24-17 win at Craven Park, with Clive bundling his way over close to the line. Rovers had shown a habit of blitzing teams in short spells, hitting them with tries and goals and leaving them with a mountain to climb, and this was no different as they led 13-2 after just 23 minutes.

The wonderful form continued as Rovers regularly pushed aside historic bogey grounds and teams. Millward became the first player to score 200 tries for the club in a 19-14 away win at Salford, the first there since 1969, his two proving the difference.

The side showed the ability to both grind out tight wins over the likes of Wigan and Salford yet let loose against teams they could dominate. They hammered Barrow 40-12, Clive completing a wonderful 50-metre move in which he exchanged passes with the rampaging Smith in the win.

Rovers then splashed a world record £32,000 on loose forward Phil Hogan from Barrow and they swept aside Leeds and Salford again, as well as Leigh. Hogan was a talented, international-calibre star and added even more nous to a pack steamrolling opposition sides as the Robins continued their soaring league form.

Yet he was also capable of covering centre when required, providing some flexibility and support for when the inevitable injuries began to bite as the punishing schedule of league and cup games mounted up.

Tight losses to title rivals Widnes and Bradford did clip their wings somewhat yet wins over Castleford and Workington helped steady the ship.

In a display of 'splendid wing play', Clive grabbed two tries in a crucial 20-5 home victory over St Helens, one of which saw him outpace the defence from 45 yards out to go in under the sticks. There was soon another crucial game as Rovers hosted nearest rivals Widnes at Craven Park as the possibility of the league title neared. Just to fray fans' nerves even more, the season had been disrupted by terrible weather, leading to fixture congestion. Yet if Rovers could pick up the points against Widnes it would provide them with a great cushion against any slip-ups as the campaign played out.

As was typical of the team of the time, they stepped up to the plate. They produced a wonderful first 40 minutes to triumph 22-7 with Clive managing to score his 99th try for the club. 'Sullivan's try was an absolute gem,' John Sexton reported, stating that it was 'showing off not only his best qualities but the almost telepathic skill of Millward'. Sexton continued, 'Rovers's player-coach … in a flash regathered the loose ball, and, ignoring the obvious pass to Agar, he threw a long ball inside where Sullivan was steaming through.'

Clive finally managed to score his historic 100th try for Rovers, making him the first to reach the milestone for both Humberside clubs, when he grabbed one in a 57-3 mauling of Huddersfield.

Although it came in rather anti-climactic fashion, one awarded for obstruction, it was a remarkable and historic achievement. The fact that it came in one of Rovers's best ever league seasons highlights the requirement for even the best wingers to be playing in a good team, which allows them the field position and quality ball to prosper.

That team ethic was highlighted again when Rovers produced a wonderful 15-8 away win over Widnes, although Steve Hubbard stepped up from the 'A' team in the absence via injury of Clive. Clive returned in a shock 13-11 loss to Workington, during which both Phil Hogan and Roger Millward had to leave the field due to bad concussions.

Clive helped the side get back on track as Rovers went four points clear in the title race in a 'shoot-out' of a game against Castleford. Rovers 'sprayed the ball round like it was a sevens contest', the pick of their tries a 50m effort from Hartley with Clive playing his part in support, after Millward took a quick tap after a penalty to go in under the sticks.

Just to emphasise the frantic nature of the contest, referee Mr Moss was knocked down by a gang of Castleford players in pursuit of Clive and actually missed Hartley placing the ball down, although he dusted himself off and correctly awarded the try anyway.

Hartley had been prolific and destructive all season and got his 35th try in a 13-11 win over Featherstone that had Rovers within touching distance of the league title. But with three games to go they actually fell to defeat in all of them, one a nailbiting 18-17 loss to Bradford preceded by a reverse at St Helens, followed by another at Wakefield.

Yet their superb early-season form had seen them amass two more points than runners-up Warrington and, after 47 years, Rovers were league champions again. The honour was mathematically confirmed as Warrington lost 16-3 against relegation-threatened Featherstone.

Rovers had scored 616 points on the pitch, 61 more than the second-highest scorers Leeds, and conceded only 344, only 22 more than the best defence in the league belonging to Widnes. The combination of an irresistible attack, with tries coming from all over the park, and a punishing defence, is ultimately what all rugby league sides aspire to achieve and Hull Kingston Rovers, with Clive a crucial cog, had done that.

The efforts had, however, been exhausting, as highlighted with the loss of the last three league fixtures. That form continued into the Premiership and they were dumped out 26-4 by Bradford, but for the fans and players at Craven Park it had been a momentous season.

How could it get any better? For Clive, at the age of 36, could he ever top it? The resurgence of Hull FC, who had gained promotion in superlative fashion by winning every league game, suggested their wilderness years were also over. Could FC challenge KR the following season? Could FC even surpass them?

Yet, as was so often the case in the career of Clive Sullivan, one had to expect the story to take yet another, dramatic, turn. This time, however, it would be for the better, not the worse.

Close to the Promised Land

ONE of the aspects of modern-day rugby league that many people bemoan is the decline in prestige of the Challenge Cup. The famous old cup, one of the most handsome in all of sport, was produced for a bargain £60 in 1897 in Bradford. With inflation it would cost around £18,000 today, still dirt-cheap for a trophy created using sterling silver and standing 38 inches tall with immaculate and intricate craftsmanship.

When people with almost no knowledge of rugby league are asked for a memory of the sport, they are almost always bringing up a Challenge Cup moment as the competition has, since technologically feasible, been broadcast on the BBC. The fact the final has, for most of its history, taken place in London, in the spotlight of the national media and with armies of fans travelling from up north, has also helped considerably in cementing it in people's memories.

Challenge Cup finals have seen some of the bravest and most dramatic moments in UK sport as players have put their bodies on the line to make the walk up the Wembley steps to be presented with the trophy.

For both Clive and Roger, despite spending close to two decades in the sport, a Wembley final had eluded them so if they were ever going to make that trip, 1980 would have to be the year. Both were the old-stagers as opposed to the exciting young talents who had emerged in the 1960s. Clive was 37, an unbelievable age to still be playing top-flight rugby league, especially after so many injury concerns during his early days and even more so for a player so often associated with pace. Roger, although younger, was becoming increasingly more prone to injuries and his prolific try scoring had started to dry up. The rugby league brain was still very much intact but the legs and body seemed to be just a fraction slower, which can make all the difference.

The game had altered in many ways since both had first made a name for themselves. The points awarded for goals, tries and drop goals had changed. The volume of tackles permitted had increased. The on-pitch violence of the 1960s still existed but in a much subtler way than the legal forearm smashes of their early years. The British game had finally begun to emerge out of a financial slump seen in the '70s as the new decade approached.

Rugby league, despite considerable social challenges, was ready to emerge from the struggles of the '70s into the eye-popping '80s and Hull, of all places, looked like it could be its epicentre.

Rugby league had never seen a situation like it as the decade dawned. Two clubs from the same city with huge support, peaking both on and off the field almost at the same time, as Hull on a wider scale battled with the loss of its traditional working-class foundations. By 1980 the fishing industry was a sad rump, a relic of times when the people of both West and East Hull had plentiful work.

The city was seeing a decline in the industries that had been its lifeblood. The chaos wrought as mining communities were placed on the economic slag heap in the '80s has already been well documented. The textile mills had long since vanished and deep sea trawling had almost gone the same way. Hessle Road itself had already lost much of its identity, from the bustling community hub of activity, to a typical commercial road found in any city or town.

Tony Collins pointed out to me, 'It wasn't just the fishing industry that was in decline. The docks – remember that for a long time Hull was the UK's third biggest port – were declining rapidly and they were a much bigger source of employment than the trawlers. The engineering factories were also rapidly disappearing. The economic destruction of Hull by "market forces" was very well advanced by 1980. You could see this by increased poverty, the closure of shops and the increasing social problems of housing estates.'

Yet a Challenge Cup could prove a brief salve from the industrial decline on a broader scale. And, on a personal level, it was vital for Clive.

'Every season, he said that was going to be his season [to win the Challenge Cup],' Rosalyn told me. 'That was his ambition. He said he wouldn't go until he played there. It went on, and on. A lot of players would go on bus trips, and Clive wouldn't go. Eventually he went on his works do, and I went with him. I was amazed, the noise around Wembley. He said he was pleased he'd been because he'd have been overwhelmed the first time he ran out. He had played an international there. Maybe 5,000, 10,000 people. But it was empty [for that game].'

Anthony also recalls the special place the cup, the final and the occasion was for his dad, and the whole family, 'I know he'd waited a long time to get to Wembley, a long time. I remember watching finals with him.'

But the early signs in the 1979/80 season were not good for Clive. Rovers flattered to deceive, being knocked out of the Yorkshire and John Player cups early on. Five early defeats in the league also put paid to any real chance of back-to-back titles.

The one good early-season run of form came in the BBC Floodlit Trophy. Rovers made light work of first Castleford then Keighley, picking up 25-12 and 41-15 wins respectively, then they reached the final with a 10-7 victory over St Helens. The Robins did remarkably well to see off a spirited Saints side despite the loss of Millward to a fractured jaw, although typically of rugby league as a sport, Millward only went to hospital after staying on the field for the game.

Hull FC also knocked out Halifax, Huddersfield and Leeds in impressive fashion to set up a 'dream' all-Humberside final.

At the time this seemed like a unique occurrence with both Hull clubs triumphing in a competition open to all clubs across the country. To make the event even more special, the final was to be held at the Boulevard. The crowd was an indication of just how quickly rugby league in Humberside had recovered from its mid-1970s nadir, as 18,000 fans, from both sides of the river, packed into the ground to see a wonderfully unique derby.

First blood was drawn by Steve Dennison of FC, who pounced on a fumbled ball on the halfway line and raced away, much to the delight of those from West Hull. Clive himself was seemingly put into the clear as the first half wore on but was ankle-tapped and brought down by Keith Boxall.

Come the second half, the game was going back and forth as the crowd's tension and anticipation only grew with the thousands in the stand creating a palpable hum.

From a scrum inside Rovers's half, the ball was moved at pace and found FC full back Paul Woods, who steamed on to it. He stepped up and shook off the despairing midfield defence of Rovers to go in under the sticks, finally breaking the tension in the terraces. Clive, as determined as always, attempted to cut in off his wing to stop Woods, but his fellow countryman's pace had already seen him cross the line before there was any chance of a tackle being made.

Rovers hit back, rather ominously for later in the season, via Steve Hubbard. Allan Agar had stepped the defence and, showing his wonderful vision, placed a pinpoint kick for the wingman to race on to and touch down. Yet FC, with Dennison also proving an accurate goal kicker, kept Rovers at arm's length with a try from forward Charlie Birdsall who burrowed under close to the line.

The final whistle saw Hull FC 13-3 winners and the Boulevard exploded with joy. Fans flooded on to the field, although it must be pointed out that this was more in celebration rather than in any real attempt to harass the distraught Rovers players or fans.

It was a terrible loss for Rovers to endure, especially with the game broadcast live on BBC2, as the rampant Airlie Birds won the arm-wrestle. It was Hull FC's first major trophy in 21 years and, as Richard Tingle pointed out in his match report, it 'demoralised and shattered' Rovers. For FC, it was a 'no-frills performance, [doing] the simple things right. In that regard, it was near perfect.'

A response was needed on the east side of the city. Rovers, in rude financial health, had already announced that they would engage in a 'spending spree' early in the year with an eye on the Challenge Cup. 'I have spent the morning ringing several clubs about players we are interested in,' chairman Land revealed.

Soon enough, hooker Ray Price was signed from Dewsbury for £4,000. Rovers then flexed their financial muscles even further when they smashed the world transfer record by paying £38,000 for Len Casey. Tellingly, interest in Casey had also come from Hull FC.

Back to having bumper crowds at the Boulevard, they had wished to continue their upward momentum by bringing back their former youth product. During his brief stay with Bradford, Casey had won a John Player Trophy, producing a man-of-the-match display in the final, and toured with Great Britain.

The investment proved immediately successful for the Robins as they began their Challenge Cup campaign with an 18-13 away win against Wigan. 'Perhaps the most succinct summing of Kingston Rovers's return to form in Saturday's Challenge Cup win at Central Park was not in words, but simply a smile from Rovers vice-captain Clive Sullivan,' wrote John Sexton in his match report. 'It was a smile that said it all. It was the smile of a man who thought his Wembley dream had been snuffed out again, but had instead the hope rekindled to burn more brightly than before.'

Millward made his first appearance since his broken jaw and Casey made his second debut as Hartley, Hubbard, Lowe and Clive all scored. Clive's was a typical poacher's effort, slipping in at the corner and, in the words of Millward, 'We got it perfectly right. The composition was right, the preparation was right, and the approach was right.'

A 'performance of superb, attacking football' was then produced in the next round as Rovers beat Castleford with relative ease, 28-3. Clive, looking a 'constant danger' and spending part of the game at centre, played his part in a physical encounter with his punishing running and tackling.

Although it was a match that Rovers largely dominated on the scoreboard, typically blitzing the visitors with 23 points in 24 minutes in the second half, it wasn't easy physically. Phil Hogan and Castleford's Gary Connell were sent off, Hogan going straight from the field to hospital following his dismissal for a badly broken nose, highlighting the ferocity on display in front of a thrilled Craven Park crowd.

Warrington were next up. They had one of the league's best defences and in Brian Bevan they also possessed one of the best wingers in rugby league. Yet, in another display of effective teamwork and ruthless finishing, Steve Hubbard ran in two tries and kicked five goals in a 23-11 win. Clive, and his centre Bernard Watson, shackled Bevan wonderfully, Sullivan receiving praise for 'keeping all danger at bay' in a display of his defensive prowess.

A showdown against Halifax at Headingley was all that stood between Rovers and that elusive cup final. Rovers were overwhelming favourites with Halifax a Second Division side. A very good one admittedly, but Rovers were the reigning league champions. Yet Millward did little to change a tried and tested routine he had used for previous rounds, refusing to take the West Yorkshire outfit for granted.

KR trained on three evenings during the week although the inclement weather did hamper preparations with a waterlogged training pitch. They then retreated to a 'secret hideaway' the night before the game, with 18 men selected for the tie. Substitutes were allowed so three men were set to miss out.

In an exotic move, Halifax coach Maurice Bamford took his players to a Turkish bath house in the days prior, presumably in a bid to keep his side stress- and strain-free.

As it was, Millward, Clive and the Rovers faithful had little to worry about as they produced a professional display to beat Halifax 20-7. Clive, one of the best and truest professionals the game has ever seen, ran in two crucial tries that helped settle any nerves.

The first was a routine effort, Agar slipping the ball out wide to a waiting Clive after Lockwood had gone agonisingly close on the previous tackle. Clive's second was a similar score as Lowe broke infield and, after the defence was drawn in, he found Clive in space to stride over.

Agar, Steve Hartley and Mike Smith also later went over as Rovers finally confirmed a return to Wembley. 'I can hardly believe it,' an elated Clive said after the final whistle went. 'I am so happy. The two tries were a bonus because I have been under a bit of pressure since it was discovered I needed three more for my 400.'

Indeed, due to the excitement of the cup build-up, the fact that Clive was so close to such a huge milestone had largely been forgotten. Yet, rather typically of him, his desire for the team to triumph rather than for him to attain personal glory was the main priority. He did eventually get his 400th try in the 23-9 league win over Castleford. With a score that 'typified the previous 399 of his 18-year career', he received a pass from Agar, beat one defender with a sidestep, and outpaced the cover defence in the dying moments of the game.

Hull FC's Challenge Cup campaign had started with a routine 33-10 win over amateur side Milom of Cumbria, then an 18-8 victory over

York followed at the Boulevard. Excitement really began to build after a 3-0 triumph at Bradford in the quarter-finals which meant that for the first time since 1961 they had reached the semi-finals.

Despite the low scoreline, the extremely healthy crowd of 22,000, 10,000 of whom had made the trip from Humberside, were treated to 'a game nobody dare turn away from, a thriller which drained the fans as much as the players', as reported by the local press. It was an encounter in which 'no quarter was asked or given by two immaculate defences'.

Sammy Lloyd had kicked a 12th-minute penalty and scrum half Clive Pickerill had slotted over a drop goal five minutes from time. At the final whistle 'jubilant Hull fans spilled on to the pitch, and carried captain Steve Norton shoulder-high off'.

It was some result as that season Bradford were a fine side, on the way to winning the league for the first time in their history. As such, it was not hyperbole of reporter Richard Tingle to describe the FC performance as them 'tactically, physically and mentally' outperforming the West Yorkshire outfit.

Lloyd, the metronomic kicker, had proved to be a shrewd and insightful signing for FC from Castleford back in 1978.

'It was a unique team [Hull FC]. I didn't realise it at the time,' he told me in a 2017 interview. 'I was getting ready to hang up my boots, I'd had ten years at Cas. I was looking to move on and look for some business opportunities; I'd had a fantastic career and no regrets.

'Then, in the days before mobile phones, I was in a pub in Halifax with family, and someone at the bar shouted, "Is Sammy Lloyd in the pub?" and he gestured "someone on the phone for you, someone called Arthur Bunting".

'I kind of knew it was coming as I'd had a few conversations with Knocker [Steve Norton], who had desperately wanted me to come. He said, "I'd love it." Arthur Bunting basically said "We need to get you signed, the deadline is tonight. Can you meet us halfway?" So, I went over to Castleford and they came over from Hull.

'I thought to myself, "What the hell am I doing? I'm injured, I'm not fit. I'm ready to retire." And they said, "Just come and play for a season and that'll be grand." And I ended up playing for five! And I shouldn't have been playing one. I just wish I could have been there at the beginning of my career, when I was younger and fitter. But that's life. To have got five seasons with Hull was just a blessing.'

Oddly enough, despite being rivals off the field, Clive and Sammy had set up a business together in the city, highlighting the mutual respect and often friendships which developed between the two sets of players.

The pressure was on to see if Hull FC could step up and match their rivals and reach the cup final, and their semi-final against Widnes was a monumental task. Widnes were pushing Bradford hard for the title, Doug Laughton's outfit nicknamed the 'cup kings' after so many Lancashire, Floodlit Trophy and Challenge Cups from the mid-to-late '70s. Indeed, they had won a cup every year since 1974, including Challenge Cups in '75 and '79, making them the holders as Hull prepared to meet them at Swinton.

Hull FC were preparing to take 15,000 supporters over the Pennines with them to continue their revival, which had been hailed as 'one of the most startling stories in the game'. Rather cruelly, Paul Woods, whose form had been a crucial part of FC's wonderful season so far, had received a nine-match ban due to an incident in an England vs Wales game, meaning he would also be ruled out of the final if Hull beat Widnes. For fans of Hull KR, the match produced a mixture of emotions. An all-Hull final seemed scarcely too big to even dare mention.

Did you want your rival to win, to set up the biggest derby game in history? Could you support your rival for one game? And, if the derby was made for Wembley, was the possible ecstasy of victory worth the risk of the agony of defeat, one you'd seemingly never live down? Tony Cope recalls, 'Some of the lads were more excited because it could be a derby. And some others said we get to Wembley and black and white gits get there as well, we can't get away from them.'

FC's clash with Widnes was every bit the intense war of attrition expected, lit up with pieces of skill and courage that thrilled the watching crowd. Widnes took advantage of a strong wind at their back in the opening half, kicking regularly. Yet stand-in full back George Robinson proved more than equal to the task, despite having some 'robust' tackling to deal with as well as the wind.

Neither side could make a dent in the other's brutal defences as both sets of forwards ripped into each other. Both teams went close with Sammy Lloyd tackled a yard from the try line while winger Graham

Bray and hooker Ron Wellman also threatened, as did Widnes via big prop Les Gorley, brought down via a miracle tackle by 'Knocker' Norton.

Eventually one side had to crack. Widnes conceded a penalty and Lloyd, always a superb goal kicker, took full advantage. With Widnes desperate to have a chance to defend the trophy, they increased the pressure, but conceded another penalty with Lloyd again converting. The travelling Hull fans were then sent into raptures as Wellman finally managed to make it over the line, a crucial score as Widnes prop Brian Hogan also crashed over in a manic closing period. It finished 10-5 to FC.

With both Hull sides confirmed for Wembley, the pressure and tension across the city began to build.

'The fact we were playing Hull, I suppose it added that extra pressure, because the city was totally buzzing from when we got through to the final,' Hartley told me. 'There was a space of some weeks. The pressure was on to win any derby game, let alone that one. But once you get on to the field, you play the game.

'It was a massive occasion. People still speak about it today. It'll probably go down in the city of Hull's history. Not only because of the two clubs, but it affected the city in general. Television crews were coming into the city and getting people's reactions and opinions, and not just for the cup final. The city was on a roll, really.'

Lisa remembers the intense media presence as both sets of players counted down to the final, 'I was privileged for the memories, like the Challenge Cup in 1980. Not many people get that. [A film crew came to the house and] we had to get dressed up, in our best clothes and play out in the garden while my mum was pegging washing out, like it was normal. And I hated wearing dresses. We were passing a rugby ball, it was really staged!'

Of course, the players, while dealing with the media and fan speculation, had to continue to work in their 'day' jobs, which was particularly odd for Clive and Sammy, business partners yet opposition for the biggest game of their lives.

'That was bizarre,' Lloyd recalls. 'We didn't give away any secrets. It was a strange yet unique situation to be in. So, Clive desperately wanted to win for Rovers and I wanted to win for Hull.

'To play against Clive, you had a tremendous amount of respect, just like every other player you play against. Rugby league, it's a big family, you have contacts in most clubs, you've either played with them at county level or at international level. Or you've been at functions when you've got to know them.

'But when you trot out on to the field, that all goes. It's about playing the game. So of course, you respect people that you know, but you haven't got to let it influence how you perform. It's all about respect. There is a tiny element where you think, "This is weird playing against a buddy." But that goes after a fleeting moment, and you just get on with the game.'

Clive himself spoke openly and honestly in the run up to the game, remarking, 'Those regular injuries [at the start of my career] took me to the edge of despair, which can only be matched by the heights of joy I have experienced in both my rugby and my marriage ... Many times I lay in a hospital bed and thought, "That's it." The credit for my new bursts of determination must go to a great extent to my wife Ros.'

Journalist David Howes, writing the piece, pointed out that the final 'provides the final instalment' of a 'life's ambition' when referring to Clive's career.

Although he played no part of the 1980 cup campaign, Hull FC also had a young, local-born forward named Lee Crooks on their radar, one of the most highly lauded young players perhaps in the history of the game, both on Humberside and further afield. Yet he was also a Hull FC fan and he remembers the feeling approaching the cup final and the knowledge that Clive could prove to be a crucial cog in a Rovers victory.

He said, 'I was ten when I started playing the game at high school and there was obviously a big rivalry between Hull and Hull KR. Clive was a big figurehead of Rovers at the time, with an iconic status. He was one player who stood out for Hull KR. And that status grew, as I got older.'

The league results, as with the Floodlit Cup Final, suggested that there was little between the two sides. In their first league meeting of the season, a record First Division crowd of 14,000 had seen a 20-20 draw with both sides showing character to overturn deficits in a thriller, played at a 'fast and furious pace ... hard without being dirty ... the players handled situations with the utmost professionalism'.

Rovers then beat Hull FC 29-14 almost one month before the cup final to tie the season record at one win each alongside that draw, although both sides were far from full strength in the latter-season clash.

Finally, the week of the final loomed.

'Turn off the lights'

ROVERS headed down to London on Wednesday, 30 April. According to Roger Pugh in his history of the club, after being seen off by hundreds of Rovers fans, the team watched *The Good, the Bad and the Ugly* on the coach, a nice treat for the cowboy-loving Clive and a nice call back to the 'cowboys of the North Sea' that had populated the city in previous decades.

Going down a few days in advance proved to be a smart move as it took the team out of the pressure cooker on Humberside ahead of the 3 May encounter.

They stayed in Surrey, also away from the bustle of London, and trained out of Windsor RUFC. Pugh states, 'This generous but simple act of hospitality would not raise eyebrows in the 21st century but such cooperation was almost unheard of in 1980 and permission had to be obtained from rugby union headquarters, who consented provided that it was kept low profile.'

According to Sammy Lloyd, the Hull FC side had a similar routine, 'Both clubs were desperate to get out of town and all the buzz surrounding the final.

'[I] can't seem to recall what we did on the way down apart from singing, outrageous mickey taking and then getting ready for the next training session as soon as we'd checked in to our hotel. We were given a police outrider once we were down south and he became adopted by our team and was invited to all our sessions. Great going through red lights as he held the traffic up for us to saunter through like temporary royalty!'

One unfortunate reality of sport is how sometimes players miss out due to injury, lack of form, or simply due to ageing. One such man was Ged Dunn, although he was still involved.

He recalled, 'Unfortunately, it came too late for me. I was 31 in the floodlit final. By 1980 I was coming up to retirement. I'd love to have been five years younger. But I went on the coaching side of things.'

Dunn can provide a fascinating insight into both Millward and Bunting as they prepared their charges for the ultimate stand-off, even if it was more Yorkshire in nature than Mexican.

He continued, 'When he [Arthur] moved over to Hull, with his knowledge of players and his connections in West Riding, he got some good, great players, like Knocker Norton … Roger was player-coach when I was playing. The greatest player ever to put a pair of boots on was Roger Millward. He could do anything. When you look at the modern-day coaches, Roger wasn't in that style. The game wasn't all about yards like it is now and completion rates. It was about the game, and your attributes, and how good you were.

'The good thing about Roger was he could get the best out of you. He could get the best out of people like Phil Lowe and Sully. Sully had his moments at his club when he was a bit fed up and not playing well. Roger was a great motivator. He worked with a guy called John Moore [assistant manager], you can't separate the two. John would take you aside and just mention something about your game, and you knew [he was right].'

Tony Cope also told me about Clive's memories when he reflected on the game and the build-up, 'Clive often commented nothing went wrong for them. They had a light training session on the Wednesday, another training session on the Thursday. They had a tour round on the Friday.

'Roger was adamant that it was treated like another game and some of the players even went for a few beers on the Friday night, because that's what they'd do before any other game. Clive always said Roger and his staff couldn't have done it any better.'

For Hull FC, a light game of football the day before the final had heart-breaking consequences, as backs substitute Graham Evans injured himself and was on crutches, ruling him out of an appearance. 'To wait 13 years for your first taste of Wembley and miss out in this fashion is heartbreaking. It's the worst moment of my career,' a distraught Evans told reporter Brian Batty.

An often-repeated anecdote that highlights the whole city's obsession with the game was the banner hung by the side of the motorway on the day of the final, reading, 'Will the last person to leave Hull please turn off the lights.'

The match had completely sold out with Wembley packed to its 95,000 capacity. While most those in attendance were fans of the two sides, the uniqueness of the ultimate inner-city derby, between two top teams, had captured people's minds with confirmed reports of Australians flying over to witness the occasion. 'It's caught the imagination,' Eddie Waring rather laconically described it in the BBC *Grandstand* broadcast.

'It was magical,' Cope recalls. 'The Holderness Road and Hessle Road were both decked out in their team's colours. Down Wembley Way, there wasn't an ounce of trouble. People, black and white and red and white, they were walking arm in arm together. Where else, in what other sport, do you see that?

'The trains were packed. We pulled into Doncaster station at about half six in the morning and a policeman, in one of those old-fashioned bobby hats, was walking down the platform. We passed him a can of long-life out of the window. He took his hat off, put the can in it and put it under his hat and kept on walking.

'I was talking to a policeman either at half-time or full time. I can't quite remember. He said, "I volunteered for this weekend. You lads, you come down, have a few beers, watch the game, go round London and have a few more beers and head back home, we are just here for your safety. It's a fantastic weekend."'

Rather tellingly, the final's matchday programme featured a large advertisement on the last page by Hull City Council, headlined 'In Hull, we're developing some winning ways' and 'Hull- a great British city'.

The ad pointed out the positives taking place in the city, such as the opening of the Humber Bridge. It also finished on a defiant note with, 'All we ask is that you share our confidence in the future, the sort of commitment that, with hard work, and preparation, has propelled our teams to this distinguished occasion.'

Another revealing advert, highlighting rugby league's new-found confidence and resurgent popularity, was one advertising 'RL' as 'the status symbol'. For only £5.50, plus postage and packaging, a sweatshirt with huge 'RUGBY LEAGUE' lettering across the front could be yours. Similarly, branded playing cards, autograph books, diaries, keyrings and car stickers were all available from the public relations department at the newly renamed Rugby Football League.

'Community singing', as it was rather charmingly referred to, was led by the rather idiosyncratic choice of Windsor Davies and Melvyn Hayes of the sitcom *It Ain't Half Hot Mum* as kick-off approached. The pair, not vocalists by even the loosest use of the term, helped hype up the crowd with renditions of 'Congratulations', 'The Happy Wanderer', 'Sailing', 'John Brown's Body', 'You'll Never Walk Alone', 'When the Saints Go Marching In', and, of course, the rugby league hymn, 'Abide with Me'. Interspersed with these were the club songs, 'Old Faithful' and 'When the Red, Red Robin'.

In the changing rooms, however, the mood was a far cry from the jovial, joyous scenes around the ground. The pressure was extraordinary although some of the players enjoyed the occasion more than others. 'We had to win that game. It was a no-lose situation. We couldn't lose. We had to win!' Hartley empathised to me, clearly the memories still vivid getting on for 40 years later. '[It was like that in] most derby games. I liked that.'

Mike Smith can, however, recall how others, in particular Clive, dealt with the occasion, 'Clive had a very nervous stomach before a game. He was always sick before a game. I don't know why the lads did it, but lots of lads tried to make themselves sick. I don't know if that was nerves or adrenaline. At the Wembley final, obviously, lots of our lads were very nervous. And I think Clive was in the toilet department the longest! He almost missed the team talk, he was so nervous.

'It was his and Roger's first Wembley final. It was mine as well, but with Clive and Roger being such icons in the game, it was the pinnacle back then, like the Super League Final. Especially against Hull, it must have meant a lot for Clive playing against Hull. The pressure he was under [to win].'

Eventually, it was time for both teams to emerge on to the field. The long Wembley tunnel had an amphitheatre-like effect as the insistent singing, whistling and cheering from crowd rolled down the entrance. Some of the players jigged nervously on the spot. Others, such as Clive, stood bolt upright, conserving energy. In the pre-match TV broadcast, he had admitted that, having had a walk around the field, it had made him 'a little bit nervous', although with a wry smile he had also said he was aiming for a hat-trick.

Finally, both sides emerged on to the field, the already impossibly loud noise rising to near deafening levels. To highlight the friendliness in evidence among both sets of supporters, as the players walked side by side around the field and waved to the stands, flags from both teams were waved next to each other, creating a shimmering mixture of red, black and white.

The tension was raised even further when the players stood for the national anthem and to shake the hand of the Queen Mother. It was a proud moment for them but it delayed the 80 minutes that had been on their minds for weeks. Could Clive and the Rovers do it? It's impossible to boil down a man of the stature and experience of Clive Sullivan to one game and one performance. But a winner's medal would prove to be the exclamation point on an already incredible career.

Finally, it was time. Many predicted an edgy opening yet that could not have been further from the truth as the players' energy exploded on to the field.

Rovers struck early after Roger Millward kicked for touch and found it 35 metres out from Hull's line. In the best piece of skill in the game, Brian Lockwood, using a move learned in Australia, shaped to throw a pass to some dummy runners and then almost immediately slipped the ball to Hubbard running an arcing line, 15 metres out from the posts. Hubbard then streaked through the defence to go in under the sticks.

Hubbard didn't manage to convert his own try but in what would prove to be a crucial call, Rovers were awarded a penalty due to a fracas that developed in the moments after he touched down, Graham Bray slipping a punch in as Hubbard celebrated. The Rovers winger didn't miss this time, sending his side 5-0 up.

The needle between the two teams then only increased after FC's Ron Wellman hit Roger Millward late. As the side's hooker, he was one of the key defensive players required to shackle Millward. The late tackle did more than just disrupt Rovers, however, as Millward's jaw was broken yet again and he was forced to leave the field briefly.

The upside to this was another penalty, which Hubbard slotted over to put Rovers 7-0 up with only a quarter of the game gone. Amazingly, Millward would later claim that a stray boot from Steve Norton helped reset his jaw after adrenaline and the desire to play at Wembley helped him to return to the field. It was a huge boost to Rovers.

As Hartley stated about Roger Millward, 'Over the years, you put players into categories in all sports. You have average players, then there's good players, very good players, great players. Then there's Roger Millward. He was above all of them. He didn't really have any faults in his game, and it's difficult to say that with anybody who plays any sport, they have a weak link somewhere.

'I saw a lot of him, just watching the game, let alone playing with him. He was so consistent with everything he did. It's difficult to say he had a poor game, although he probably did by his own standards.'

Despite Millward's return, FC finally found a way back into the game as the half wore on with prop Tim Wilby crashing over, but Lloyd sent the convertion attempt wide. Just to help stamp KR's authority back on the game as the first half wound down, Millward slotted over a 30-yard drop goal after Phil Lowe had made a break and that sent them into the dressing rooms 8-3 up.

The second half was an even tighter affair as Lloyd added another penalty to leave the score at 8-5 with 30 minutes to go. Both sides concentrated on attritional defence and kicking for territory as the minutes ticked by. FC eventually managed to find a chink in KR's defence but it was snuffed out well. 'Graham Bray made a break and Clive came across and tackled him,' Mike Smith recalled.

'People said he lost some of his pace, but he was fantastic at reading a game. And that saved us a little bit in that game. That one instance.'

The tackle was picture perfect. With Hubbard writhing in agony on the opposite wing after pulling off a crucial tackle himself and badly injuring his ankle, the ball had worked its way out to Clive's side of the pitch. As Bray attempted to turn him inside out, Clive had wrapped him up around the legs and forced him into touch. Even Bray was moved to congratulate Clive as they both lay on the turf. 'Still a good footballer,' Waring uttered on commentary.

With only five minutes to go, FC were penalised again and Hubbard added another two-pointer for 10-5. It seemed too big a mountain for

FC to climb but they did get a penalty with literally seconds remaining. Rather than try an elaborate move, the ball was simply trundled up, the Rovers defence arriving en masse to meet FC's captain Farrar. As the ball was played and the ball moved on to the next FC receiver, the hooter went. Hull Kingston Rovers had won their first Challenge Cup, and so had Clive. Brian Lockwood deservedly received the Lance Todd Trophy.

'[It was] more than a celebration, it was more a sense of relief. It was very nerve-wracking,' Anthony recalled.

'As supporters we were disappointed, but in retrospect, it was nice of both of them to get a win.' Crooks told me, 'There was a part of all Hull supporters that was pleased that Clive was a part of that.'

The joy etched on the face of Clive, and indeed all his teammates, still radiates off pictures and video footage. Clive climbed the steps second only to the captain and coach, the irrepressible Millward. 'Clive was a very, very happy man,' Lloyd told me. 'I, like half of the city, was despondent. I was rather miffed at my own performance that day, which wasn't up to standard. Not up to my standard, anyway.'

The game had not been a classic in the conventional sense, but the passion, emotion and camaraderie between both sides' fans and players highlighted the very best of rugby league. Rugby league was and still is a community, and both sides of Hull had provided the code with the greatest advertisement. When television reporters went into the dressing room after the game, they found both sets of players sharing beers and chit-chatting. Indeed, it was even reported that Roger Millward bought Wellman a pint, showing what happened on the field stayed on the field. In a moment that summed up the whole occasion, after a BBC reporter asked Millward what he and the team would go and do, he simply replied, 'I think I'll go get drunk', although qualified that he'd probably have to use a straw' referring to his badly damaged jaw.

'There is a great rivalry, but it's a good rivalry. There's no hatred. There's respect there. And it generates great humour as well', Hartley told me, referring both to supporters and players of both sides.

Unsurprisingly, both teams were given a brilliant reception back in the city, Rovers parading the trophy in the east of the city while FC were congratulated for a supreme effort in the west. Both teams were treated to civic receptions.

Yet the salve on the city proved only temporary. Away from sports, plenty of Hull's social issues remained. The cup final was a bittersweet occasion on a wider scale, according to Collins, 'I'm not sure that the 1980 final gave the city confidence – unemployment continued to rise and industries continued to disappear. But the fact that Hull was for the late 1970s and early 1980s the rugby league capital of Britain meant that ordinary working people could be proud of their traditions and culture … rugby provides the city with its cultural pulse, both for daily social interaction and as something that gives Hull its unique character.'

But, for one day, Hull was not only the most important city in rugby league. It felt like the most important city full stop.

The 1980 Challenge Cup Final proved to be both the end and the start of an era. But, for many supporters of a certain age, it's the defining moment of not only Clive Sullivan's career but of their life as a rugby league supporter.

Moving On

THE Challenge Cup Final did little to suggest that Hull would lose its place as the biggest city in rugby league. But sport is without sentiment.

Before the dust had fully settled, the comings and goings at both clubs began. Roger Millward hung up his playing boots for good but was unsurprisingly rewarded with a long-term contract to continue his role as coach. Allan Agar, such a brilliant purchase, left for Wakefield. Brian Lockwood, another excellent signing, moved to newly promoted Oldham.

On the other side of the city, Lee Crooks signed on pro terms for FC. Only 16, his signature was celebrated in the *Hull Daily Mail* as Crooks, a captain of Hull, Yorkshire, and England youth teams, was expected to be a future star and immediately became the key man for the 'A' team.

FC also broke the transfer fee record set by Rovers when they spent £40,000 on Wakefield's Trevor Skerrett, a builder by trade who at the age of 25 had matured into one of the game's best utility forwards. Arthur Bunting, who was adamant he would step down at FC regardless of the cup final result, decided to stay.

For Clive, approaching 38, his future was also uncertain. 'Hull KR are a go-ahead club, and it is obvious from recent reports that they are on the lookout for wingmen,' he stated. 'That can only mean they intend to replace me. I feel that I have something to offer to the game, and that I can continue to play first-team football, if not at Rovers then elsewhere.'

In total, Clive had made 213 appearances for Rovers, scoring 118 tries. He had won a Yorkshire Cup, a Floodlit Trophy, a league title and a Challenge Cup, to add to his previous Yorkshire Cup and World Cup. That haul, along with the age of 40 approaching, suggested that he could retire. But such was his overwhelming love for the game that he wanted at least one more season and he was allowed to join Oldham for £2,000.

The move was his first outside of Humberside in terms of club rugby and, all told, was not a huge success. The brightest point was the fact that Lisa and Anthony, growing older and more aware of the game, regularly made the trip over to Lancashire to see their dad play, according to Rosalyn, who said, 'We went every Sunday when he was at Oldham. It was a nice drive and everything.'

It was not that Oldham weren't a club with some upward momentum. They recruited well in a bid to consolidate in the First Division. But the results never arrived, and they struggled on the field for most of the season.

Alan Smith, also in the twilight of his career, recalled scoring a try against Clive in one fixture, 'I played opposite him in a game against Oldham. What I remember was the game was a see-saw. We weren't having a great season; we were around the bottom four. We were all getting older. Oldham got ahead, then John [Atkinson] got a wonderful try, then Oldham, we just let them in. And then I get the ball, and who's opposite me but Clive. And I just huried for that corner, and somehow, I managed to just get it down, before I got out into touch.'

Clive, like the rest of the side, struggled to get going. Following his Oldham debut in the Lancashire Cup against Swinton, the injury curse of his youth began to strike again. First he broke a jaw against Bradford and while out of the team he was approached by Doncaster, although the move came to nothing. The transfer was partially scuppered by another unfortunate injury.

'One day I had a really bad feeling; I knew something was going to happen,' Rosalyn said. 'Anthony and Lisa were with me. At one stage, he went down like that [keeled over] and Anthony said, he's hurt his stomach. I said, he hasn't, he's hurt his arm. He badly broke it in two places. We went to hospital in Oldham, they said we can't do anything, go to your local A&E. It had swollen all up by the next day and he was getting tingling.

'The bone was displaced and he was losing feeling. They had to operate straight away. That was sort of the end of his season there. He was in hospital and he was in agony. He said, "That's it. I'm never playing again ever. This is the end."'

With Oldham's season not going well, they began to search for a new coach. Clive applied following his stint at Hull FC but was unsuccessful, pipped to the post by former Great Britain stand off Frank Myler. Seemingly set on not playing again, he also took an interest in the coaching position available at Huddersfield, although he also lost out again.

Almost inevitably, it was Hull FC who provided him with a lifeline. After only 18 games and three tries for Oldham he re-joined FC for £2,000 on 17 July 1981. Although signed on a player-coach deal, the suggestion that Clive would play regularly for a high-flying team seemed highly unlikely. The deal seemed more designed to bring him back into the fold as an assistant coach for the 'A' team to pass on his knowledge to others.

It goes without saying that FC had changed immensely since Clive had left in the mid-1970s but, despite the 1980 Challenge Cup loss they were still a team in the ascendancy.

Clive's return to the Boulevard created no ill-will on the part of either FC fans or KR fans. Indeed, his return was met with open arms. 'To play with Clive, he was immensely influential because of the years he had played at such a high level, with Wales, Hull, Rovers and Great Britain,' business partner and teammate Sammy Lloyd told me.

'That experience really shows. He was great at passing that on to younger players. But Clive would never shirk anything; he always tried his level best. That was a part of his character. I think that's one of the reasons that he's loved. He is probably one of the few people who could play for Hull and Rovers. People of both sides of the city held him in such a high regard. He was able to make it work.'

Aside from the fresh faces such as Skerrett and Crooks and the return of an old one in Clive, Hull had also shown just how much the rugby league world had been turned on its head with an outstanding triple signing. They secured the services of three Kiwi tourists, winger Dane O'Hara, centre James Leuluai and stand off Fred Ah Kuoi. 'They are three world-class players and we have repeatedly said that this club will always be on the lookout for top-class players,' announced Hull chairman Charles Watson as they were unveiled.

Although it was then revealed that Ah Kuoi had decided to join North Sydney instead during the build-up to the new season, his absence did not dampen expectations too much. The fact that two of the very best players from Australasia were willing to relocate to Humberside further solidified the belief that East Yorkshire was at the pinnacle of the game.

Watson's promise of bringing the very best players to Hull was not just lip service as the stars continued to arrive. They signed British tourist Dave Topliss from Wakefield for £30,000, a stand off at the peak of his talents.

Hull then smashed their own record, paying £70,000 to Featherstone for 23-year-old utility back Steve Evans. Just for comparison's sake, when Hull FC sold young back rower Joe Westerman to Warrington in 2015, he cost £150,000. For rugby league in the early 1980s, these were serious amounts of money.

The spending added further fuel to devoted crowds at the Boulevard. A thrilling derby against Rovers, which FC lost 17-16, was seen by a then-record First Division attendance of 18,500. Unfortunately crowd trouble, not something ever really seen in derby games, also flared up as 40 people were injured during running battles and brick throwing from both sets of supporters. The presence of 'bunker hill', a mound of debris at the Boulevard because of construction work, only added to the availability of missiles and weapons.

It must be emphasised this that was an anomaly with condemnation from both clubs and most supporters ringing out after the violence, even local MP James Johnson asking for a 'return to sanity'. Yet it is an indication of just how much not just derby but any match for either FC or KR meant to their fans. Success is a positive but it can occasionally bring a negative element along with it.

FC's season was a mixed bag, however. Despite a somewhat poor league form that saw them finish in seventh place, it was a very competitive season and although they were nearer to the middle of the table they were only seven points adrift of Bradford, who won the league again. FC also lost in the Premiership Final against Rovers in another tight affair, although Clive was not selected to play.

With so much headline-grabbing transfer activity in and out of the Boulevard, Clive had rather gone under the radar and a pre-season hamstring injury had put any suggestion of a return to first-team rugby on the back burner.

'Clive came back as a coach more than anything else, to play in the "A" team now and again to sort of bring on the younger players such as myself,' Crooks told me. 'He got on with everyone. He spoke to people on his level. And I think from a coaching point of view, he'd have gone on and made quite a good coach if he'd have had the opportunity. He had the respect of everyone at the club. When you've got that, it makes everything easier. He was one of the few people who gained that respect straight away due to what he had achieved in the game.'

Yet an injury crisis and a return to fitness prompted a first-team recall at the age of 38 for an away fixture against Leigh. The game finished 16-16 and Clive was denied a fairytale return as his apparently legitimate last-minute 'winner' was ruled out due to his foot being in touch. 'I was right behind Clive and not once did his foot go in touch,' teammate Tony Dean remarked in the game's aftermath.

Still, Clive continued to plug away in both the 'A' team and first teams. Never a first choice as such, with a rib injury also bothering him, he did add to his FC try tally which had been stuck at 247 since 1974 by scoring his first since then against Castleford in the 1981/82 season. At the Boulevard, appropriately enough, in a frantic game, he went in six minutes from time in a 42-24 win. 'This game had everything, including nostalgia,' was how Richard Tingle memorably described the occasion.

The 1981/82 season would prove to be memorable for the Airlie Birds as the expensively-assembled side supplemented with prodigious 'A' team talent gelled into a cohesive unit. It would be disingenuous to suggest that Clive, on the field, played a huge part. Yet his recruitment by Bunting, to provide a steadying hand off the field as a coach and on it on the occasions he was needed, was a masterstroke.

It's hard not to reflect on how someone like Johnny Whiteley had been a friend and mentor to Clive's generation. Now Clive was fulfilling the same purpose, stepping in for the likes of Dane O'Hara when he was sidelined with a mid-season injury.

FC were in wonderful league form and the first sign that they were on the verge of doing something special was when they finally gained some measure of revenge on Rovers. In the John Player Trophy at Headingley, in front of over 25,000 people, FC toughed out a 12-4 win. Yet just as the spectre of the Challenge Cup had haunted Clive, Roger and Rovers, it now did so for FC. Aside from not having won it since 1914, they had lost in all five visits to the final since, in the 1920s, '50s, '60s and the '80s. Indeed, their Challenge Cup Final record was one win and eight defeats.

The draw was somewhat kind to them in the early rounds as they knocked out Second Division Salford, 29-15. Then came another symbol of rugby league's brave new world as Hull travelled down to Craven Cottage in west London to face Fulham, who had played their inaugural season the previous year and gained promotion, drawing very healthy crowds of around 7,000.

Such was Fulham's impact on the game and, perhaps more importantly, the club's impact on the bank balance of Fulham's soccer club colleagues, that numerous soccer clubs openly discussed launching rugby league sides in non-traditional areas. Carlisle, Cardiff, Maidstone and Mansfield Town all dipped varying degrees of toe into the world of league, some turnaround for a sport apparently on death's door less than a decade previously.

Cardiff 'Blue Dragons', the rugby league side launched by Cardiff City, apparently actually tried to recruit Clive back when he was at Oldham. A move to the short-lived side, however, came to nothing.

As it was, Fulham pushed Hull very hard but the Yorkshiremen, expecting a tough fixture, were not to be denied, winning 11-5. Their next opponents, Halifax, were also a Second Division side yet on a waterlogged quagmire of a pitch, FC were dragged into an arm-wrestle. Their big-name backs and half backs were hamstrung somewhat and 'plucky' Halifax produced a gutsy performance to push them close. Yet eventually the class of the home side came through and they secured a place in the semi-finals with a 16-10 win.

The performances had not been the best but FC had shown the clichéd yet true traits of champions; the ability to win even when playing poorly. Yet everything snapped into place in the semi-final at Headingley against Castleford when, as reported in the press, Hull 'tore the Castleford defence to pieces' in a 'three-try blitz in the opening 20 minutes'.

Showing the potential of the likes of Luluai, Topliss, Evans and the ball-handling Crooks on firmer pitches, the opening 20 created too great a hurdle for Castleford to battle back from. O'Hara, another who preferred the harder pitches, went the length of the field in the most memorable score as FC returned to Wembley with the 15-11 win.

Full back Gary Kemble, another Kiwi import who had previously turned out for Hunslet, was named man of the match, as much for his defensive heroics with Castleford rallying late in the game as for his destructive running early on.

Laying in wait in the final were Widnes. Although FC and KR were the key teams of the late 1970s to mid-'80s, Widnes had proved a constant thorn in the side of both clubs and were the defending cup holders having beaten Rovers in the 1981 final.

The 'Chemics', who had beaten Leeds 11-8 in the semi-final, had a great mixture of youth and experience. Individuals such as Keith Elwell and captain Mick Adams were in their primes with crucial big-match experience, Adams having been voted First Division player of the year in 1979 and 1980. Add in prodigies such as David Hulme, Andy Gregory, Mike O'Neil and the Myler brothers, and they presented a formidable challenge.

Just to add to that blend, Clive's former teammate Brian Lockwood had joined them from Oldham. At the age of 35 he was on the cusp of winning a historic fifth Challenge Cup winner's medal having been part of successive victorious sides – first with Rovers and then against them for Widnes.

In a cruel blow, FC lost out in their league title bid a week before the final when they played Widnes of all teams. Although they won their game they also needed KR to beat Leigh, who were top of the table. On an afternoon when even those on the west of the city supported Rovers, Leigh just about hung on and, due to a fixture in hand, secured the league title three days later after a win over Whitehaven.

The cup final, however, was what everyone was focusing on, at least at the Boulevard. Realistically, Clive had no chance of playing. With Kemble, O'Hara, Leuluai, Evans, Welsh international Paul Prendiville and former Wakefield captain Terry Day vying for selection, it would take a catastrophic injury list to allow a chance.

Such was Hull FCs depth in forwards and backs that even Lee Crooks, who had shown a wonderful ability as a goal kicker as well as a metre-making forward, was set to be relegated to a bench spot.

Despite his absence from the team selected, Clive travelled down, along with almost the whole squad, on the week of the cup final. They stayed out of London, in leafy Windsor. Bunting, a stickler for detail, an essential quality for a top-level coach, had already scouted out locations to stay in during the weeks prior. Such was his attention to detail he even decided on what kind of club-branded clothes the players should wear in the build-up, choosing burgundy pants and polo shirts.

Although lacking the uniqueness of the 1980 cup final, the tension was still unbearable as the seconds ticked down on game day. The crowd were provided with the another rather dubious 'pleasure' of 'sing along with Doddy' as comedian Ken Dodd was the master of pre-match ceremonies. Perhaps driven to despair by the musical stylings of Dodd, one FC fan, decked out in a full ape costume with a Union Jack flat cap and Hull scarf, proceeded to invade the pitch during half-time.

As downright bizarre as Dodd and the ape costume were, the game was all business once it began.

Perhaps mindful of their slow start in the 1980 final, Hull exploited the goal kicking of Lloyd whenever they could to chip away at Widnes. However, the Chemics dominated much of the game and veteran centre Eddie Cunningham carved open Hull twice. But the try of the match was when Widnes winger Stuart Wright intercepted on his own line and went the length of the field to seemingly add another trophy to his club's cabinet, outpacing a despairing O'Hara in pursuit. It was a try that 'you can go to Wembley for 50 years without seeing', as David Miller of the *Daily Express* described it.

Hull needed something huge and with Crooks brought off the bench, the momentum began to swing. 'I can remember getting up and sitting down and getting up and sitting down,' Crooks told me. 'Actually running out on the pitch for the first time, I just remember feeling like I was running on sponge, it was so draining and energy-sapping for your legs. It took some time to get used to. The atmosphere was electric, and just the experience alone was fantastic.'

Although no longer the captain with the armband instead on David Topliss, 'Knocker' Norton fashioned a half break for himself and managed to crash over to leave the game at 14-11 in the last quarter. Crooks then made a break and managed to slip the ball out of the tackle to O'Hara, who beat the attentions of the covering defence to go over.

At 14-14 the outcome was down to Lloyd's kick. It missed, according to the touch judges, although Lloyd is adamant to this day that the ball went over the posts.

The final hooter sounded to bring the curtain down on an enthralling final that was the first to go to a replay in a generation. Although a draw wasn't a win, the dramatic comeback from Hull created a sense of momentum going into the replay, set for Elland Road 18 days later.

For Clive, who had finally got his 250th try for FC having 'outplayed and outclassed' Leigh's Jamaican-born Great Britain winger Des Drummond, the replay would present one last, unbelievable, opportunity.

The Ecstasy

JUST to highlight how close rivals Hull FC and Widnes were, they met in a Premiership Final at Headingley before the Challenge Cup replay. Hull's team was changed slightly from the cup final but the backline remained intact, presenting no opportunity for Clive to feature.

Any momentum that Hull had from the closing stages of the cup final seemed to evaporate as they lost 23-8, although Crooks again proved how dangerous a player he had become by scoring all of his side's points. Suddenly a season that had promised unprecedented success, with four trophies possible, was on the way to becoming a relative failure if the cup final wasn't won.

Elland Road isn't Wembley but for many sports fans and players in the north it is up there with Old Trafford and Anfield in terms of iconic status. The fact that the replay was played midweek, under floodlights, added another unique twist to the occasion and 41,000 was an excellent crowd for a fixture few had expected to see, requiring short-notice arrangements. But even with that in mind the stadium was almost sold out.

'We played Widnes in the Premiership Final. I kicked a couple of goals and managed to secure my place in the [Challenge Cup] replay,' Crooks recalled.

'The build-up to the replay, we went away on the Monday night and stopped in Harrogate. We did some training and a light run before the game. I remember getting in the bus, as we were coming into Leeds, the amount of supporters we had was phenomenal.'

Aside from Crooks, Bunting had made some alterations to his team, many enforced rather than a result of selection. Hooker Ron Wellman, a key cog, was ruled out with injury. It gave a wonderful opportunity for Tony Duke, a 37-year-old warhorse who had been involved with the club for years, occasionally as first-choice hooker and often as an understudy. Indeed, he had even spent some of the previous season on loan at Workington Town.

As remarkable as Duke's opportunity was, it was more than matched by another last-minute call-up, as Lloyd recalls, 'Remarkable how life can turn round ... Clive is back at Hull FC. And a fluke opportunity, he was working hard in the "A" team. He basically wasn't in the first team squad. The chips were down and lots of us were injured, we were playing twice a week. And had been, it was at the end of a long, long session, lots of us were coming towards the end of our career, plus injuries. The story goes, on the morning of the game, the replay, Clive gets a call, and he's delighted to hop over to Elland Road in Leeds to play.'

At the age of 39, Clive had gone from waiting 16 years to play in a Challenge Cup Final to playing in two in three years. And at the ages of 37 and 39! To be still considered able to play at the top level at such an age, when sportspeople as a whole were largely written off by their early '30s, shows the mark of Clive as an athlete. The fact he was a winger, a young man's position if ever there was one, further solidifies just how great he was.

Clive had been selected over Dane O'Hara, such a significant strike weapon for FC. Exactly why O'Hara was out of the team is still a matter of conjecture to this day with some claiming he was injured and others saying he was dropped due to a 'discipline issue'. Despite the elation for Clive and Tony Duke in being given an opportunity to crown a whole career, their selections did dampen expectations of a Hull FC victory.

'People had sort of written us off because Ronny Wileman had got injured, Clive had come in for Dane O'Hara and Arthur had changed his half backs around [Tony Dean replaced Kevin Harkin at scrum half],' Crooks said.

'So, people had put the pen through us. But the self-belief as a group of players we had was incredible. Everyone performed to the best of their abilities. And the support we got was unbelievable.'

In the minutes leading up to kick-off, confusion reigned as Hull produced a team sheet showing that Gary Kemble had been replaced by Barry Banks at full back. It seemed another blow but when Banks emerged from the dressing room in his club slacks and blazer ten minutes before the first whistle it became apparent that Kemble had overcome an ankle issue to be able to play.

It was reported that 45 coaches and nine double-decker coaches left Hull, carrying around 3,000 people, plus all those making the shorter trip via car over to Leeds. 'The Hull exodus began with most fans making a late-afternoon start. A handful even set off early yesterday morning,' an unnamed local reporter stated.

Such was the rush over to Leeds, and the amount of people at the turnstiles, that some supporters only managed to see the second half, as fans 'were still filtering through the tunnel and on to the edge of the pitch at half-time, hoping to force their way on to a few spare inches of terracing'.

Those that were late had missed a first half that continued in the vein of the first final, and that of the Premiership Final. It was a take no prisoners' mentality from both sides.

Despite Hull FC's rejigged line up, they started the stronger. They threw themselves into Widnes in both attack and defence, roared on by the vocal black and white fans. But Widnes met them head-on time after time.

The earliest chance came to 'Knocker' Norton, charging on to a ball by Topliss to go 30 yards. He was brought down inside the Widnes 25 but the ball found its way to Crooks who went close. Widnes, defending wonderfully, snuffed out the chance, and a Crooks drop goal sailed wide. Both sides uncharacteristically dropped the ball as the atmosphere continued to build before Widnes drew first blood, Mick Burke slotting over a penalty from just inside Hull's half.

Clive looked perfectly at ease with the pace of the game despite its end-to-end nature as both sides made half-breaks and chances. He fashioned one of his own, going on a mazy run deep into Widnes territory before being brought down. Perhaps, ten years previously, he would have pulled away to finish the chance. But his innate understanding of the game, of what lines to run, still took him within 25 yards of the Widnes line. The chance was fluffed from the resulting play of the ball but Hull were gaining some traction and beginning to make dents in their opposition's defence.

Finally they made a breakthrough. Norton and the sublime Topliss exchanged passes to send Kemble, showing no signs of a damaged ankle, steaming through a gap to score, which added to the Hull voices 'in full cry'. Crooks then added the goal to open up a 5-2 lead.

FC had Widnes on the ropes and regularly gained ground as the Chemics made uncharacteristic handling errors. Coming inside, Clive again looked dangerous, stepping infield rather than attempting to go around the defence close to the line and cleverly avoiding any risk of being tackled into touch. Shortly afterwards, Kemble, Leuluai and Duke combined to send Topliss into a massive gap to score for a wonderful try. Although Crooks missed the kick, a half-time lead of 8-2 was more than satisfactory.

The second half was much the same as the first as Hull kept up the pressure. Some credit must go to Prendiville, whose rugby union background had equipped him with an accurate kicking ability, and, rarely for a rugby league winger, he often kicked for territory along with Hull's half backs, creating an extra outlet that Widnes struggled to shut down. Duke was also having a fine game at hooker, proving a menace in the contested scrums.

Duke was not the only one of the old gunslingers impressing. Clive again rolled back the years to produce a stunning tackle on Andy Gregory as the young scrum half made a break, desperate to drag his side back into the game. But Widnes were now beginning to get the bit between their teeth, and Burke added another penalty to close the gap to 8-4.

Nerves really began to fray when Stuart Wright went over in the corner for Widnes, Burke's missed conversation leaving it at 8-7 with 20 minutes to go; 20 minutes for Hull FC to hold on, to put the 1980 cup final behind them, for Clive to win his first major honour at the club he had long been synonymous with.

Lots of sides may have panicked or produced the 'up the jumper', safety-first style rugby. But this Hull team was exciting and attacking. After a Widnes kick sailed into touch, FC worked the ball forward ominously before Topliss received the ball, produced an outrageous sidestep, and crashed in under the sticks to help settle the nerves, the score extending to 13-7 up after Crooks had converted.

Burke slotted another penalty soon after with Widnes desperate to find a way back into the game. Crooks, still only a teenager, then interjected himself into the action. Picking up a ball from dummy half, he ran hard and true at the line and crashed over in front of the Kop end of the stadium, where many of the Hull fans were based. To further cement an iconic moment, Crooks, the youngest player on the field, turned to be first congratulated by Clive, the oldest.

'To score the try in front of all of the Hull supporters was a great experience. To celebrate that with Clive is just a memory you'll keep forever,' Crooks told me. The young forward then converted the try and added another penalty for an 18-9 lead.

It led to a glorious close to the game, from a Hull perspective at least, as the cup was all but secured. Mick Crane, another player to have played for both Rovers and FC, came on as a substitute in the dying moments for Norton as the final hooter rang out. Hull FC, with Clive playing a major part, had done it.

'He [Clive] played a significant part. It was a fairy story,' teammate Lloyd recalled. 'It couldn't have happened to a finer man. I was just delighted for him. It was a dream come true for him.'

In the joyous scenes on the field, Clive was pictured holding the base of the cup aloft with his famous radiant smile spreading across his face. Rather comically, Clive did not have his two false front teeth with him. For the 1980 final he had stashed them with a club member of staff but in '82, due to his last-minute call-up, such arrangements had not been made. So he sported a distinctive and iconic gapped-tooth look as he and his teammates basked in the adulation of the crowd.

'This means more to me than anything I have achieved in the game,' he remarked to pitchside reporters. 'Winning the World Cup and that medal with Rovers was great, but this was something special, and I can now retire from the game a happy and contented man.'

Typical of his humility, he was quick to downplay his own contribution even when basking in the glow of victory, 'Winning was all-important. After the boss had shown faith in me, I was determined not to let anybody down. I did not have a lot to do, but I was more than happy with what I did. I knew I could do a good job, but it's ironic really, I spent 13 years at the club, and only won a Yorkshire Cup winner's medal.

'I was with the club in those bad days. This is something else and the memory of tonight will stay with me for the rest of my life. Winning with Hull has been a lifelong ambition.'

'The Challenge Cup win at Hull was a great moment for him. He spent so long at Hull,' Rosalyn told me. 'I was there watching the game. You see them on the pitch, celebrating and cheering. Then they go in the dressing room, all the lads together, and then they get the coach home all the lads together. By the time they get back home, you've started coming down.'

It appeared that Clive was done for good as a player due to his retirement talk. And while both Hull clubs would continue chasing leagues and cups in the coming seasons, it can't be denied that Clive had played a key part in their progress.

'The domination of the game by Hull and Hull KR in the late 1970s and early 1980s helped raise the profile of the sport,' Tony Collins wrote in *Rugby League in the Twentieth Century*. 'Partly this was because of the uniqueness of a sport being led by two teams from the same city.'

One of the most fascinating elements of that era was the subplot involving Clive, and his glorious, seemingly happy ending as a player.

The Agony

LIFE, like sport, is largely devoid of sentiment. Clive's suggestion that he was set to retire remained semi-true as he turned out a few more times for Hull FC in the worst of injury crises. Indeed, on one occasion, he was described as 'being dragged away from a warm fireside chair' to make an appearance against Halifax at Thrum Hall, scoring the vital late winner after Crooks put him in the clear close to the line. His defensive prowess was also still with him, described as wonderful, as he 'missed nothing' in the tight 8-2 win.

In a nice reunion, Mick Harrison also re-joined the club in a similar deal to Clive's as an 'A' teamer recruited to bring along some of the youth players. 'It's nice to be back,' the prop announced.

The 1982/83 season was perhaps the pinnacle of the domination of the Hull clubs as FC finished top and KR were runners-up. FC also lost the Challenge Cup Final to Featherstone and the Premiership Final to Widnes.

Yet Clive was still an ambitious man and was certainly not one to take a backwards step from a challenge. While Hull FC were at the pinnacle of the game, he had taken up the post of coach of Second Division Doncaster at the back end of the 1982/83 season. They had only won one and drawn one game, losing 25 other fixtures when he took on the appointment.

To say Doncaster were a poor side would be something of an understatement. Despite being from Yorkshire, rugby league territory, being more specific they are from South Yorkshire, outside of that traditional area. Only in a sport with such geographic quirks as rugby league could the south of a county be considered out of the main catchment area for the code and Doncaster Rovers Football Club was considered the town's premier sporting attraction.

But it has also to be pointed out that they were a well-run, friendly club and had the potential to be a solid team, if a manager could get the blend correct. Even to this day, Rosalyn still speaks very highly of Doncaster and how the Sullivan family was welcomed with open arms. The hope was that, with Clive in the dugout, the club could enter a 'new era' with a more professional outlook and a more visible presence.

Clive proved an immediate success as they beat Dewsbury at home 15-12, their first home win for 11 months. It was called a 'revival' but Clive was quick to dampen too many expectations, pointing out, 'There's a lot of work still to be done.' Doncaster did have some good existing players for him to build around, such as playmaking goal kicker David Noble.

Shortly after the Dewsbury game, Doncaster then played against Hull FC's 'A' team in a 'special' fixture, to allow Clive to evaluate more of his players. Doncaster, down 13-2 midway through the second half, ended up winning 19-18. Hull had 'reckoned without the fighting spirit that Clive Sullivan seems to be grafting on to Doncaster's game'. Indeed, the *Hull Daily Mail* headlined the result as 'Sully's spirit defeats Hull'.

Away from the pressures and spotlight of playing for the Hull clubs, Clive the coach created a team mainly made up of older players coming to the end of their careers, such as Ron Wileman, and he even occasionally made appearances although they were usually from the bench.

Clive also invested in youth by signing 'A' teamers from other sides who were keen to play first-team rugby including Ray Atkinson from Hull FC. 'All I had for Clive my whole life was admiration, even when he played for Hull KR. He was one of my favourite players in rugby league,' Ray said.

'When I first met Clive, I was a young Hull FC "A" team player. Clive had re-joined Hull FC. Unfortunately, I had a few ups and downs in my younger life, and I had left Hull FC. I had taken up athletics and Clive's young son Anthony was down at the athletic track at a meet. We had Australian and American colleges there. We ran 200 metres and although I came last I ran my personal best, still about fourth fastest in the country. Clive asked me to go down to Doncaster with him. I went down with Tony Banham [an 18-stone prop forward]. We joined Clive at Doncaster.'

Looking at Clive as an individual, he clearly had two sides. One was the ultra-competitive win-at-all-costs athlete who had been such a success. Yet, he was also, especially as he grew older, a man who clearly relished the role of mentor and father figure as well. As such, many of the younger Doncaster players became regulars in the Sullivan household.

'He used to take the lads from Hull, they were all young lads,' Lisa, then a teenager, remembered. 'They used to sit and watch *Grange Hill* with us before my dad took them training. I remember that really vividly. They wouldn't leave until *Grange Hill* had finished!'

It's something Ray himself remembers with affection, 'I used to spend many a Tuesday and Thursday having tea at Clive's house before training, because I was a little bit short of money. They really did look after me. My life was a little bit upside down. I was dark-skinned like Clive, and rugby league still had very few dark-skinned players.

'I had a chip on my shoulder. Clive told me there were two roads in life you could take. One was a hard road, where you worked, and you were honest, and you struggled. And the other was the criminal road, and he said that is a much easier road for you to take. He said this is the hardest road. But I stuck on it due to Clive.

'But he was one of these guys who inspired young men like me. Clive used to say, "If I can make it, anyone can make it." So, he put himself down a little. Or maybe he made you feel as important as anyone else.'

Unfortunately Clive's bright start did not continue and after beating Hull, Doncaster did not win another game in 1982/83. They were, however, never beaten badly, often pushing decent sides like Salford and Wakefield very hard.

One could argue that the presence and prestige Clive brought the club was just as important. It was not that Doncaster got worse as a team under his command, they simply remained in the same place. His presence did have a major impact on young players such as Ray Atkinson.

He said, 'I was brought up in Hesslewood orphanage, a Barnado's home. Clive got to hear about my life and he said, "Dry your eyes son. Dry your eyes." He said, "Don't try that with me. Dry your eyes."

'You know when someone stands you up straight, and you think, "Jesus Christ. I'm not going to get away with that one." Clive sat me down and told me some home truths. He told me to take that chip off my shoulder, mould another one, and put it on my other shoulder, so I'd be the most balanced person on the pitch.

'I took that; I actually did stuff like that. I thought about it. I always wanted to try new things on the rugby pitch. Clive was always someone who said, "Have conviction. I'm not going to say to you at the end of the game, why did you do that? If you think you can do it, do it."

'And a lot of coaches wouldn't allow you to express yourself like that. They'd want you a lot more structured. Clive gave you the reins ... he showed me all these little tricks as well. How to stand a player up. He said, "Dance down the touchline. Take a footstep in and half a step in, make them stop. As soon as they stop, run away from them."'

Clive also showed a keen understanding of how to get the best out of his players, according to Atkinson, even if it had worse consequences for some of them than others.

Ray continued, 'Tony Banham was a really huge, powerful guy. He didn't like training much. We were playing a game of touch and Tony handed me off in the face. Later, Tony came running through. I let him run past, and then I chased him and pushed him over, much to the disgust of Clive.

'He said, "You two, 20 press-ups each." I said it wasn't me! And Banham said the same thing. I went down and did them. Clive, knowing he [Tony] wasn't going to do them, let him get away with doing five. Later on, he said, "If I had pushed Banham to do more than five he would have refused and it would have undermined me."'

One issue still a factor in the sport, although nowhere near the extent it was when Clive started, was racial abuse of players.

'Clive always taught me, "Don't let that phase you,"' Atkinson told me. 'They are trying to get under your skin. He said, "Turn round and smile. The best way to silence them is by scoring tries." I remember playing in one game, and I scored three tries. I said in training, "I'm sorry for being a bit greedy with the ball." He said, "You can come and score three tries every Sunday."'

Clive's legacy as one of the best wingers to play the game, and his reputation as a gentleman off it, preceded him at both home and away games, according to Atkinson, 'He never put a stranger down. When we used to play away teams, like Barrow and Whitehaven, Clive was respected throughout the game. Even in those clubs in Lancashire and Cumbria. You didn't really know people in those teams but you could be assured you'd get a warm welcome if you were with Clive.

'Everyone wanted to speak to Sully. All the opposition players, the supporters. Clive Sullivan! Clive Sullivan! They all used to ask him, "When you got that interception in the World Cup, why didn't you put it under the posts?" His answer was, "I had no need to!"'

Doncaster's poor end to the 1982/83 league season carried on to the following year and they won only two games, both at home. The first was an impressive 30-0 scoreline against Keighley and the second came against Batley, 21-10.

It wasn't all doom and gloom. Clive did sprinkle some of his cup experience on to the club. They picked up a 16-12 first-round win in the Yorkshire Cup against Bramley, their first victory in the competition since 1971. They then advanced in the John Player Trophy against Batley, 12-11. Although they were knocked out in the next round of both cups the wins still highlighted some progress, especially as they gave First Division Salford 'all they could handle' in the second round of the John Player Trophy.

Yet Doncaster's challenges were actually highlighted by the victory over Batley with *The Rugby Leaguer* pointing out that while the wins helped earn a 'heartening degree of self-respect', the bonuses and sparse crowds actually cost the club money rather than made it. 'Some success can be a problem, but we have to look at the future ... the one thing is certain is that there is no future in losing all the time,' Doncaster's chairman John Barron told the newspaper.

But more cup success occurred and it was particularly close to Clive's heart. Doncaster managed to overcome Batley yet again, this time in the first round of the Challenge Cup with an 11-8 scoreline. They were then knocked out 40-7 in the next round, ironically by Hull KR at Craven Park, but the first-round success was apparently one of Clive's favourite in the whole game. Rosalyn can still recall 'the happiness on his face, that he'd achieved something with that bunch of lads' following the final whistle against Batley.

Ultimately, however, the success was fleeting.

'We weren't the best rugby league team,' Atkinson told me. In a revealing anecdote that followed, perhaps Clive, so renowned for his amiable nature, did not quite have the killer instinct in the dugout he had shown on the field.

Atkinson said, 'We once played Hunslet, who were unbeaten at the time. Everyone expected them to beat us by 50 or 60 points [but] they beat us 12-10. The only reason they beat us was because they kicked a goal in the last ten minutes. The week after, we went to Batley who were only a few places above us and they beat us by 40 points. He [Clive] was sat in the changing rooms with his head in his hands. And he said, "Guys, where am I going wrong?" We turned round and said, "It isn't you; it's us who go wrong." He was so disappointed for us.'

It's a matter of opinion how good a coach Clive could have been. Most of his friends and family believe he could have made a success of it. Perhaps, on reflection, his charismatic presence and immense likeability, alongside his humble nature, would have made him a perfect assistant coach, a foil for a disciplinarian head coach. He would have made an excellent good cop to someone's bad cop.

As it was, he left Doncaster at the end of the 1983/84 season having made a lasting impression on the club, fans and players, but not on the league table. A perfectionist and a born winner, he was open and honest about why he decided to leave in an interview following his resignation.

He told the press, 'It's been a struggle without the right backing and you can only grin and bear it for so long ... the habit of losing has become ingrained at the club and the biggest difficulty has been trying to achieve a more professional approach.'

But, keen to remain in the game, he also conceded that the experience of being at the wrong end of the table rather than the top end had proved invaluable.

'Despite the occasional win and several close calls, usually against the better teams, he found it an unequal battle,' was journalist Don Field's summation of Clive's stint.

He did remain in the game, returning to Hull FC to help with the 'A' team. On one of those occasions which is so surreal it seems made up, he made one last appearance for Hull FC in 1985 against Bradford at Odsal, the team that had turned him down over two decades previously after a game at that exact ground. Even more bizarrely, Martin Clawson, son of Terry, the goal kicking forward for the 1972 World Cup Final, played for Bradford.

Rugby league records are notoriously patchy but it is believed that at the age of 42 Clive broke and still retains the record for the oldest player in a First Division fixture. Even in the modern, professional era, the only comparable player would be Steve Menzies, who was 41 when playing for Catalan Dragons, and a forward.

Clive was called up amid a brutal injury crisis and Arthur Bunting, still in charge, remarked, 'Clive's offer was a great gesture.'

After Clive had come on as a 55th-minute substitute, stand off Steve Portz, another older player drafted in, put him into space and he went over, seemingly breaking another record for the oldest ever scorer. Yet the referee had not read the script and the try was ruled out for a forward pass.

Although it really would have been a fairytale end, rugby league, like all sport, doesn't work that way and Clive's final game of rugby league was that 26-12 loss against Bradford in a valiant effort by an injury-hit team.

Never Forgotten

LIFE is like a good game of rugby league in many ways and momentum swings back and forth. One minute you're behind, the next you're ahead. It's exciting, painful, exhausting, invigorating. Everyone goes down, everyone makes it back up, eventually. It is, of course, completely without sentiment. And, eventually, the final whistle goes.

After hanging up his boots for good, Clive had returned to one of his off-field loves, running a club and bar, appropriately named 'Sully's'. The venture allowed him to also combine rugby league as a side was formed from the bar.

'Clive got in touch with me and told me he was opening Sully's club on Chamberlain Road,' Tony Cope told me. 'He asked me if I would go on the committee with him and would I start a rugby team. It was a no-brainer to have a team with the name Sully's. There was one or two other ex-Hull KR players.'

Unsurprisingly, Clive still dabbled in training. 'Even in his 40s, he still had speed, he'd leave us for dead. He was a gazelle, he really was,' Cope recalled, still clearly in awe to this day.

Clive also reunited with some faces from the past, playing in charity games for an 'All Stars' team set up with old running mate Alan McGlone. Typically for a generation of men who had lived and died for rugby league with a win-at-all costs mentality, the 'friendly' games began to take on a competitive edge, according to McGlone.

He said, 'Sully would turn out for us if he didn't have anything to do. When he turned out with All Stars, we never got beat, we played 19 games. But it ended up that all these amateur teams wanted to set their stall out, look at these old men.

'But no matter how old you get, you never lose the will to win. The last game we played, [it was against] a top West Hull amateur team, who won everything in amateur rugby. They wanted to take that scalp. It turned into a knuckling match … There were five sent off and three serious injuries. And we decided not to do it any more.

'The last game Sully played was at Everthorpe prison. He said, "My back's killing me. I must have twisted it." He said, "I'll do ten minutes." He did that and came off with me, and he said, "This is serious, it's killing me." And I said, "You're doing a lot, doing this, doing that. You've got to slow down; it might be a slipped disc." It was only two or three weeks later he was in hospital and got told he had cancer.'

Clive was diagnosed with an aggressive form of liver cancer in the summer of 1985. He met the challenge head on, refusing to feel sorry for himself and battling to recover just as he had done from the numerous injuries.

Sammy Lloyd recalls, 'Clive was upbeat as his numerous friends and teammates rallied around him. I remember him telling me, "This isn't going to beat me, Sammy." And I said, "If anyone can beat it, you can."'

The cancer was proving to be a tougher hurdle than any opposition winger, or thigh or neck issue ever was, however.

'When I retired in 1980, I ended up assisting Roger [Millward] in 1985/86, the last few years of Roger's time at the club,' Ged Dunn said. 'It was fantastic being with Roger. It was around the time Clive got ill. It was a sad, but happy time. I can still see Clive in the clubhouse. He'd had chemotherapy, he had a hat on and he wasn't looking good. Me and Roger and him were stood at the bar, the three of us. We knew it was the end for Clive really. But we had a great time reminiscing, a catch up.'

Many others shared off-the-record memories of Clive, with his luminous smile, a sense of humour, putting on a brave face as his condition worsened. But he dealt with his illness in the dignified way he did most things. Ultimately, it was one fight he could never overcome, and he passed away at the age of 42 in Hull General Hospital on 8 October 1985.

'I used to say, "You'd die without your rugby",' Rosalyn said. 'It was said as a joke. But I can't put into words how much he loved the game.

That was Clive. He didn't like training, but he loved the game. And he did die without his rugby. He played in the April, his last game ever anyway.

'Someone said to me, you get these prophecies, and you don't know where they come from. He was always on the dot or early. He'd say, "We have to be ready 20 minutes before we had to." He'd be saying, "Are you ready yet?" while I was doing my hair or getting the kids ready. I also used to say to him, "You'd be early for your own funeral, you." And he was. The hearse came, it was unbelievable. They came to the door and said, "We are really sorry, but we are early." So, we had to wait 15 minutes. He was a stickler for being on time.'

The news was understandably greeted with shock and an outpouring of grief from the whole of Hull, as well as the whole of rugby league. At his funeral, with crowds lining the streets outside Hull's Holy Trinty Church a small moment of celebration was caused when it was announced that the main road into Hull would be renamed Clive Sullivan Way. KR chairman Colin Hutton, and his equivalent at FC, Roy Waudby, both delivered readings. Waudby's, from 1 Corinthians 9:24-274, proved tragically appropriate. 'Do you not know that in a race all the runners run, but only one gets the prize? Run in such a way as to get the prize,' it states.

For the family, the tragedy was made tougher in some regards by the fact that Clive was such a visible, public figure, so beloved by so many. 'When he died, it's on the front pages and on the news. But it's our time. It's our dad,' Lisa said.

The family, highlighting their resilience, did rally, raising thousands in Clive's name for cancer research. Just as Clive had attended a vast number of functions during almost all of his life in the public eye, Rosalyn held fundraising events all over the city.

Cruelly, all of the Sullivan siblings also went on to pass away much too young and cancer was a factor in the death of Brian, his big brother, teammate and friendly rival.

Perhaps an indication of the traits that had defined Clive as a person, his competitiveness and caring nature were reflected in Anthony and Lisa. Anthony became an elite rugby league player, a winger of course, for Hull Kingston Rovers, then St Helens. He played for Wales and Great Britain, winning a Lancashire Cup, a Challenge Cup, and a pair of Super

League titles as well as being selected on numerous occasions for end of seasons 'best of' teams. He also played rugby union for Cardiff RUFC and even appeared for the Welsh national side, making him part of a small group of players to have represented the country at international level in league and union.

'I played with his lad Tony, when he first came to us,' Mike Smith told me, reflecting the circular nature of sport. 'He was just like his father, the way he conducted himself. He was a gentleman. And he's still the same now.'

Ray Atkinson, who knew the young Anthony, echoed those sentiments, 'Anthony turned out to be a chip off the old block, a fantastic young man. Clive taught him well.'

'When my dad was playing I'd never wanted to play rugby,' Anthony told me. 'I always wanted to play soccer. I kind of fell into a little bit. Then I played Colts and 'A' team then found myself in the first team. I played with some players my dad played with. It was odd for me, and I'm guessing it was a little odd for them as well!

'But running out at Craven Park was great for me. I'd been in the stands, watching. Going into the first team dressing room and hanging my clothes up was nice because I remembered going in as a kid after games. Craven Park was a friendly, home from home atmosphere for us. I got the chance to play for Wales, and it was a great honour for me.'

Lisa, meanwhile, became a nurse. 'My dad died when I was 13, which was sad. But he's kept alive in a way,' Lisa said. 'He pops up everywhere. I suppose in that way I am really, really fortunate.'

'Whenever Clive is brought up, people come with the stories,' Rosalyn said when reflecting on his untimely passing. 'What a legacy that is. It'll be 32 years this year [2017] and there is still interest.'

Legacy

IT'S easy to look at the story of Clive Sullivan and consider it a tragic one or a case of 'what if?' But, on the flip side, 'what was' is the more appropriate and positive issue to reflect and ponder on.

His longevity, his intelligence to adapt his game as he aged and slowed down is the greatest riposte to the fact his early days were injury-ravaged. He was an extremely determined, talented rugby league player, not one defined and destroyed by injury.

'When you talk about wingers, he has to be up there with the best there has been,' Hartley said in 2017. 'Opinions are opinions, statistics, they are the truth. They don't lie. After all the opinions are given, his try-scoring records and his longevity speak for themselves.'

Alan Smith, one of the very best wingers of his era, rather humbly pointed out, 'I'm prepared to be the great pretender me, to John Atkinson and Clive [Sullivan]. I know! I know [I was there and played with them]. Whatever I did, I did to the best of my ability and I loved it. But I think it's fantastic people felt I was as good as them.'

What if rugby league had capitalised on his World Cup triumph better in 1972? While it didn't to anywhere near the degree it could have, perhaps the better way to look at it is the ray of light which shone during a tough decade for rugby league, and it created the last great moment of success for a British side to this day.

What if Clive's career prime coincided with Hull FC and Hull KR being the dominant forces in the game? Well, his successes would not have been quite so sweet and well remembered.

What if his historic act of becoming the first black Briton to captain a sports team had been recognised more at the time? Perhaps, if more had been made of it, it would have drawn attention away from Clive's substantial achievements as a player, and that team's wonderful victory.

He also left a legacy as a new generation of black British rugby league players began to make their mark, the prolific winger Martin Offiah and loose forward Ellery Hanley becoming cross-over stars in the late 1980s and early '90s. Clive's own pioneering achievement was recognised when he was named as one of the 100 greatest black Britons in 2004.

The saddest what if, of course, is what would have happened had he still been with us?

'Anyone who's anyone always seems to die young,' McGlone commented. 'He would have been huge [had he lived]. Because of who he was, and how he was. He would have been an ambassador, like Bobby Moore or Trevor Brooking [for soccer]. I think he'd have been the first knighthood. We've never had one in rugby league.'

'It was a tragedy that he died so young, just as an ambassador,' Whiteley, who knows plenty about being an icon himself, told me.' 'He had that kind of intelligence, that he could have been a formidable ambassador for his code [rugby league]. He made a big mark on this city. The road shows that even at council level he made an impact.'

Clive's mixture of resilience and amiable, humble nature, aligned with his generosity of time and spirit, make it seem very likely that he could have had an impact on the game in some way or another.

'I think of his smile,' Sammy Lloyd reminisced about Clive. 'He had just a wonderful, charismatic smile. He was ever so friendly. I got to see that as a player and working with him. I worked with him for a considerable length of time, and you get to know someone very well. When you get to play with them you get to know them even better. But in all moments, when the chips were down, in difficult moments, Clive would have a smile. A real cheeky smile. It was a real part of his personality.'

'He was so modest,' Rosalyn said. 'He'd be amazed at what has happened and the esteem he is held in.'

The legacy Clive left has been matched by very few sportsmen or women across all disciplines, not just rugby league. He was a husband and a father. A pioneer in the social history of British sport. A supreme talent. But above all, he was a winner. He was a true professional.

Bibliography

The Rugby League World Cup: An Illustrated History of Rugby's Oldest Global Tournament (Brighouse, League Publications Ltd, 2009)

Richard de la Riviere, *Rugby League: A Critical History 1980-2013*, (Brighouse, League Publications Ltd, 2013)

Phil Holmes Jr and Sr, *Reluctant Hero: The John Holmes Story* (Leeds, Scratching Shed Publications, 2010)

Phil Caplan, *Shoey The Lion Heart: The Mick Shoebottom Story* (Stroud, Tempus, 2004)

Bev Risman, *Both Sides of the Fence: A Life in Rugby League and Union* (Leeds, Scratching Shed Publications, 2016)

Malcolm Reilly and Harry Edgar, *Reilly: A Life in Rugby League* (Edinburgh, Mainstream Publishing, 1999)

Joe Latus, *Hard Road to the Top: The Clive Sullivan Story* (Hull, Boulevard Stadium Publications, 1973)

Eddie Waring, *The Great Ones and Other Writings* (Leeds, Scratching Shed Publications, 2010)

David Storey, *This Sporting Life* (London, Vintage, 2000)

Bill Dalton and Michael Ulyatt, *Old Faithful: A History of Hull Football Club 1875-1986* (Beverley, Hutton Press, 1988)

Brian W Lavery, *The Headscarf Revolutionaries: Lilian Bilocca and the Hull Triple Trawler Disaster* (London, Barbican Press, 2015)

Lee Crooks, *From Hull to Hell and Back* (Leeds, Scratching Shed Publications, 2011)

Tony Collins, *The Oval World: A Global History of Rugby* (London, Bloomsbury, 2016)

Tony Collins, *Rugby League in Twentieth Century Britain: A Social and Cultural History* (Abingdon, Routledge, 2006)

Garry Schofield OBE and Paul Challenor, *Tries the Limit* (Edinburgh, Mainstream Publishing, 2000)

James Booth, *Phillip Larkin: Life, Art and Love* (London, Bloomsbury, 2015)

Alec Gill, *Hull's Fishing Heritage: Aspects of Life in the Hessle Road Fishing Community* (Barnsley, Wharncliffe Publishing, 2011)

David Bond, *Legends: Hull FC 20* (Skipton, Vertical, 2015)

David Bond, *Rivals Across the River* (Great Britain, DB Publishing, 2015)

Roger Pugh, *The Robins: An Official History of Hull Kingston Rovers* (Leeds, Scratching Shed Publications, 2016)

Malcom Andrews, *Hardmen* (Sydney, Allen and Unwin, 2012)

Anthony Clavane, *A Yorkshire Tragedy* (London, Riverrun, 2016)

Phil Caplan and Peter Smith, *Leeds Rugby League Football Club:100 Greats* (Stroud, Tempus, 2005)

Rugby League Journal, *Rugby League in the Sixties*

Rugby League Journal, *Rugby League in the Eighties*

Henri Garcia translated by Roger Grime, *Champagne Rugby: The Golden Age of French Rugby* (London, London League Publishing, 2007)

The Julia Lee Collection at Huddersfield's Heritage Quay